Karina Machado was born ~~~~~~~~~~~~~~ er family moved to Australia, w~~~~~~~~~~~~~~~~ er mother's psychic gift, igniting a life-long ~~~~~~~~~~~ ra-normal. After graduating from the university of NSW she began her career in journalism as editorial assistant at *Time* magazine in 1994, and is now a senior editor at *Who* magazine. Karina, who lives in Sydney with her husband and two children, is also obsessed with the Tudors. She's even been known to dress up as Anne Boleyn, whose ghost she's sadly never seen.

SPIRIT SISTERS

True Stories of the Paranormal

KARINA MACHADO

headline

Copyright © 2009 Karina Machado

The right of Karina Machado to be identified as the Author of
the Work has been asserted by her in accordance with the
Copyright, Designs and Patents Act 1988.

First published in 2009
by Hachette Australia
(An imprint of Hachette Australia Pty Limited)
Level 17, 207 Kent Street, Sydney NSW 2000
www.hachette.com.au

First published in the UK in 2010
by HEADLINE PUBLISHING GROUP

1

Cataloguing in Publication Data is available from the British Library

978 0 7553 6093 2

Text design by Bookhouse, Sydney
Typeset in 11/16.46 pt Sabon LT Std

Printed in the UK by CPI Mackays, Chatham, ME5 8TD

Headline's policy is to use papers that are natural, renewable and recyclable
products and made from wood grown in sustainable forests. The logging and
manufacturing processes are expected to conform to the environmental
regulations of the country of origin.

HEADLINE PUBLISHING GROUP
An Hachette UK Company
338 Euston Road
London NW1 3BH

www.headline.co.uk
www.hachette.co.uk

For my mother, Silvia Machado

'Strange and dark is the night! Whither go we?
Are we on earth or in heaven?
Upward or downward our flight? What mysterious
Spaceless and boundless abyss!'

JUAN ZORRILLA DE SAN MARTIN

'I shall but love thee better after death'

ELIZABETH BARRETT BROWNING

CONTENTS

INTRODUCTION

One night, when I was eight years old, I saw a man in military regalia standing in my bedroom doorway. In the dim light of the hallway of our two-bedroom apartment in Sydney's Eastlakes, I could see his medals gleaming and the broad bulk of his silhouette.

Or could I?

Almost three decades later, if I close my eyes, I can see him again – 'the Colonel', as he came to be known in our family folklore.

My enduring fascination for the paranormal owes much to seeing, dreaming, or – will I ever really know? – imagining, the Colonel. Yet it goes deeper than that. I grew up hearing stories of my mother's sixth sense, including the time that, as a young woman making *tortas fritas* at home in her native Uruguay, her belly blooming with me, she blurted, 'Turn off the radio. Uncle is dead.'

The words made no sense. Her forty-four-year-old Uncle Americo, a dead ringer for Errol Flynn, had just finished helping her dad build a room out the back. He'd worked hard and had only just returned next door to his house, keen to relax and watch the bull fight on TV. When his wife began calling for my grandfather,

her voice calm at first, then ever shriller, like a gathering storm, my mother and her parents rushed over. There lay Americo, felled by a massive heart attack. The family watched in mute horror as my grandfather – furious with grief, tears fleeing his face – stubbornly massaged his dead brother's heart until he'd rubbed every hair off his chest.

Around the time of the Colonel, we'd visit friends in inner-city Dulwich Hill, run rampant with the family's four children up and down the hallway and through the bedrooms of their rambling Federation home, squealing and spooking each other while our parents held impromptu séances in the living room. We'd spy on the grown-ups, hear their laughter or sense their nervous silence, watch in awe as an upturned wine glass glided around the dining table, spelling out messages from an unknown world.

I remembered that feeling in January 2006, when my husband, Anibal, looked me in the eye and told me that a semi-transparent little boy had stood at the threshold of our kitchen and lounge room, peeked his head around the corner and watched him for a few seconds. Enough to make eye contact. Anibal hadn't been asleep; he's a night owl and was up watching his usual late night sports. At that moment, I realised that the cliché of every hair standing on end is accurate. I almost swooned, because I understood that this person I trusted implicitly had witnessed something out of this world.

That reminded me of something I'd learned as a child: a paranormal experience is a great leveller. After all, if my grounded tradesman husband could see a ghost, couldn't anyone? Spooky stories are universal; a ghostly tale can even work as a social ice-breaker. On the other hand, sometimes these experiences are rarely revealed secrets: cherished encounters held tight and close for fear that exposure will dim them, as daylight fades a precious old photograph.

In the following pages you'll meet ordinary women with an extraordinary story to tell. From a twenty-two-year-old criminology student who will never forget the night a ghostly colonial family crashed her childhood sleepover, to a woman who has come face to face with her own doppelgänger and a mother of seven who was held and soothed by her husband five days after she'd buried him.

While many of my interviewees refused to label something which is as much a part of them as the colour of their eyes or their shoe size, they're nevertheless likely to be psychics and/or mediums – and there's a difference: only mediums are in touch with the spirit world. It's possible, therefore, to be psychic without ever tipping your hat to the dead.

Parapsychologists, who investigate and weigh up the evidence for life after death and paranormal phenomena – known as 'psi' – such as ESP and psychokinesis (mental influence on matter), have long been on a mission to understand encounters such as those described in this book. Is that eerie mist a spectral visitation, or just a foggy trick of the light? Are those bangs and knocks communication from the spirit world, or simply an old house creaking and shifting? It's their job to figure that out.

'A phenomenon is paranormal if it cannot be explained in conventional scientific terms,' says Adelaide parapsychologist Dr Lance Storm. As to whether he believes in ghosts – known to these academics as 'discarnate entities' – Dr Storm is undecided. But he offers two theories to explain them. The first is straightforward: 'That any kind of experience of a discarnate entity can, within reason, be taken literally as proof of an after life,' as long as the likelihood of hallucination, delusion, day-dreaming or fantasy have been ruled out. The second possibility has the futuristic-sounding name of 'the super-psi theory' and proposes that ghosts 'result from a strange blend of the imagination and an advanced form of psychic ability, such as telepathy.' In this scenario, people who've seen a ghost 'are producing [the vision] in the same way as the mind produces characters in dreams and if any new information is provided by this entity, it is coming via telepathy from someone who is still alive, or one's own clairvoyant ability,' the parapsychologist explains. In other words, the super-psi theory gives a tick to psychic ability, but crosses out the after life.

In *When Ghosts Speak*, Mary Ann Winkowski, the Ohio housewife whose life inspired the TV hit, *Ghost Whisperer*, puts it like this: 'Ghosts are just regular folks – who happen to be dead.' Sydney paranormal investigator Robb Tilley, who's seen the dead since he was a teenager, agrees: Ghosts are merely 'dead people', he says. The erudite fifty-eight-year-old public officer at the Australian Institute of Parapsychological Research fields an average of two calls a month from frightened people from all walks of life who are sick of living in a haunted house. Not unlike Mary Ann Winkowski, Robb (charging only enough to cover costs) will visit the home to 'clear' it. Aided by 'a whole team of good spirits', Robb moves the ghost – also known as an earthbound spirit – along.

'Mostly, it's dead people with a high emotional attachment to the house and a new family moves in and they resent these people and their kids being in the house,' he says. 'It's quite rewarding to successfully clear a place. I check in the next day and people say, "We all slept beautifully and the house feels peaceful and safe. The whole atmosphere has changed."'

But it's common, he adds, for people to wait two or three years before they pick up the phone. 'People feel embarrassed; most of them don't want anybody to know that they've had to call me in,' he says with a chuckle. 'Because this stuff isn't supposed to happen.'

But it does.

I have interviewed or corresponded with over two hundred women – aged nineteen to eighty – who wanted to share their stories with me. Too many, in fact, for one book. These women would not stand out in a crowd; they could be your sister, your mother, your aunt or your best friend. The vast majority do not publicise their gifts or work as psychics; on the contrary, many keep their experiences hushed inside them, and only decided to speak out because the time was right, or because they're passionate about creating a sense of community for other women who might be struggling with their own experiences.

Time and again, they'd preface their words with, 'I've never told anyone this, they'd think I'm crazy . . .' but then, the stories would tumble out: they would give up their ghosts. 'People are so scared to talk about it, they don't want to be laughed at,' says author and publisher Maggie Hamilton, who's had many profound experiences. 'I think of myself as a very normal, average person. I think what I've learned from all the things that have happened is that these things are *not* paranormal. They are actually normal.'

Here I must point out that *Spirit Sisters* is not a scientific treatise. I did not set about testing these women in a laboratory, nor am I qualified to do so. I listened to them in good faith and, in turn, their experiences chilled me, moved me and made me weep. I felt privileged to have met women like the feisty Kath Campbell, who picked her life up again after losing her two little girls in an horrific car accident, and Angela Wood, whose young daughter, Anna, became a household name following her death in 1995. Their stories are a powerful testament to the idea that love survives death and that frightening experiences with spirits are relatively uncommon.

Where some of my interviewees had only the one indelible encounter to share, for others, life itself is an ongoing paranormal experience. Ultimately, all of their stories reignited my childhood quest for answers about the afterlife, and I'm hardly alone in my curiosity.

'More people say they believe in ghosts than at any time in the last sixty years of professional opinion polling,' British academic and author Owen Davies, told ABC Radio National. 'They act as anchors of spirituality ... perhaps there is a subconscious fear that if we lay the belief in ghosts we will lose an element of our humanity. Some of us evidently need ghosts to live as much as they require us to die.'

A recent US survey found that three out of four people believe in some aspect of the paranormal. Of these, forty-four per cent were women (compared to only 29% of men). I could find no similar Australian poll, but a three-year study of youth spirituality by Melbourne's Monash University found that seventeen per cent of our Generation Y (born between 1979-1990) pursue an 'eclectic' spirituality, which includes belief in reincarnation, psychics and ghosts. Again, this was more common among young women.

While there's no concrete proof that women are more likely to have a paranormal experience than men, it's the girls who seem more willing to talk about it. 'Generally, women may be more prone to having psychic experiences, or are more emotionally free than men to share them,' says Dr Storm, 'because their female peers are more sympathetic and supportive.'

The disparity may be cultural, according to medium Mahta Manzouri, twenty-nine. 'In Western society, masculine energy is more preoccupied with the world of the "now" – economics and technology – rather than the spiritual world. So females tend to dominate these fields. But psychic ability is not mutually exclusive to either gender.'

Marie D. Jones, a California-based journalist, paranormal investigator and author agrees, suggesting that 'women are biologically more apt to sense changes in the environment, and to be attuned to intuition, both of which seem inextricably linked to paranormal events. Changes in the environment require a brain that is able to focus on many things at once, and absorb a sort of "multi-tasked" reality that makes up our day-to-day lives.'

As a flock of unsung mediums in our midst tend to their quiet lives – going to work, looking after their families and speaking to the dead – a new generation of ghost-busters is craning for a glimpse of what they live with every day. Pay TV reality shows like *Most Haunted* and *Paranormal State* are all chasing ghost-hunting's Holy Grail – an apparition caught on camera – while psychic sleuth programs like *Psychic Detective* and *Sensing Murder* abound. In 2008, thousands tuned in to watch the Seven Network's *The One*, a viewer-voted search for Australia's most gifted psychic. Hit TV dramas including *Medium*, *Supernatural*, *Ghost Whisperer* and *Fringe* are also helping quench the public's appetite for all matters other-worldly.

'I have been in this a long time and have seen cycles of interest,' adds Marie D. Jones. 'The UFO field was exploding during the 1980s and 1990s, and then died down. Now we have ghosts taking over! But there is a definite drive to understand the unknown and the media is right there reflecting that drive. People are coming to realise, amidst economic turmoil and global challenges that cause stress and fear and discomfort, that there is 'something else' to life, and it involves our ability to connect not only to each other, but to the vast other realities we have long sensed existed, but only spoke about in hushed voices.'

And women are at the heart of it. At book groups, on lunch breaks, girls' nights and coffee mornings, women are exchanging ghost stories, much as our mothers and grandmothers may have done before us. 'It's like "secret women's business",' says Sydney mum and medium Naomi Kalogiros, who regularly puts on morning tea for a clutch of girlfriends to share paranormal experiences.

In an age when psychics are the new therapists and buying your own high-tech ghost-hunting equipment is just a click away on e-Bay, this book is a celebration of the one thing that hasn't changed in hundreds of years. When a friend draws close, lowers her voice and starts to unravel her ghost story, as her eyes widen and her smile fades, as the very air around you seems to thicken and the back of your neck begins to tingle . . . isn't it delicious?

STRANGERS IN THE NIGHT

Ghost Stories

'A spirit glided past my face; the hair of my flesh bristled'
BIBLE: HEBREW, JOB 4:15

Here's the thing about writing a book like this. It makes it hard to sleep.

After hearing so many stories of women waking to the sight of a ghostly stranger, I've changed my after-dark ways. Now I hardly ever risk a 2 am bathroom call and I'll suffer a parched throat instead of walking through the sleeping house for a glass of water. Should I dare, the living room seems a black maw, a perfect spot for a spirit to perch on his travels between dimensions. A dead room.

I have nothing to worry about, according to Hans Holzer, arguably the world's most famous ghost hunter. Ghosts are not 'dangerous, fearful, and [out to] hurt people,' he writes in his encyclopaedic *Ghosts: True Encounters With the World Beyond*. The eighty-eight-year-old German parapsychologist says 'ghosts – apparitions of "dead" people or sounds associated with invisible human beings – are the surviving emotional memories of people who have not been able to make the transition from their physical state into the world of spirit.'

Holzer believes that ghosts exist in a state of 'shock induced by sudden death or great suffering.' They'll stay that way, he believes, until a medium can make contact and explain what has happnened. It's a process, he claims, not unlike psychoanalysis.

In keeping with the general concensus among mediums and spiritualists, he points out the crucial difference between earthbound spirits (ghosts) and 'free spirits', who are 'in full possession of all mental and emotional faculties and memories'. Ghosts are essentially trapped on earth and not from the spirit world, unlike free spirits who have crossed into the light and may return at will, to offer comfort to the grieving or to pass on a message.

Apart from ghost and spirits, experts suggest two other theories to explain an apparition: a psychic imprint and an 'apparition of the living'.

A psychic imprint, or replay, is where an emotional event has 'imprinted' itself on the environment and remains accessible to sensitive or psychic people, whilst an apparition of the living (also known as a 'crisis apparition') is a situation where a living person, usually unknowingly, projects his or her form to a loved one when in fear, in an emergency, or on their death bed.

One of the most famous instances of a psychic imprint occurred in the English city of York – nicknamed the most haunted city in the world – in 1953. Apprentice plumber Harry Martindale was halfway up a ladder installing central heating in the cellar of the historic Treasurer's House when he heard a trumpet blare. The apparition of a Roman soldier astride a horse then came through the wall – trailed by around twenty dishevelled foot soldiers shuffling along in pairs, carrying daggers, swords and shields.

The young tradesman fell off his ladder in shock and watched, dumbfounded, as the troops filed by, keeping to what would have been the ancient Roman road. 'I could see them and all they had to do was glance at me and I'd had it, but not one of the soldiers looked in my direction,' Martindale told UK historian Richard Felix in a recent interview. This experience is up there with my favourite ghost stories of the twentieth century, not just because of the details Martindale provided – his photographic descriptions of the mens' costumes and armaments helped date the soldiers to the fourth century – but because it is a marvellous example of how the paranormal can march its way into our humdrum present when we least expect it, and wear a plumed helmet to boot.

It's important to note that while the following accounts take place at night, it's not to say that an apparition can *only* be seen under a blanket of darkness. I've interviewed women who can spot an apparition just as easily in aisle three at the supermarket at 2 pm. Perhaps it is only more common at nightfall, because that's when our conscious minds are quietened.

Emma Snowden's poignant little apparition was probably not a replay, because in interacting with Emma, she evidenced consciousness. She didn't utter a sound, but Emma had a powerful understanding that she was communicating with her. (It will become apparent as the stories proceed that during these encounters, thoughts are often transferred telepathically).

Emma is a film publicist who lives with her husband and son in a restored nineteenth century workers' cottage in the historic inner-Sydney suburb of Balmain. Emma and her husband, Paul, sleep in the home's handsome front room, complete with original beams and fireplace, that would have once been used as the sitting room.

In 2002, Emma's son, Ted, was only three, so she was very familiar with the feeling of being summoned by a child in the early hours. It was exactly this sensation that awoke her one cold night. 'I remember being deeply, deeply asleep, and then widely awake in a way that a mother is – instantly operational,' she recalls.

'There was a little girl next to my bed. It was less a kind of vision and more a kind of emotion for me. She wasn't frightening me and she wasn't demanding anything from me but she was needing my attention, my mothering. It was just her saying, *I need you to be awake and I need you to be with me for a moment.*'

As usual, I am gobsmacked by the details Emma remembers of the little ghost's appearance. 'Her clothing was very grey and she had some sort of scarf or a muffler around her neck. She had a very round face and her blonde hair, which was very fine and pushed away from her face, was tucked into this scarf.' The girl, who looked no more than four, wore something that resembled 'a coarse, thick dressing-gown,' says Emma. 'There was nothing shiny or glossy about her. Everything she was wearing was very matte. That's what I mean by "grey", she was muted, as if someone had drained her of colour.'

Despite the sharp portrait she paints, uppermost in Emma's memory is the *emotion* of the encounter. 'I wasn't overwhelmed or frightened. It was like a call from a child in the middle of the night. Then she didn't vanish into a puff of smoke or anything, it was just like this intense feeling dissipated.' She has never experienced anything like this since.

Real estate office manager and Sydneysider Robyn Levett, thirty-four, also had an 'interactive' experience, this time with a maternal ghost: 'My family and I had moved to a house in Glenorie, in semi-rural Sydney. It was February 1998 and it was a hot, sweaty day. The house we were moving into was 110 years old and had recently been renovated. Like most old houses, there was an old part and a new part. My bedroom was in the old part.

'After moving boxes all day, I was knackered. I went to bed early and decided to read for a while. Whilst lying there, I thought I felt someone or something looking through the window at me, but I dismissed it, thinking to myself that I was just super-tired. I turned off the light and went straight to sleep.

'It was a hot night, but it was getting pretty chilly closer to dawn. I woke up cold and I really wanted to sit up and put the doona over me, but I thought to myself, *the sun will be up soon and it'll be hot, so I don't need it.* As I lay there thinking this, something was on the other side of the room, just near the bedroom door. I switched on my bedside light and had a quick look, nothing there. I turned off the light and rolled over to face the middle of my double bed.

'Whatever was over the other side of the bed was now standing behind me.

'I was so afraid, I was paralysed. Either through fear, or the ghost paralysed me, which I think I've heard of. I kept thinking to myself, *Oh my God. What is happening? Please don't hurt me.* As I'm thinking this, she's knelt (or sat?) down on the side of the bed, and despite being paralysed I could feel myself moving with the mattress. She then pulled the doona up and tucked it up under my chin!

'As she gets up, the mattress moved with her and she whispers, "Shhh, go to sleep," and repeats this until she leaves via the bedroom door.

'Like the good girl that I am, I go straight back to sleep.'

At first, I thought this story might have been a 'replay', where Robyn's psychic sensitivity somehow triggered a re-enactment of an event that would have occurred umpteen times in the century-old bedroom; a mother tenderly tucking her child into bed. Then again, the spirit seems to have tuned into Robyn's unvoiced sense of feeling cold, and reacted accordingly. As for the paralysis Robyn describes, this seems to be a recurring theme, and is explored in depth in the conclusion.

Sydneysider Rhonda Rice, sixty-nine, is one who wakes in fright to the sight of strangers in her room. Rhonda began to see 'the visitors', as she calls them, when she was in her fifties, but is only now becoming accustomed to the silent figures who materialise only centimetres from her nose. As soon as she screams, they disappear. 'I saw one, a farmer with khaki overalls on, and the check shirt. He was just standing beside the bed. They don't talk, they are just *there*. A lot of the time they seem to be looking at me, which is worse in a way, because they are so real, you are sure they are going to grab you.'

Three weeks after I interviewed Rhonda, she emailed me with news of her most recent experience: 'My latest visitor was a young, handsome guy wearing a light-coloured shirt and dark pants. When I opened my eyes, he was standing by my bed, right near the bed-head, in line with my face. He was just gazing down at me in a friendly way. As usual, I yelled and he disappeared. I was able to get back to sleep after telling myself I needn't be scared, but it really is scary to find someone there like that. I just realised something . . . when I see my visitors, even though the room is dark, I see them clearly, and they usually appear quite solid.'

The Catholic scripture teacher consulted her doctor, who diagnosed hypnagogic hallucinations, a condition when one may experience visual and/or auditory hallucinations at the onset of sleep, though Rhonda's experiences are always in the middle of the night.

Sometimes, Rhonda sees inanimate objects – once, a 1.8 metre painter's ladder right by her bed – and one of her most unforgettable encounters with visitors is possibly a replay situation. 'There was a woman in her late thirties and a teenage girl in colonial clothes – I could see their bonnets – just strolling across the bottom of my bed. They just walked through, laughing and talking as though out on a street somewhere.' The women, says Rhonda, simply vanished through the wall.

Living in a house dating back to 1897 in the inner-Sydney suburb of Marrickville in the 1990s, full-time mum Naomi Kalogiros had a similar experience – but the apparition would appear to her at precisely the same time *each* night. 'I was seeing a man in a black coat and a big wide-brimmed hat walking a dog, a Pomeranian. He would appear out of the wall, into the doorway and disappear straight into the bathroom. It would be 11 pm every night without fail.' Naomi, thirty-seven, says in the five years they lived there, her husband never saw the man, whom she presumes was a rector, and only one other person – a friend of the couple's – described, without any prior information from Naomi, seeing exactly the same tableau.

The bathroom was a hot spot, says Naomi, for the spritely vicar and his pet. Showering, she would often feel an icy hand at her back – her husband also complained of this – and when pregnant with her first child, she would be in the bathroom in the small hours and see, but not hear, the Pomeranian barking at her. A search at the land titles office revealed that the block had belonged to the rectory of the local church.

Like Naomi, freelance writer Frances James was not in bed when she saw her stranger. In 1996, the nineteen-year-old was supporting her studies in English literature and sociology by waitressing part-time at a Port Melbourne restaurant. 'I was clearing away the last few plates after a function. As I walked down a hallway towards the kitchen, there was a service hatch to my right, about 3-4 feet [90-120 cm] away. I had a strange feeling and looked to my right and saw this blonde man look up, very alarmed,' says Frances, who noticed his fair skin and pale eyebrows. 'I thought, *who is that*? There was a shelf in the hatch so his expression was partly concealed, but his eyes looked shocked, opened wide in surprise, and I could see his mouth open.

'He wore a white shirt, open at the neck, no tie. He seemed about thirty, about five-foot-ten [1.77 m]. He looked solid. It was a matter of a second by the time I'd walked into the kitchen, which was completely empty and the window was shut. I felt cold and very goose-bumpy all over. The atmosphere felt very charged, very strange. I dumped the plates, turned around and felt myself running from the room.

'I had no knowledge of anything in that building, no expectation of it,' says Frances, who asked not to work in the function room again. 'I had never seen anything before, or had anybody in my life who believed in ghosts or experienced them. It wasn't like the apparition had any significance to *me*, it just felt like I'd walked in on it. I surprised him – he was going about his business and he wasn't expecting me.'

They fill me with a panicky curiosity, these unearthly strangers. I yearn to know who they were in life, how they died, why they're still around us and what, if anything, they want . . . but I never, ever want to meet them.

THE FAMILY

'They were dressed in their Sunday best, staring at me.'

Little girls love a sleepover. It's so much fun to swap secrets, giggle about the cutest boy in class, give the Barbies an extreme makeover. It's also a rite of passage, proof that you're growing up, a way to show Mum and Dad that you can sleep away from your bed and blankie, can face alone those fears that creep into your room, cloaked in moonlight. Once the muffled giggling and whispering fades out, when eyelids begin to droop, lashes quivering over peachy, pillow-warm cheeks, then little girls sleep like the dead. Not with them, usually. But not all sleepovers are the same.

Amy Shepherd loved hanging out with the girl across the road. Her friend, Martha, had four brothers, and Amy, being much younger than her two half-siblings, was effectively an only child. Growing up together in rural Wellington, between Dubbo and Orange in western New South Wales, the third graders zigzagged between each other's homes, playing tips, building cubby houses and enjoying the comfortable routine of life in a typical Australian country town.

One autumn evening in 1993, when Amy was seven, she toted her nightie to her friend's house. It wasn't her first time sleeping over. Martha's place was practically a second home, but that didn't diminish her excitement. Before bed, there was time for a game of hide-and-seek, the girls' laughter filling forgotten corners of the 1960s weatherboard house. Then they played dolls and brushed their teeth. When it was finally time for lights out, Amy fell into a peaceful sleep, nestled beside her friend in a king-size single bed.

In the middle of the night, her eyes snapped open. She needed to use the bathroom. Grumbling inwardly, because she'd been nice and warm, the child got up and padded through the silent house, sensing a shift in its rhythm. In the hush of the early hours, it is sometimes possible to feel a house breathing, to tap into its resting pulse – especially in the country, where the darkness and silence is so dense you could almost scoop it into your palms. All finished, Amy returned to the bedroom, where her friend's bed was flush against the wall, Martha fast asleep on the far side. She climbed in beside her, turned back around to regain her comfy position . . . and there they were.

'A family of three – a mother, father and a little boy – dressed in their Sunday best. And they just stood there, staring at me.'

Sitting in a café in Sydney's Queen Victoria Building, Amy's raisin toast goes cold as she unspools a story that makes me want to stop the shoppers around us, shake them out of complacency, alert them to mysteries snug inside their loved ones. Now twenty-two, the criminology student has a kind, open face, with watchful green-blue eyes and dark brown hair. When she smiles, which is often, the corners of her eyes crinkle, spilling the warmth inside her. But there is something else in her expression, something disconcerting. It is fear. Even fifteen years later, the memory of what she saw that night still terrifies Amy Shepherd.

In the darkness of the small bedroom, as her friend slept on, oblivious to Amy's attempts to wake her, the family inspected Amy with detached curiosity; they could have been on a stroll at the zoo, and she the exotic import. 'They looked like people, but you could tell they weren't,' recalls Amy, because of their 'glowy' quality. The trio stood side-by-side, the parents in their thirties, their son around ten. All were dressed in what appeared to be the fashion of the early 1900s, the males in dark-coloured suits, the brunette woman in a long-sleeved dress with a scarf tied neatly under her chin. 'Her skin was very pale,' says Amy, diving deep into her memory for the details I'm hungry for. 'That's probably what gave off the glow.'

Clearly in command was the father, who was 'straight-faced and very tall', says Amy, reluctantly agreeing to try to sketch the scene in my notebook. The picture she draws is of three stick figures standing in a line between a doorway and a bed, with another stick figure lying on the half of the pillow closest to the people. What it points out is that it must have been a very tight fit in that bedroom that night.

'I don't know how long we stared at each other for,' she says, in a low and even voice, 'but eventually the mother bent down and whispered something to the little boy and he nodded, then came over to my bed. He reached out to my leg and went to touch it. That's when I freaked out and threw the blankets over my head.' The whole episode lasted between five and ten minutes – an eternity for such an uncanny exchange – but the questions it raised will haunt Amy for the rest of her life. 'Who were they? What happened to them? Why haven't I ever seen them again? Did they give up on me because I didn't help them? Did they find someone who was able to help them?'

It's a story that 'freaks people out', admits Amy, who learned this the hard way the next morning. 'The first thing I told my friend's parents when I woke up was that there were three people in my room. They thought I was crazy, but when I told Mum and Dad, I was so adamant, they believed me.' Amy's mum Judy remembers it well: 'She was telling me about a mummy and daddy and a little boy there in the bedroom with her,' says Judy Shepherd. While meeting 'the family' is Amy's earliest memory of seeing spirit, her mum says she was younger when she first showed signs of psychic awareness. 'Countless times, she'd sing out to me, "Mum, what are you doing?" and I'd wake up saying "What?" and she'd say, "You're crouched down in the hallway." But I wasn't. I was in bed.'

Two years after the ghostly family, Amy saw a teenage boy in her lounge room. She caught him out of the corner of her eye, whipped around and watched the stranger make himself comfortable in one of the family's chairs. Growing up, Amy was plagued by a litany of strange events: being poked in the side, seeing balls of light travelling through the house, feeling her bed move – once, so forcefully that the headboard was shoved against the wall – and hearing voices. 'I've gotten into the habit of listening to music when I go to bed, otherwise I can't sleep,' says Amy, who'll pop in her iPod to avoid the chatter. 'It's nothing really clear, it's like hearing a group of people, a gathering of sorts. I could always hear it in my bedroom. Last time I was home, they were all talking rather loudly.'

'Amy is a very level-headed, sensible girl,' says Judy, the friendly forty-eight-year-old herself very much a straight shooter. In a matter-of-fact way, she tells me about the night her husband awoke to a feather-light touch on the forehead from a blonde, six-year-old boy: 'The little boy ran down our hallway, through the front door – with the noises of the front door opening and closing – and my husband just lying there, stunned, and this voice in his head saying, *Get up and have a look*. Then he heard the footsteps, the little boy running down our driveway, barefoot.'

Intriguingly, but certainly not atypically in these accounts, Judy – who like Amy has felt her bed shoved roughly against the wall – has also heard the muffled speech that her daughter describes. One night, she awoke at 2 am to the sounds of music, chatter, a gathering in full swing. 'I thought, *Who'd be having a party in the middle of the week?* and being a sticky-beak, I got up to investigate.' She followed the sounds to the bathroom, where it seemed to be loudest, stood on the bathtub and opened the window, but it wasn't coming from outside. 'It wasn't deafening. If you can imagine someone in the other room has the radio on and there are two men in conversation, but in the background, there's a party going on? That's what it was like.' Baffled, she swivelled slowly around in the glare of the bathroom, trying to pinpoint the source. It made no sense, but the noise seemed loudest the closer she stooped to the ground. The din, she discovered, was snaking up the bathtub drain.

A year went by, and Judy organised for well-known medium Deb Webber (who appears on the TV show *Sensing Murder*) to take the stage at the Wellington Soldiers Club, where Judy worked. 'That was the interesting part,' says Judy. 'She knew nothing about me, but said I've got several ghosts in the house and that they're channelling through a drain in my bathroom.' Four weeks before my conversation with Judy, Amy was home from uni and mentioned to her mum that she had not been able to sleep for the incessant chitchat in her room. 'I thought, *Well, maybe they're channelling through the air vents now because it has to come from somewhere!* I mean, you tell people this and they think you're crazy. We are *not* crazy people.'

In fact Amy, who hopes to join the Australian Federal Police, is the poster girl for a happy, functional upbringing. The single student speaks lovingly of her mum and dad, her siblings and 'awesome' extended family. It is mainly her loved ones she confides in when she experiences something she can't explain, and her eyes still get moist when she remembers a recurring nightmare that sickened her as a child. Night after night, she witnessed her parents' execution in a Nazi concentration camp: 'I watched them being shot to death, over and over and over again. The camp was lit up. I was on the outside of the fence and they were on their knees. I'd wake up crying, sobbing. I didn't even know what a concentration camp was when I was little.' She shrugs at the suggestion that she may have been glimpsing a past life. Deciphering the dream is not a priority for Amy. She's just relieved to have left that deathscape behind.

Since Amy has moved to the city to study, things are considerably quieter at home in Wellington. 'Now they're with Amy. She's the one with the special gift,' says her mum. Though it's not a particularly *welcome* gift, bemoans her daughter, since 'I just don't know what to do with it.' And who could blame her? A busy young woman juggling a demanding course, part-time work, family commitments, and as many crime thrillers as she can squeeze into her scant leisure time, Amy could probably do without phoning her mum at 2 am because 'my whole bed just jolted and it scared the crap out of me!'

Sometimes, it's worse than that. In December 2007, fourteen years after an anonymous turn-of-the-century family branded her girlhood, Amy woke to find another uninvited guest, this time inside her uni dorm. 'I jolted awake and there he was. He was tall, he was solid, just standing next to my bookcase, looking at me.' Who was this shadow man, and what unearthly terrain do these drop-ins populate? Amy wasn't about to ask. 'I just said, "Oh God, not again", and threw the blankets over my head.'

Perhaps it is wiser not to look at them. Best not to think about how long they linger, watching, wondering if they'll step closer. Tut-tutting at the gall of these fleshly intruders who steal into their world.

A PROPER GREETING

'It was like I was a ghost in his world.'

When a house is asleep, some of its inhabitants wake up.

Not those who are cosy in their beds, their minds drifting through dreams, warm bodies at ease. But the others: the ones who linger in the walls and crevices of a building until darkness beckons, whispering that tonight they can dress their spirits in the clothes of their old lives and come out. Tonight, there is one who can see them.

Like Judith Parker. In the daylight hours, the Melburnian is a graphic designer. From Monday to Friday, she is familiar with the rhythms of her working day, the routines of her colleagues, the job she must perform. No surprises here. But night upends all protocols, Judith has learned. This is what you know when you have locked eyes with the afterlife, watched it step forward in a khaki shirt, shake your hand and bid you, 'Good morning.'

Judith was in her late twenties the first time she was woken up by a spirit, a prim lady in the buttoned-up fashions of the 1950s. 'I was apprehensive,' says the eloquent thirty-eight-year-old, measuring her words. 'You're taken unawares. You're not expecting it and I wasn't sure what was going on. Then I described her to my mother and she thought it sounded like my Aunt Margaret who died when I was two. She would often baby-sit me.'

On that night, Judith was asleep in the home she shares with her mother, Lynette, the home she has lived in since birth. She was sleeping on the left-hand side of her bed, facing the window where moonlight pours in, often interrupting her sleep. But the moon was blameless this night – what woke her was the feeling that someone was watching. Her eyelids opened and there stood the lifelike figure of a woman, barely a metre away, 'between my knees and my feet at the bottom of the bed,' recalls Judith. 'Her hands were by her side. She was quite still, quite motionless.'

Trim and neat in a Peter Pan blouse, fitted jumper and pleated skirt, the woman appeared to be in her forties. Judith could trace the contours of her silhouette; admire the way her short, wavy hair was swept across to one side. I ask how long she watched her and Judith smiles. 'Well, I'm not very brave because when it happened I was really scared stiff and I closed my eyes and prayed. When I opened my eyes, she wasn't there.

'I sound very cowardly and it's kind of funny, because I think it's intriguing – all this – but on the occasions that I have experienced these things, I am actually quite scared. I suppose they don't mean you any harm, but you don't really know how to react.'

Throughout our conversation, Judith, who has also heard the spirit of her late father playing with her beloved cats, plays down her stories. She explains she has had only a handful of experiences and doesn't believe they warrant much fuss. Even after she tells me about the man in the khaki shirt.

In January 2006, Judith took a week off work and went to stay with her cousin and her husband in their 1850s-era home in the Victorian gold-mining town of Beechworth. Judith was staying in what once would have been the dining room. 'Now, my cousin's husband has a really off-beat sense of humour, so when I woke up at about five o'clock in the morning and someone was shaking my hand really, really hard, I said, "Oh John, it's really early!" Then I realised it wasn't John.

'He was of average build with a tanned face, and short, crisp sandy-blonde hair. He was quite good-looking, but he didn't have a specific "look", I couldn't say whether he looked like an eighteenth-century man or a nineteenth-century man. He just looked like a man! He was in a khaki-coloured shirt. And he was shaking my hand and kept saying, "Good morning." He had my hand and was continually shaking; you know how when you meet someone you really like and you're like, 'Hi, hi, hi! Haven't seen you in ages!" That's what it was like. And then I realised he wasn't looking *at* me, he was looking straight through me. That's when I felt him go over my head and disappear into the wall behind me.

'I was so scared I couldn't get out of bed to tell my cousin. I just lay there for half an hour until it got light. For the rest of my time there I felt really uncomfortable, I didn't feel happy, and I'd have the light on to go to bed because I just couldn't sleep in there.'

Judith has never forgotten the way it felt exactly as if a living man was shaking her hand, excitedly flinging it up and down: 'You know how you can feel the bone in someone's hand? He had a really firm handshake.' She is also haunted by the memory of his gaze. 'It was like when someone looks you straight in your eyes and you have the experience of someone looking at your face, but they're looking a little off to the left or right. That's what it was, and I thought, *He's not actually realising that I'm here.*'

Who *was* he seeing? Did Judith's latent psychic abilities somehow trigger the replay of a happy, but long-dead moment in the course of one anonymous life? 'That was the weirdest thing,' she reflects. 'He wasn't really aware of me at all. It was as if he was shaking someone's hand in his world, not mine. He just walked through me as though I didn't exist – *like I was a ghost in his world.*'

MOONLIT OFFERINGS

'He was staring straight at me. I could see the whites of his eyes.'

There are two ghost stories Sophie Masson likes to tell. The experiences are like night and day. Fear did not figure in the first, while in the second she was fear made flesh. She never tells one story without the other, because they work in tandem to spark a sensation in the listener that anything is possible.

'I've always felt pricklings in the air,' says the forty-nine-year-old French-Australian author of popular fantasy novels for young adults, and mother of three. 'I always used to feel that that this world is a façade and that there is something else there which you don't necessarily see, though out of the corner of your eye you might catch something. I'd always wondered how I would react if one day I was to see something . . .'

Her first opportunity to find out came in July of 1998, when she was away from her Armidale, New South Wales, home at a week-long series of workshops. Deep into a story that would become a three-part novel set in the middle ages, Sophie was not sleeping very well, as happens when she works. On TV, she watched an interview with the heavy metal band Black Sabbath, who were unapologetic about their use of the occult as a stage prop. 'They thought it pulled the punters in,' she recalls, 'and I remember thinking, *Idiots! You should never use these things in that way.*'

The novelist went to bed, her brain a jumble of thoughts and images. That night, she dreamt of a rickety timber house where a woman sat writing at a weathered desk. 'Suddenly, the screen door creaks and something hurtles into the room where she is sitting, a tiny triangular face with red eyes ablaze,' says Sophie. 'It rushed straight for her throat.' Gasping, she awoke, unsure what to make of it.

The next night, another obscure dream. This time of a man walking into a shimmering lake whose beauty is deceptive, for with every step he takes into the water, he transforms into something green and bronze, 'something less than human,' says Sophie, who again woke with a thudding heart, her skin chill to the touch. The following morning, she took the train to Sydney, where she would stay with her brother. His house backed onto a vacant block of land, the bare yard punctuated by a lone tree.

It was the third night.

No nightmare this time, only the barking of the family's dogs to slice her sleep. 'It was the kind of bark that tells you something is wrong, the sharp short sound that tells you their hackles are rising,' she says. Instantly alert, Sophie got up to look out the window. In the light of the full moon, there was no mistaking what she saw only a few metres from where she stood: 'A young man, standing absolutely, perfectly still. He had one hand on his hip, the other one facing down, with the index and third fingers making a V, as if he was holding a cigarette, but there was no glow. He was staring straight at me, I could see the whites of his eyes.'

Transfixed, Sophie held his stare, utterly fearless – *so* this *is what it's like*, she thought – only fascination nailing her to the spot. She noticed he wore a jumper, jeans and sneakers, but her writer's mind could not decide their colour. Grey? Silver? The shade of a moonbeam? 'He was so sharp, I can't say he looked unearthly,' she remembers. 'The only thing that was really strange about him was that he was standing so still, not moving a muscle.' Then something snapped in her conscious mind, and her thoughts were full of her brother, his family, of an intruder outside. She roused the household, spreading panic, and the sleepers tumbled, red-eyed, from their rooms, to witness a strange man on a winter's night. They all saw him. 'I said to my brother, "Yell at the dog! If he hears you, he'll realise someone is awake and run away."'

Then – the oddest thing. Suddenly, there was no man, only a stunted eucalyptus tree. He was gone, and the people poured back into their rooms, perplexed, even the dogs were silenced. A part of Sophie was outraged. 'A tree? I saw a tree? No, I did not, it was no tree I saw then,' she fumes. 'This night, the dogs barked differently, and I saw someone. It was something I may never understand, but it was there.'

In the daylight, her analytical mind tried a trio of theories on for size: 'That it was my mind that projected that being out on the night. That it was a kind of vision of my animus, as Carl Jung might have said. That it was a product of three disturbed nights,' Sophie mused. 'Whatever. I still do not know what it was that stood there, looking at me, with such a remote, liquid gaze that night of the full moon.'

Somehow, the vision powered the writer's work, which now flowed stronger and more inspired, she says. Ever prolific, she tapped away with renewed impetus and by the time of her next encounter, four years later, Sophie had long since filed away the mystery of 'Third Night'.

Once again, she was off to Sydney, to launch a book and catch up with a dear friend and her husband. Over a cheerful restaurant dinner, talk turned to spooky matters, and Sophie leaned in as her friend's husband spun a yarn about a witch who'd enchanted children in the village in the central European country where he'd been raised.

Back at their place, where Sophie was staying, she closed the door of the spare room, which was right by the front door, and went to sleep. At 2.30 am, she woke up with a start. The front door was open, the low buzz of voices coloured the night. 'Oh, hello, how are you?!' she heard, clear enough to detect puzzlement in the voice she couldn't recognise. Was it male or female? Telling herself it must be her friend or her husband, she listened, worrying over what could draw visitors at this hour.

A breeze tickled the wind chimes hanging outside the spare room.

She was drifting back to sleep as she heard the voices fading, then heading outside down the steep garden path. 'Suddenly, I heard a gunshot and a scream,' says Sophie. 'When you live in the country, you hear gunshots,' she says. 'I knew what it was.' Now she was wide awake and sitting up in bed, thinking somebody had just killed one, or both, of her friends. Petrified, shaking, her heart slamming, she sat, straining to hear. 'Then I heard the upstairs sliding door open, slowly, deliberately. I thought, *Oh my God, this person is now coming into the house to see if anyone is left!*'

On the end of the phone, I think of Truman Capote's *In Cold Blood*, the classic non-fiction account of a family slaughtered by two gunmen in the middle of the night. In the thick of the instant, for Sophie too, everything she'd read and watched which had unfolded in this way flashed before her.

'But nothing had prepared me for the fear. I was *beside myself* with fear, I was so afraid, I was almost not afraid, if you know what I mean?' she explains. 'I was just sweating from every pore. I thought, *I can't stay here and not defend myself.*' She quietly slid to the wardrobe and pulled out a coat-hanger. Above her, she could hear footsteps, the steady paces of the shooter planning his next move.

'I straightened out the coat-hanger. I was thinking in that cold, clear, insane way that when they come in, I'm going to jab them in the eye. I thought, *I am not going to let them kill me*.' Behind the door, she waited. And waited. The wind chimes sounded high and clear, like a child's laughter. 'Finally, I thought, *I'm going to have a look*, I couldn't bear to stand there any longer. I opened the door very quietly and looked out into the corridor. The moonlight was streaming in. It was perfectly quiet and still.' Checking the front door, she was shocked to find it shut and locked. Her friend's bedroom door was closed, all silent within.

Still in 'this heightened state of bizarre fear', she crept upstairs to try the sliding glass doors. They, too, were shut and locked. Now, the chimes were still and not a sound punctured the slumbering house. 'I stood there feeling stupid,' says Sophie. 'Stupid, but relieved.'

When the sun rose, Sophie wondered if she'd dreamt the terror. 'But then I looked down and there was the coat-hanger, and I knew it wasn't a dream.' Over breakfast, her friend flinched at the story, and said she had no knowledge of a murder in the home she'd adored for thirty-five years. It would be easy enough to find out, but Sophie is not digging for it. 'Something uncanny passed me by that night, and I find myself not wanting to know what it was,' she says, adding that the only time she has ever been as petrified was when she thought the light plane she was travelling in was about to crash.

'One good thing: at least now I'm not scared by horror films,' she sums up. 'Nothing can match the reality of it – the strangely ordinary face of extraordinary terror.'

THE INTRUDER

'I didn't think for a second he was a ghost.'

It was a golden time in the life of book publicist Emma Rusher. The career woman was busy planning her wedding, her mind brimming with fabric swatches, seating plans and the challenge of finding the perfect gift for guests. On this autumn night in 2007, she decided to turn in early, her account manager fiancé, Alex, still out on the town at a swanky fashion launch.

At 10 pm, she climbed the stairs to the loft bedroom of their little sandstone house, looking forward to losing herself in one of the tower of books perched on her bedside table, and then sweet dreams. Built in the late 1800s, their home was a narrow workers' cottage – 'as wide as a Volkswagon Golf,' says Emma, with a laugh – in Balmain, one of Sydney's oldest suburbs. Formerly a working-class hive of dockland workers and labourers, today the area is a bustling, affluent pocket of the harbour city, a magnet for artists, writers, professionals and young families.

When Alex arrived home an hour later, he had a surprise for Emma. Smiling sleepily, she propped herself up on an elbow to see. 'Look,' he said, and slivers of light poured out of his pockets. He explained that the party organisers had offered fistfuls of tiny Swarovski crystals as a little something for his upcoming wedding. Delighted, Emma fell back asleep, imagining her guests' tables twinkling with the scattered gems.

But another surprise lay in store.

'I woke up, and leaning over Alex's bedside table, there was a man,' says Emma, who'd been plagued by broken sleep since the couple had moved their bedroom into the loft. 'He was looking at Alex's watch.' Her husband wears a large, eye-catching wristwatch with an interchangeable 'stamp-like' face, explains Emma. People often ooh and ahh over it.

She drew in her breath with a gasp. She summons the sound for me and it's loud, like wind whistling through a gash in a window pane. 'He was so real I actually thought we had an intruder, I really did. I didn't think for a second he was a ghost.' Though the stranger didn't pick up the watch, Emma could see him peering

22

at it, inspecting the twenty-first century curio. She could sense his interest in it. 'Alex was quite happily sound asleep,' she laughs, 'and this guy was quite happily checking out his watch, and his hand was stretched towards it. I got the feeling that he was a bit of an opportunist, a bit cheeky, thinking *Oooh, I could have that.*'

Lean and muscly, but not very tall, the forty-something man stood only centimetres from her partner's head. With a swoop of her stomach, she realised, by his overall 'greyish colouring', that he wasn't alive. She sat up, her blonde hair in a tangled tumble around her shoulders, and stared at him. Heart racing now, a staccato 'oh oh oh!' fled her throat, verbal hazard lights. Hearing Emma's voice, he calmly turned his head in her direction.

In her polished tones, Emma brings to life her unexpected guest. 'He had very short hair brushed forward, sort of like a bowl cut, and steely blue-grey eyes. He was wearing a heavy cable-knit jumper and he had a pattern going around from the shoulder down across the chest and back around to the other shoulder. He wore fitted, worker-type trousers with boots that came halfway up his legs. He was a wharfie or a worker. I could draw him, if I could draw!'

At this point, it dawned on Emma that she could somehow pick up on the personality of the intruder. 'I knew that he just didn't really care about me seeing him, because I was a woman. He wasn't scared, this wasn't *my* house. I felt like I was inconsequential to him.'

Then, as if he had an eternity (which he may well have), he made a move. 'He backed away,' says Emma. 'It was a very tight room, our bed basically filled the mezzanine floor, and he backed away. Then, because I was making so much noise and poking him, Alex finally woke up and went "Huh? Huh?" By this stage, the ghost had started walking down the top three steps and I looked at him. As soon as Alex said, "What?" he disappeared, and he was looking at me when he vanished. It was like a switch was flicked off.'

23

Next to evaporate was Emma's fear, bulldozed away by anger and outrage. 'I just couldn't believe the audacity! That's what I was thinking. I went from shock and fear to *How dare you fossick about in our bedroom while we're sleeping and not care that I saw you!*'

If Alex wasn't yet wide awake, hearing his fiancée exclaim, 'Oh my goodness, I've just seen a ghost!' is sure to have done the trick. He listened to Emma's eerie bedtime story, then shared one of his own, proving perhaps this hadn't been the first time the wharfie had snooped around their home. As Emma learned, Alex also had broken nights, often waking bleary-eyed to what he thought looked like a man in 'chain mail'. As the intruder's jumper was such a heavy cable-knit – 'like something from Ireland,' she says, 'a hundred per cent wool' – Emma speculates that Alex may have been describing the weave of the garment.

Intrigued, Emma broached the subject with some long-time residents of her close-knit cul-de-sac, and found out that a previous tenant of her home had also sworn to have seen a ghost. Also, a large timber yard had once stood across the road from the house, its driveway – where scores of blue-collar workers filed in and out each day – directly opposite their house.

Emma accepts that she must have the medium's knack, because there have been other encounters. In the winter of 1997, she was living and working at a boutique hotel in Scotland. When a baby's shrill cry wrenched her from sleep one night, she assumed a guest's child was restless and thought nothing more of it – but then came the dreams. For the next week, Emma had a recurring dream which placed her on the hotel's second floor, dashing down the corridors, searching for the wailing infant.

Oddly, in her dream, the hotel's walls were covered in green, fleur-de-lys wallpaper, quite unlike the building's present-day, contemporary finish. 'I mentioned my dreams to the landlady,' says Emma. 'Though flustered, she wasn't surprised. Before renovations, the corridors had just that wallpaper! Over the years, many guests reported a crying baby disturbing their sleep. But there were never any children checked in on the nights of their complaints . . .'

A couple of years later, back in Sydney, Emma unwittingly invited a ghost home with an art deco dressing table she dragged from a Bondi street at a council clean-up. 'She was a very sad girl, I was quite upset by her,' says Emma, of the forlorn young flapper who materialised by the dressing table when she was home alone one night. 'She really wanted to tell me something, but I was too scared and told her to go away. I wasn't ready for that kind of experience, then.'

As for her brazen Balmain intruder, though she has flipped the moment over and over in her mind, Emma has come to no firm conclusions. She wonders if the crystals, with their supposed mystical properties, might have lured him to her room that night? And despite her previous experiences, she cannot help second-guessing herself. 'You do start to doubt yourself. You think, *Was it just a dream? What was it trying to tell me?*'

'But the thing was, I went to bed so happy that night, we were about to get married and it was just a really nice time in our lives – we were thinking about the future. Something like this would have been furthest from my mind. But I do believe that I saw a ghost. I really do.'

∽

Is your heart beating a little quicker? Don't be surprised. Ghost stories are as much about what is felt as what is seen; shared sensations that knit together the storyteller and the reader. When Emma Snowden pinpoints the sense of being needed that woke her that chilly night, many of us are sure to relate. As a mother, I know exactly what it's like to snap awake, alert to the slightest change in the atmosphere that tells me that one of my children wants me by their side. Robyn

Levett's story turns this idea on its head: here a ghost responded to her unvoiced desire for warmth by pulling up her quilt, before hushing her back to sleep. And Robyn didn't fight it, or shrink with fear; she merely answered the tenderness of the gesture.

It was a revelation to me how large a part emotion plays in these ghostly tales, and how perceiving the emotion may take precedence over the stunning visual aspects of the experience. Warmth, compassion, maternal care, familial unity, haughtiness, surprise and bald terror all play a part in these stories. Even though Emma Snowden and Emma Rusher can describe their phantoms in minute detail, it is the memory of knowing how their ghost felt that resonates most powerfully.

However, for those of us who weren't there, it's the appearance of the spectres that haunts. After all, when we're resurrecting the experience in our minds, these are the details we'll call on: a chubby-cheeked toddler with pleading eyes and wispy, blonde hair tucked into her scarf. A stocky fisherman wearing a woollen jumper with a weave like chain mail. A perfectly still lady in a pencil skirt and buttoned-up blouse. And a dead family, wearing the long-rotted fashions from a costume textbook. Stowaways from history. Stowaways from death. Are you still thinking about how that little boy crept closer to Amy Shepherd, his bony finger crooked towards her?

You're not the only one.

AWAKENINGS

Triggering a Psychic Gift

'There was something awesome in the thought of the solitary
mortal standing by the open window and summoning in . . . the
spirits of the nether world.'
SIR ARTHUR CONAN DOYLE

I have been intrigued by the idea of what may trigger a dormant psychic gift and/or mediumship ever since my husband suddenly began to see full, *Sixth Sense*-style apparitions in our home soon after he began to meditate. Apart from the small boy I described in the introduction, he saw a woman in a red nightgown stride down our hallway, and later, a solid little girl he was certain was our daughter, Jasmin, until the real Jasmin stepped out of another room. It was a summer's evening and we had just finished having dinner outside. The sun was still up when he charged into the bedroom, where I was folding laundry, to tell me in a shaky voice – his green eyes big as saucers – what he'd seen.

All of these sightings occurred over a period of around four weeks. During this time, I didn't see a thing, but toys would crash to the floor in the middle of the night in my son's room and I could feel a charge in the atmosphere within our four walls, like the air before a thunderstorm. Once, a heavy wooden candleholder perched atop a tall cabinet in our lounge room fell with a clatter onto the floorboards a second after I'd walked past. If it had hit my head it would have left an angry bump. Startled, I flicked the light switch – it was morning, but it's a dark room – and the globe exploded!

Neither of these events ever happened again (despite my jumping up and down on the floor to see if I could make the candle-holder fall). So to have them occur in sequence at a time when my husband said ghosts were roaming our little Californian bungalow – dodging toys and baskets of washing, no doubt – seemed very strange to me.

The full materialisation is said to be extremely rare, so why then was Anibal suddenly witness to this prized paranormal event? Was it because he already had the potential and meditation somehow freed it? If I start meditating, will I too lock eyes with dead people in my hallway? Not exactly, though it would be a step in the right direction because, 'the main way in to developing your psychic functioning is quietening the mind, developing your spirituality,' says investigator and psychic medium Robb Tilley.

So, while my third eye might begin to flutter open if I take up meditation, the signs of my psychic awakening are likely to be subtler than my husband's, because my natural gifts are simply not as powerful as his.

'Anyone could learn to do what I do, in the same way that anyone could learn to play a piano,' continues Robb, 'but there are always going to be some piano players that are much better than the rest of us.'

Eminent US doctor of parapsychology Jeffrey Mishlove has explored ancient and modern methods for cultivating psychic ability, and lists three principle routes to psychic development:

'Accidental' – occurring after events including accident, illness, surgery or near death experience; 'Non-intentional' – the consequence of another kind of training, such as yoga or meditation; 'Intentional' – occuring during training specifically aimed at developing psychic skills.

However, after decades of research, 'I am not convinced that these abilities can be developed,' Mishlove explained some thirteen years later. 'I think they are *natural*, however. And I think that we can learn how to stop blocking these natural abilities.'

Australian psychic Mahta Manzouri agrees. 'Clear and strong mediumship is only truly passed down from one generation to another,' she opines. 'You cannot learn psychic mediumship, but this is not to say that no individual does not have an instinct for intuition. In fact, we all do.' Debbie Malone concurs. Though conceding that 'some people can bring it through via learning or development,' the Sydney psychic medium, whose own gifts emerged after a series of near-death experiences and a miscarriage, believes 'some people are born gifted.'

Of these, some remember being three years old and stretching pudgy fingers towards spirit playmates. For others, as Debbie puts it, 'a light bulb goes off at certain times in their lives' and rough patches, like health crises and the loss of a loved one, may spark their ability to 'see'. Anne Kidd can certainly relate to that theory: despair over the deaths of her mother and unborn child threw open the gates of her psychic ability, and it flooded out, thick and fast and uncontrollable. 'Trauma can awaken a strong intuitive and psychic ability,' explains Kerrie Higgins, a Sydney healer who studied parapsychology for six years and teaches courses for developing spiritual awareness.

Alissa Pantazis, a twenty-nine-year-old supermarket manager from Newcastle, New South Wales, also found that her psychic medium skills flourished following a traumatic event. Prior to this astonishing awakening, Alissa had only experienced the odd premonition:

'After my father passed away from cancer in April 2007, I had a number of things happen that were out of the ordinary, but what was to come was totally unexpected and life-changing for me. At first I thought these feelings, such as my arms moving almost involuntarily, were signs of my father still being around, but as time passed I began to think otherwise and went to see a medium, who was able to tell me that a man who'd died the same day as my father, named Paul, had stepped into my aura. The medium asked me if I knew of the man, and yes, I did. He was a rep who'd visit my workplace regularly to take orders, though I only knew him by face. He'd died [aged forty-one] in a car accident on April sixteenth, the same day as my father.

'The medium tried to move Paul's spirit on, but within twenty-four hours, he returned. I suddenly began to do automatic writing [when a medium channels information from a spirit using pen and paper, often in the spirit's handwriting] with Paul, who gave me family names and phone numbers. It was like being on MSN with him! When I asked him what he wanted from me he told me he wanted to go home and say goodbye to his family, as he hadn't expected to die. My next question was, 'Why me?' He told me I had the ability, he recognised me from my workplace and he knew I would help him.

'I spent the next ten days trying to contact his family in Melbourne, finally finding the words to explain why I was calling. The first name he gave me was Daniela, who turned out to be his sister, the same age as me. On the phone with her, I felt foolish at first, because she was asking questions about relatives who'd passed and Paul didn't know the answers. He said, "I don't know that because I'm not there yet," meaning the spirit world. He was an uncrossed spirit. 'Get her to ask about what happened yesterday, get her to ask about the funeral,' he said. [I spoke to Daniela Lucciantonio, who says she was alarmed when Alissa, a complete stranger, described in detail the cemetery where her brother lay, though she'd never clapped eyes on it. Alissa was also able to tell Daniela that Paul was always with her in her car, sitting in the back passenger seat on the right. 'That was the spot where the window would always fog up,' says Daniela, 'though nobody, bar a few close family members knew this.']

'After a long phone conversation, during which I answered detailed questions I had no way of knowing,' continued Alissa, 'his sister agreed to meet me at Melbourne airport, so that I could take Paul "home". I insisted on paying for my own flights, to show that I had no other intention than to do the right thing by Paul.

'His mother and two sisters met me at Melbourne airport four days later, and we sat for eight hours as Paul talked through me. By the time he crossed over at 3 pm that afternoon, there were at least twenty of his family members there, a big Italian family who all got to say their goodbyes. It was an emotional, yet amazing, experience for me and his family; more importantly, it showed the power of spirit to everyone that was there to witness it.

'After I returned home, I had an intense three months of tutoring to learn how to control my new ability. I am now a psychic medium, connecting people with loved ones and I get to talk to my father every day. People close to me now also have a new perspective of the afterlife. Paul's family and I are still in regular contact, and I still talk to him every day too. In fact, I know him better now than I did before!'

Retiree Yvonne Saunders, fifty-eight, from regional Victoria, found her way into herself via a different kind of trauma. Like Debbie Malone, a near-death experience during major surgery was the catalyst for her awakening.

'I died on the operating table in 1993. I was floating in a dark tunnel but was not game to venture further. As I lay there, wondering what could be happening, I put my hands to my face and moved my jaw back and forth; I felt completely whole, but very light in body. When I realised that I must have had a cardiac arrest during the operation, an immense fear came over me and I just sang out aloud for God to help me. Then all I remember was a *swoosh*, then doctors covering me in foil blankets. I did not regain awareness for another sixteen hours.

'Since then, over the years, I have seen my deceased parents – my father about five times, and once, my mother and father together – been visited by 'light beings' [enlightened spirits], and seen three of my past lives in my sleeping state. To this day, I continue to have dreams that come true.

'I have finally come to realise that I am a 'light worker' [a spiritually evolved soul whose purpose is to help others] and my NDE [near death experience] was part of my life plan.'

Many spiritualists, mediums and healers agree with Yvonne and Alissa that uncovering and embracing a psychic gift happens as part of a greater plan. 'For the individual who has this gift and is not fully aware of it, their life path will eventually intervene to where they find themselves in the position of removing their "seals" in order to face and explore their gift,' continues Mahta Manzouri, who has extensively studied the psi realm.

Kerrie Higgins expands on this idea: 'Women go through many cycles of change in their lives, and change can push us to uncover new abilities in order to allow us to cope with circumstances,' she says. This was the case for Queensland schoolteacher Isabel (who requested that her surname be omitted). Divorce steered the thirty-four-year-old toward her psychic-medium calling, as she writes below:

'I have been working as a clairvoyant on weekends for the past four years. My work as a spiritual reader began after a divorce and a need to find myself. Rather than taking anti-depressants or jumping into another relationship, I ventured into my spiritual side and found a part of myself that had been lost in childhood: my ability to communicate with the dead.

'I am constantly amazed with my readings for others and my own personal experiences with spirits trying to communicate with me or through me. It began as a "feeling" and developed into more physical communications.

'I believe that it is important for people to develop their spirituality and not to be afraid of what cannot be seen. There is so much good in the world for people to tap into in order to understand themselves and their journey in life.'

Spirituality can also be boosted in pregnancy, when 'there is a growing awareness of the new life and the responsibilities that are ahead,' says Kerrie. 'Women begin to tune into this new energy within them, to communicate, perhaps through dreams or somewhere in the doorway as they drop off to sleep or awaken from sleep. She might become conscious that she has this ability to speak telepathically with the spirit of her unborn child, and begin to use this ability in other areas.'

'My life has been a paranormal experience since the birth of my son in 2001,' writes Larna Bruzzese, thirty-eight, from Victoria. 'I had some stressful moments while pregnant and decided to start meditation. After he was born, I started to notice things. It all started at night, when I would hear my baby cry and I would get up and find him sleeping, then return to bed and hear voices, like a dream, but I was awake. It has increased to seeing and even helping people make contact with the other side.

'Early one morning I had a little boy visit me, telling me he drowned in a pool. I asked him who he belonged to, as in who

I needed to contact, and he said "Sharon." I had a friend named Sharon and I assumed it was her. He continued to tell me he'd died from a seizure, not from not being able to swim. He talked about his mum and gave me a few other details.'

Soon afterward, Larna bumped into an acquaintance called Sharon and understood that this woman, not her friend, might be the person the child was trying to contact.

'I pulled her aside and asked her if she knew of a boy who'd drowned in a pool. She said yes. I explained what had happened and continued passing the messages on and she confirmed my description of the boy. Ten years ago she'd been a police officer and he was a case that she'd been called to – it really shook her up.'

Just as we unconsciously encourage a psychic gift to flower, we also consciously turn away from it. 'I chose to shut down,' is a common refrain among my subjects. (Incidentally, my husband stopped meditating after his experiences. He too chose to 'shut down' and hasn't seen them since.)

Sometimes, a terrifying experience with a ghost or spirit in childhood scars us and we choose to reject our psychic awareness as a way of coping with what frightens us. 'It's not uncommon for people to shut down their awareness following a traumatic experience with a spirit at an early age,' says Kerrie, who helps her clients uncover these memories, heal and move on, usually with a renewed enthusiasm to explore their psychic side. Occasionally, we shut down because it's just too much to juggle, on top of our hectic lives and the demands of partner, family and work. 'People martyr themselves and their opening to spirit in order to keep everyone happy, to avoid losing a partner or dividing the family,' she says.

I asked Debbie Malone what advice she'd offer to all the real-life ghost whisperers among us, especially those who are at odds with their burgeoning gifts. 'You have to really learn to work with them because the more you try to turn it off, the worse it gets,' she says. 'It's almost like they become frustrated with you and will do anything they can to make you work with it. If the ghosts or spirits can see you, they're all just going to go to you. You're like a lighthouse and there are all these lost ships out at sea.'

Set rules, stresses Debbie, work with it on *your* terms. Anne Kidd, whose story follows, eventually realised that it was in her power to set boundaries with the dead who'd stand shoulder to shoulder around her bed every night, drawn like moths to her incandescent psychic light.

That was just one of the many lessons her awakening had in store for her.

OPEN ALL HOURS

'I had dead people turning up everywhere.'

Every night for six weeks, always in the dense dark of 2 am, Anne Kidd woke up shrieking and drenched in sweat, her bedroom a mosh pit of dead people. Silent and watchful figures of all shapes and sizes would crowd around her bed, then vanish with her screams. Something was happening to the advertising executive that she couldn't harness, something beyond the teachings of her conservative Christian upbringing. Desperate for answers, desperate for sleep, Anne knew that if she didn't get a handle on the situation, she was in danger of falling apart. 'I was really frightened, this wasn't *fun*,' she says angrily. 'This wasn't, "Ooh, wow, I'm a cosmic person." My life was completely out of control.'

Sitting in Anne's tasteful period home in Adelaide, it is difficult to reconcile that image of confusion and fury with the softly spoken, urbane forty-year-old sipping wine and stroking her cat on the plush chair in front of me. Only her hair, a halo of burnished ringlets, is unrestrained. Then again, she has come a long way since those broken nights in 2005 when her budding psychic-medium abilities were almost her undoing. 'I've now learned that when this happens to you, you're like a beacon, you're a light, and they can *all* come to you. They just want you to help them, but I didn't know that. I just wanted them to go away.'

You cannot blame Anne for feeling less than hospitable. At the time, she was flailing in a mire of grief following the sudden death of her mother, and the miscarriage of the child she and her husband, Michael, an architect, had longed for. Trauma was the culprit. Pain was to blame. Suffering had somehow activated a powerful dormant gift inside her. It was a gift she didn't care for. 'I didn't see it as a gift or a talent or a blessing, I saw it as a burden,' she says. 'And my poor husband didn't sign up for any of this: Normal girl becomes psychic. *Hello*?!'

What Anne endured in the small hours was astonishing, but so was the trail that led to those six haunted weeks. After years of trying for a baby, Anne and Michael turned to IVF treatment. Not long after starting the physically and emotionally taxing process, Anne's world began to tilt. 'It sounds very strange, but I started to notice really weird things,' she says, looking down at her pale, manicured fingers. 'I'd be typing at work and I'd see colours coming out of my hands.' In 2000, during an acupuncture session, 'a baby appeared in front of me,' she says. 'It was the face of a newborn, a beautiful, perfect baby girl.'

Weeks later, Anne discovered she was pregnant. 'It was wonderful,' she whispers, but an accidental fall seven weeks into the pregnancy robbed the couple of the chance to be parents. Anne was broken, but determined not to lose hope. She decided to see a 'spiritual healer', who advised her, 'You need to evolve more spiritually before this child will come,' which inflamed her. 'You expect, "Your fallopian tubes need seeing to," or something logical like that,' she fumes, 'but I said, "Tell me what I need to do to do this," because you know, I was prepared to do *anything* to try and achieve the dream of a family and children.' The woman suggested Anne join her on a course to develop her psychic abilities. 'I thought, "Oh bullshit, but okay, I'll do it." I was really angry, the *grief* . . .'

To her amazement, Anne enjoyed the course, agog at being granted a pass into a bizarre parallel universe where drawings on display charts leapt to life and mythical creatures danced around the room. 'The strange thing was,' she says, plucking an olive from the fruit-and-cheese platter she'd prepared, 'that I could see the same things as the lady who had brought me. We were comparing notes: "Did you see that? Did you see that?" . . . It's almost like *The Matrix*, there's this world, and then there's another that most people can't see or feel or interact with. I was seeing glimpses of that.'

It was only the beginning. Her abilities were about to burst forth in a way she would never have imagined or wanted. In 2003, her mother, a vivacious and caring pillar of the family, was diagnosed with depression and took her own life.

Anne and her sister, Judy, who'd been staying with their mother and were the ones to find her body, were inconsolable. Weeping, Anne relates a remarkable moment in the hours before her mother's death: 'I was at the shops with Judy, at the check-out, when I'd said to her, "I'm going to have to sit down, I'm going to collapse." So I went and sat, thinking I'm going to faint, and as I was sitting there, I saw a golden cord and it just went *woosh woosh woosh*; it just unwound and disappeared. I thought, *Oh God, what was that?* Later I was told it was my connection with my mother being severed. When we found out the time of death, it correlated.'

For a month, the sisters remained at their mother's home, seeing to the heartbreaking task of packing up what's left behind when life stops. It was when Anne returned to Adelaide, her psychic light charged by a torrent of tears, that the 2 am wake-ups began. 'I was stressed, upset and emotional. I was trying to get my life together and heal body and soul, I was coping with one of the biggest things anyone has to cope with in their life, and I had dead people turning up everywhere!'

Can you imagine?

'Sometimes they were just shapes. Other times, they were so solid, I'd think we were being robbed. I had a woman with a long pigtail, and she had my drawers open and she was going through them . . . Sometimes, my mother was one of the people, which was particularly hard. It was like the channel had opened and I couldn't manage it.' Driving home from work one day, an exhausted Anne was ranting, swearing and sobbing in her car. 'I am so sick of this! It's not fair! I've had enough!' she yelled, thumping the steering wheel. Then a car pulled up in front of hers. What happened next was, 'one of those moments,' says Anne, 'it was vibrant.'

The car's number plate was ASK. A-S-K. So she did. 'I said, "Right, I don't want to be woken up in the middle of the night anymore by these people. I've had enough. You can come between six and eight and after that, it's not on."' She snaps her fingers. 'That night, nothing. I thought, *Ooh, I actually have some say in this!* I found out you can set boundaries.'

Anne believes this was her first lesson. The second was about to unfold. After much ringing around and seeking recommendations, Anne had arranged for a grief counsellor to visit her home for weekly sessions. As soon as she opened the door, Anne knew that the warm and maternal sixty-something Sarah would be perfect for the job. What she didn't expect was that she would bring company.

The trio, including Anne's husband, Michael, was sitting around the lounge room, getting to know each other at their first session, when a heavy, cast-iron candelabra, one of two that perch at either end of the sofa, began to rock from side to side.

'That candelabra?' I ask, pointing. It seems so foreign that such a tall, weighted thing could move of its own accord. Anne nods. Michael must have had the same idea because Anne remembers him saying, 'Has anyone else noticed the candlestick's moving?'

'Then the other one started swaying. Everybody stared at each other but nobody said much.

'Next thing, there was a young man standing next to me, I couldn't see him but I could *feel* him,' says Anne, and something inside me churns. At first, Anne didn't let on, worried about what Sarah would think of her. But the spirit of the youth would not be dissuaded – Anne could feel his hand gripping the flesh of her upper arm.

She blurted, 'There's a boy standing next to me, and he's holding my arm.' Without flinching, Sarah said, 'Oh my God, it's Peter.' Anne had not yet mentioned a word about her psychic abilities, she explains, and had no idea that Sarah's own son had committed suicide two years before. After all, this was their first session. What followed was an impressive display of natural mediumship, with Anne relaying, among other things, a feeling of having her ankles 'wrapped up in plaster casts.' Sarah blanched. 'Do you know what?' she said. 'Six months before he died, he broke both his ankles and he was in plaster.'

This was something. Until that day, Anne had only *seen* the spirits, most of them the colour of skimmed milk. Now they were communicating with her. 'Do I need to see a psychiatrist?' she asked her counsellor. 'No,' Sarah shook her head, smiling. 'You've got the gift.'

Looking back, there had been clues in her past as to what she was capable of, but Anne had ignored them. As a child, she can remember feeling the familiar bulk of her cat, Misty, curled at the end of her bed long after he'd died. Years later, as a twenty-year-old university student, she walked out of her room and screamed at the sight of a slightly transparent, caped, male figure who had 'an elegant and protective' presence, standing at her flatmate's door. Today, she believes this was her friend's spirit guide, but at the time, her first thought was that someone had broken in. 'For six months, I slept with the sheet over my head. But even though it scared me, I never thought I had anything special. I just thought it was there and I happened to see it.'

Anne says she is still an apprentice, still stumbling through the lessons 'the universe' dictates. She now knows how to free earthbound spirits, which she learned serendipitously during a pedicure. Dabbing cherry polish on Anne's toes, the beautician casually mentioned a cranky ghost in the salon who was troubling the staff. 'I can see him,' Anne told her, her eyes clapped on a frowning old man. 'He's standing next to you.' She began to talk to him telepathically, gently explaining that his body had died, that the building was no longer his home, coaxing him into the light. At her next appointment four weeks later, the staff marvelled: 'What did you do? Our ghost is gone!'

'I believe that when people die in trauma or not at the right time, or children are separated from their parents, it's like a mix-up happens,' says Anne. 'They get stuck. And then they're too scared to move on, or they don't realise they're hanging around for years, or even centuries.'

Meanwhile, at her development classes, she is fine-tuning the art of receiving messages. 'They show you how they died through your body,' she explains. 'Sometimes it's a bit scary, but they're only trying to show you. As soon as they get the message across, the feeling goes.'

As for the dead people breaking curfew, for the most part, 'I've got it under control, but sometimes, they just turn up,' she sighs.

'I was lying down on the couch one day when this man walked in and I thought, *Can you get* out? *What are you doing in my lounge room?* He just walked off. I have no idea who he was. It's like the more you learn, the less fear you have, but then there's always more to learn. It's never-ending.'

GRAFFITI

'I could feel it pulling towards me, like a magnet.'

Climbing the stairs to an office in Sydney's bustling Glebe, where I'd arranged to meet advertising sales rep Michelle Garcia, I look up into the face of a pretty young woman whose features are lit by a certain twinkle in her chocolate eyes, like a discovery still unfolding. 'I knew it would be you,' she says, beaming. 'I saw you walking down the street earlier and I said to myself, "I bet that's her."' We shake hands and slip into a neighbouring cafe. We have exactly an hour, and the stories banked inside Michelle flood out.

In 2003, when Michelle was twenty-three, she tried meditation for the first time, with the encouragement of her partner, primary school teacher Trevor. '"It's good for your soul and spirit,"' he promised. The first time she tried it, sitting quietly with her eyes shut, purple light blazed where she expected only darkness. She thought that was 'bizarre', but still had no cause to think the ancient practice would do anything other than help her relax. 'I was well aware of ghosts, it wasn't something I didn't believe in, but I had never had experiences with them, though Mum always believed in ghosts. She used to say, "There is nothing to be afraid of, they are out there."'

Her mother, Leonie, had first-hand experience, having once seen her best friend, who'd died as a teenager in a motorbike accident, eyeballing her from a busy sidewalk. Now, thanks to meditation, her daughter's own sixth sense was inching forward.

In bed, on the verge of sleep, 'I felt like there was definitely someone standing in my doorway. I couldn't see them, but I could feel them. I got all these prickles on my arm,' recalls Michelle. 'I could feel it pulling towards me, like a magnet, it wanted me to know it was there. I felt like I was being drawn to it.'

'It made its way over to me, I could feel it coming closer . . . then I felt like my whole body was shaking. I thought I was having some kind of fit, it lasted about five seconds. I thought I might have epilepsy.' Sipping her juice, Michelle adds, 'there was a really tight feeling, like someone held a rope around my stomach and was tightening it.' Over a period of about six months, this happened at least five times. She says she didn't consult a doctor because she didn't feel the answer lay there. Instead, she visited a spiritualist church. She sought only guidance – she didn't expect an epiphany.

As the medium who ran the service told the congregation about her work and her abilities, realisation crept over Michelle like a lengthening shadow. 'She explained how when you are channelling, it may feel like there is a band around you, and it's tightening. I thought, *Oh my gosh, they are trying to contact me!*' Now, Michelle actually couldn't wait for it to happen again – could she too be a medium?

Two weeks later, she had her answer.

'This time, instead of being afraid, I spoke to it in my mind and said, "You don't have to do this to my body if you want to talk to me." When I said that, everything stopped and released. As it released my body, I just rolled over – I don't know why – and on the right side of the wall behind me, there was writing.'

The name 'George' was materialising in a flowery, cursive script.

'My room was dark but there was some light coming in from the window,' continues Michelle, 'and this was no dream state, I could physically see writing, about fifteen to twenty centimetres high, as clear as I'm looking at you. The writing was calligraphy-style and it spelled George.'

'There was also a date, nineteen-something to nineteen-something, like what you'd find on a tomb. It was pretty quick, it just came and went. I didn't get a proper look at his last name or the exact dates. I just thought it was so strange. After that, a song popped into my head, "Don't Worry, Be Happy." It was as if someone had turned on a stereo! I thought I was going insane.'

But there was also relief. The visits, with their disturbing physical effects, stopped after the writing on the wall. But Michelle was full of questions: why was it her lot to solve this celestial riddle? Who was George? More importantly, what did he want from her? She thought about the house, a modern, non-descript dwelling in leafy Heathcote. There'd never been anything vaguely paranormal there, why now? The questions were paper airplanes drifting in circles inside her head.

Two years later, Michelle met Marcelle, who became a good friend. A year into knowing her, she saw a photo of Marcelle's late father for the first time. Staring at his framed portrait, 'I had an urge to ask, "Is his name George?"' Her friend paled, whispering, 'How did you know that?'

It turned out that George always used to sing 'Don't Worry, Be Happy' to his daughter when she was a little girl.

It turned out that Michelle was an apprentice medium.

If, as some have theorised, the laws of time, space and physics do not apply in the spirit world, could her friend's father have recognised her ability – mediums are said to glow like lightbulbs to the dead – and somehow 'known' that she would befriend his daughter? Here was one who could carry his message of survival to his daughter: the small matter of their meeting being two years away inconsequential, if we consider that to a spirit two days, two years, two centuries is apparently much of a muchness.

Since then, other spirits have singled out Michelle to carry, like a homing bird in flight, their messages of comfort to loved ones. Often when she least expects it. Once, she was searching her database on her computer at work when the name Lynette refused to be found, to Michelle's immense frustration, since she knew it was in the system. Instead, the name kept flashing on the screen as 'search not found'. 'Then I felt a presence standing next to me, and my head drawn to the computer screen. I remembered my aunt's mother had passed away about a month before and her name was Lynette. You get the words as thoughts, even though they are not your own thoughts, that's how they communicate.

As the message came through, 'I had an urge to write down everything she was saying. As I did, I was thinking, *I don't know if my family is going to believe in this stuff*, and I asked her to give me some kind of proof. She said, "Write down that I was there the other day when my daughter was putting new flowers on the "table." I wrote that down. She said, "I have a gold tooth." She kept bringing up aprons. I wrote it all down and thought my aunty can make of it what she wants.'

Her aunt was floored. A few days earlier, she had been arranging newly bought fresh flowers, her mother's mouth had glinted with gold, and her nickname had been 'Linny in her Pinny' for her love of aprons. 'It was confirmation,' says Michelle, 'a way of saying, "Hey, I'm still here. I love you, I care about you."'

Thanks to her newfound skills, Michelle was getting to know another side of her family. Though she has a degree in business marketing and writes music and sings with a band, Michelle is happy to sample a career as medium-in-training. Her tutors have all the time in the world for her, and there are no deadlines. 'Psychic ability is like a muscle,' she says. 'The more exercise you give it, the stronger it is going to get.'

HOTLINE TO HEAVEN

'They watch you. They know where you are. They know what you're doing.'

Debbie Malone is one of Australia's best-known mediums. She has appeared on TV as a psychic sleuth and has done the rounds of talk shows, sharing her passion for snapping spooks with her digital camera. The chatty, auburn-haired mum of three from Sydney's Sutherland Shire would not look out of place selling cakes at the school fete, but what you would never know, as she hands you your lamington, is that she can see the dead who hover at your shoulder.

Chances are she will also hear them murmur in her ear and feel the sting of their last corporeal moments. 'I'm clairvoyant, so I see things; I'm clairaudient, so I hear; I'm clairsentient, so I feel and I'm psychic, so I can see past, present and future,' explains the fast-talking forty-five-year-old former graphic designer. 'But I'm also a medium, so I talk to dead people.'

Debbie believes a series of six near-death experiences – beginning when she was three and hospitalised for bronchial pneumonia – gave flight to her psychic gifts, which she chose to 'shut down', until two murdered women hijacked her dreams and sent them crashing back into her suburban life. One of the most vivid NDEs occurred when she was thirteen and her heart stopped during surgery to remove her appendix. The little girl floated up into the corner of the room and watched with detached curiosity as doctors laboured to bring her back.

But it was not until she had a miscarriage in September 1992, aged twenty-eight, that her gift blossomed; an unstoppable force that would change her life's purpose. 'That was more or less when I woke up and could see dead people,' she relates cheerfully. First came the voices: since a scuba-diving mishap when she blew out her right eardrum, Debbie has suffered tinnitus, a condition character-ised by hearing a constant sound like crickets chirping. Suddenly, unknown voices began to whisper underneath the familiar drone.

Then came the nightmares.

That same month, a trio orienteering in the Belanglo State Forest, south of Sydney, discovered a decomposing body. The next day, another was found, only metres from the first. Police soon confirmed that the bodies were those of missing British backpackers, Caroline Clarke and Joanne Walters. The doomed girls were the first to find their way to Debbie Malone's dreams. 'I knew they were dead but they were alive in my dream. They kept showing themselves walking away, and there was a man with a gun who was making them walk away from me,' says Debbie. 'They were pleading with me to stop it, they kept saying "Please help, *please help*."'

But Debbie 'had no idea what to do,' though she was haunted nightly by ever more detailed dreams of the slain friends. The dreams would differ in perspective – sometimes, she might watch omnisciently as the hellish scene played out; at other times, she would feel the victims' terror, or stare out from the killer's soulless eyes. 'I'd go to bed and see the next chapter and the next day I'd watch the news and the next chapter would be on,' says Debbie. She contacted police, but was dismissed as a 'fruitcake'. Then, a curious turnaround: eventually, what Debbie knew was far beyond the scope of what had been made public, which in turn cast suspicion on *her*. But finally, 'after many months of contact with the police, a breakthrough'. Debbie was assigned two detectives and asked to keep a diary of her night visions.

Belanglo gave up seven battered young bodies in total, and four years later, road worker Ivan Milat was found guilty of the murders (though Debbie is convinced he has killed up to fifteen others). The four-year role she played in the backpacker investigation, though never acknowledged, signalled an important new phase in her life: the acceptance and embracing of her gift.

Raised in Sydney's western suburbs with her parents and younger brother, Debbie knew that she was never alone, even when she lay down to sleep, but when she spoke of it to her parents, she was told she had an overactive imagination. 'I used to feel people in my bedroom,' she recalls. 'I used to always hear voices. It's like hearing a muffled conversation, and I always had to sleep with the radio on.' When she was fourteen, her grandfather died and he would regularly manifest 'like a glow, sitting on the bed.' Though the teenager had made a conscious decision to set aside this aspect of herself – to concentrate on life among the living, not the dead – her grandfather's presence was soothing. 'I just thought that he belonged to me, so that was alright.'

Today, Debbie no longer struggles against her abilities. She has written a memoir, and continues to assist grieving families and police on missing person cases (since the backpackers, she has looked into twenty cases). When she can snatch a moment's peace, this harried mum, whose children range in age from twelve to eighteen, likes to soak her limbs in her backyard 'Swim Spa', a basin halfway between a pool and a spa. But the bulk of her time is spent in another halfway place, a scented room tucked away in suburban Sutherland where she passes on messages from the spirit world to bereaved family members, friends, husbands and wives.

'I think the readings help people move on,' says Debbie, who'll hear the spirit's voice through her right ear (the one affected by tinnitus) and must interpret the image that flashes in her mind. 'Sometimes it's like playing charades because it's like watching TV or video screens going across and if I don't get the message clearly enough, they'll show me again. When I do a reading I have to repeat the exact words I'm told, not like on *Ghost Whisperer*, where she changes it. They don't like that!'

Big personalities don't diminish because they've crossed over, Debbie has found, and a spirit's sense of humour is often the first thing to cross the divide: 'Some people come in and think they're going to need the tissues, but half the time they need them because they're crying from laughter, not because they're sad.' Debbie has many a story to illustrate this lighter side of her work. 'I said to one lady, "Is your father Scottish?" She didn't have a Scottish accent, and said, "Yes, how did you know?" I said, "He's dancing around in a kilt and then he lifted it up to show me and he had no knickers on!" I thought, hmm, right!'

Similarly, she 'saw' a man wearing only a towel, so Debbie asked his loved one if he'd died shirtless, but that was not the message, as both soon realised: 'I just started laughing, and she was looking at me, asking why was I laughing. I explained that he'd dropped the towel and flashed me! She said, "He used to drop the towel in front of me all the time ... You've got him, you've *got* him".' In communicating the particulars of their personality, a spirit can validate their survival.

The only problem is, not all spirits stick to business hours. For instance, 'I'll be standing in the Medicare queue and somebody's tapping me on the shoulder saying, "Tell 'em I'm here, tell 'em I'm here!" It's like, go away!' Asked to sum up what it's like inhabiting her skin, Debbie pauses for thought. 'Interesting, I suppose!' she says with a laugh. 'It's just, oh, it's trying, it's tiring. They're around me all the time, you can't go in the shower without them being there sometimes. Doing readings during the day and then they're all still with me. If they feel they have unfinished business I'll be in the shower and I can hear them, or they'll be there, tapping on the window. And I have to say to them, 'If you're that desperate to see me naked, you can just wait till I get out of the shower!"'

Debbie says her life is just like the TV show *Medium*, where Patricia Arquette – playing real-life Arizona psychic Allison DuBois – receives messages and bumps into ghosts at any time of the day or night. The hit drama was a godsend for her marriage, says Debbie. Her sceptical husband of twenty years, 'understands now. He says, "Is that what you see? Is that how it works?"'

Now, there is harmony in her home life, but coming to terms with her gift proved an unsettling time for Debbie and her family. In 2000, she spent a night alone in a cell in Maitland Gaol for the reality TV show, *Scream Test,* and endured a physical attack by two spirits. 'They just picked me up by the throat. I thought I was going to pass out. I had strangulation marks on my neck,' says Debbie. Even when she got home, 'I had them around me, I was terrified. I couldn't sleep.'

With a sigh, she adds, 'I didn't choose this. It's hard, it's draining, it affects my health. I'm sick a lot, but I wouldn't change a thing. I used to feel sorry for myself but that didn't make it any better. It's like, if you can't beat them, join them.'

Ultimately, Debbie is proud to be a bridge between two worlds. 'I'm the channel receiving their information. I'm not this super-duper smart person, I'm just privileged to be their antennae. It's like working as a team. Everything happens for a reason, and I actually think this has made my life better. If I help people, that's all it's about for me – making a difference. And the amazing transformations I see in people after they've had a reading!' she whoops. 'They might be so completely devastated and for them to get a glimpse of their loved one still being alive, just in another place, that can be an amazing experience and I feel so blessed to be able to give the person that link.'

With six NDEs behind her, Debbie has glimpsed that 'other place', and the memory of an exquisite green meadow bathed in an all-encompassing sense of love and peace will comfort her forever. 'I'm not frightened to die, but I'd like to stay here a bit longer. I figure I'm like a cat, I've got three gos left so I will make the most of those. I think it's a matter of knowing that yes, we do live on, we're not just dead in a box or scattered out in the garden. They watch you, they know where you are, they know what you're doing. They don't miss out. They are around.'

A BIRTHDAY SURPRISE

'This runs in our family – you've got the gift.'

In certain South American countries, the most important milestone in a young woman's life is when she turns fifteen, or *quince años*. Usually, there is a big party to celebrate. Guests dance, dine and honour the teenager who is coming of age, showering her with roses, snapping photos as her father twirls her around the dance floor in a traditional waltz, her gown as white and puffy as a cloud.

For Sydney mother of two Johanna Miscichowski, whose parents emigrated from Argentina in 1970, her fifteenth birthday is doubly sacred. It was the year she learned that, like all the women in her family, she'd inherited psychic gifts. As if teased hair and shoulder pads weren't enough to deal with in 1986, that was also the year the schoolgirl saw her first ghost.

It happened when the family home in Five Dock, New South Wales, swarmed with relatives from Buenos Aires. Johanna's aunt, uncle and two cousins were all staying in the front sunroom. One night, Johanna was going over her Year Ten maths in her bedroom with the door closed and the radio on for company. 'I just couldn't concentrate,' says Johanna, thirty-seven, a warm and cheerful brunette whose anecdotes mingle with her cigarette smoke, so that her words follow me home, clinging to my clothes. 'I kept getting these strange feelings, this pulling, buzzing feeling. It was like someone was pulling me, not from the shoulders but from the inside. I had this feeling I should get up.'

Unable to sit still any longer, though she didn't know why, Johanna got up and walked to the lounge room. 'I was just standing there, I felt so foolish, you know if someone is sleepwalking and they wake up? It was the same. I stood there and looked around, and there he was: my family friend, Eddy. I called him *tio*, uncle, but we weren't related. I knew who he was because it was clearly him as he'd been in life. I could see through him but he was shadowy white, there was shadow where it should be. You could see the detail, it was just perfect.

'Do you know how in the cartoons they look at what they are seeing, then they look away, rub their eyes, then look back and it's still there? I did that. In my mind, I thought *Who are you?* just to confirm I'm not going crazy, and he said, "It's Eddy."' The spirit then motioned for Johanna to come closer. 'He said to me, "It's all right. Go and tell your auntie I'm here." I said "What? I can't do that!"' But she did as she was told, and ventured into the kitchen where the adults were talking loudly over each other around the table. Sheepishly, she tapped her aunt on the shoulder.

'"*Eddy dijo que te diga que esta aquí.*"'

'"Eddy said to tell you that he's here."'

The teenager could not have predicted her aunt's reaction. 'She looked at me and said, "Oh yes, okay, I know."' Puzzled, Johanna looked from her aunt to her mother and back. With no explanation forthcoming, she returned to her room, her head crowded with questions. The next day, she learned from her mother that Eddy, a chef and good friend and colleague of her mum's who'd died of cancer only a few months earlier, had already communicated a specific message to her mother and aunt. His appearing to Johanna was further proof for the women, a gentle reminder of what he needed done.

'Your mother needs to talk to you,' her aunt later confided. 'This runs in our family – you've got the gift, and it's stronger than your mum's.'

At the same time, Eddy was taking a forthright role in guiding his surrogate niece's understanding of her nascent abilities. On another typical weeknight, as Johanna sat at the kitchen table with her homework, her dog Ronny began to yelp and lunge at a dining chair. When he wouldn't stop, she banished him outside, but still he barked. 'Then I got this chill, the same feeling as before,' says Johanna. 'I recognised it now. It's like, if you've ever heard a nice song, or something moves you and you've got tingles all over your body, *that* kind of feeling.'

'So I sat there quietly and thought for a minute. In my mind, I said, *Is that you, Eddy?* He answered, "Yes, I've just come to tell you to look after your mum." At the time, I didn't understand why he said that, but later it all made sense; my parents split up, Mum was on her own, there were health issues I hadn't known about . . .' This time, Johanna couldn't see her *tio*, he spoke through her mind as she sat silently and still with her eyes closed. Then he began his goodbyes. '"It's time for me to go. I've got to go back, they're calling me."' The girl pelted him with questions. 'He knew his answers weren't going to stop my questions, so he showed me, he put a picture in my mind. What a wonderful experience this was!

'What I saw was space, stars twinkling, then a door to a room. People were walking through that door and I was looking through his eyes. I saw all these people just shuffling towards the door, not in any orderly fashion. They were white figures, like Eddy, they were clothed. They all knew where they had to go, that was the feeling I got.' When it was his turn to step through, Eddy looked over his shoulder to signal a final farewell. She never saw him again. 'It was really one of those moments that's never been duplicated,' says Johanna with a little shake of her head.

Thrilled with the encounter – 'I was flipping! Doing somer-saults!' – she innocently told her friends and soon, word had spread throughout her all-girls Catholic school that Johanna had seen a ghost, which alarmed the nuns. 'I was so excited, I didn't think it was anything so unusual. I couldn't understand why I kept on getting blank looks and weird stares. A teacher asked me if everything was all right at home, she thought I might have been a little bit crazy, or maybe making it up to get attention. That's how I learned the hard way – I just had to be quiet.'

Though she tried darting into the tuck shop or bathrooms to escape the religious coordinator, the teacher tracked her down. '"That kind of thing is not normal, you should not be telling the other kids about it, it's unholy . . ."' she lectured. 'I was defiant,' says Johanna. 'I said, "Excuse me, this kind of thing happens in my family, it's not unusual. There's nothing wrong with me." I was so disappointed I wasn't supported.'

The confusing aftermath of seeing Eddy set Johanna on a lifelong quest to learn more, especially as her abilities strengthened. 'A whole bunch of things started happening, and I had no control over them,' says Johanna, who found, for instance, that by touching people's palms, she could describe intimate details about their lives, a talent which scared off at least one potential boyfriend who chatted her up on the steps of Town Hall Station.

Desperate for a sense of belonging, she lost herself in libraries and bookshops. 'It would have been so helpful,' she says, 'if someone had sat me down and said: "This is what happens, this is what we do."' She dabbled in different churches, married her childhood sweetheart at nineteen and became immersed in a born-again Christian off-shoot church that her then mother-in-law favoured. It wasn't the right thing for Johanna, and, eventually, neither was the marriage.

Only now that she has spent more than two decades unwrapping Eddy's fifteenth birthday gift – with the gamut of uplifting to terrifying experiences behind her – does the former flight attendant feel like she knows how to use her ability. Just as well, since she's now herself the mother of a fifteen-year-old daughter, Jessica, whose intuitive gifts are blossoming, right on cue.

Says Johanna: 'I want my kids to know the truth.'

∽∞∾

One day, not long after I finished writing *Spirit Sisters*, I answered my mobile at work. An elderly lady said she'd heard, belatedly, of the stories I was collecting for my book. She explained that, a few days after the headline-making abduction of a child some years ago, the missing child appeared to her and said, 'Tell my mother it's all over.' The woman asked, 'Why me?'

'Because you're the only one I could get through to.'

Spirits are single-minded, as shown by the testimonies in this chapter. If they have a point to communicate, and a medium flicks on her light (or it's switched on for her through any of the various means we've explored) then they won't stop until their message gets through. It's telling that interviewees used similar language to describe a spirit trying to nudge them into action: Michelle Garcia says it was 'like a magnet . . . I was being drawn to it.' Johanna Miscichowski describes a 'pulling, buzzing feeling, like someone pulling me from the inside', and Alissa Pantazis says her limbs moved 'involuntarily' when the ghost was trying to grab her attention.

Their efforts must have worked, because the mediums took up their causes with gusto, at considerable personal cost. Debbie Malone was ridiculed after she called police with information from murdered girls who were steering her dreams; Anne Kidd, who was driven to the brink of a breakdown by the demands of her clamouring spirits, felt compelled to relay messages from the son of the grief counsellor she'd only just hired; and Alissa Pantazis risked humiliation and travelled interstate in her dogged attempts to give strangers parting thoughts from their dead loved one.

Though it may feel like it's out of our hands, the awakening of a psychic-medium gift – or the decision to 'shut it down' – is actually the result of a dainty dance between our inner world and the spirit world, says healer Kerrie Higgins. 'Our feeling and sensing, personal dreamings and considerations that are underlying situations of tension, stress, change and celebration are often not consciously realised,' she explains, 'and yet it is the language that spirit hears.'

Call it heart speak.

TO SLEEP, PERCHANCE TO KNOW

Dreams, Premonitions and Warnings

'Is all that we see or seem
But a dream within a dream?'

EDGAR ALLAN POE

In the introduction, I described my mother Silvia's premonition of her uncle's untimely death. Yet that was not the first time she'd had access to the future. Some years earlier, when she was sixteen, Mum worked in a swanky childrenswear boutique in the Uruguayan capital of Montevideo.

Her working hours were 11 am to 7 pm, but at around 1 pm she began to feel anxious and flustered. She couldn't explain the sensation, but it grew busy inside her, pumping a blunt message to her every nerve ending: GET OUT OF HERE. Finally, she had to act. 'I have to leave now,' she told her boss, who stood blinking in a jasmine-scented cloud as she swept by him, her handbag tucked firmly beneath her arm.

In forty-five minutes, she was home. 'Let's go and see Yolanda,' my mother told my grandmother, mentioning, out of the blue, a four-year-old cousin who hadn't been well of late. 'Good idea,' said my grandmother, Alba, and after picking up Tia Nelly, my mum's aunt who lived next door, the trio hopped on the bus to the humble outer suburb where Yolanda lived with her parents.

Staring out of the window, my mum took in the scenery of her melancholy city: the rusty national coat of arms on the wall of a public school, homes without windows, homes without doors, and vacant blocks of land. Her gaze drifted to her mother and aunt, deep in conversation. Both had painted their small mouths red for the outing.

Finally, they arrived. Yolanda's mother was sitting in the sunshine, sipping *mate*, a South American tea. She looked up and smiled. The ladies stopped to chat, but my mother went straight to Yolanda, who lay in bed, her ginger hair a sunburst on the pillow.

'It was the strangest thing,' remembers my mum. 'I had the fiercest need to be with her.'

The child soon stirred and asked to go to the bathroom. Mum offered to help her, but she shook her head. Swinging her legs over the side, Yolanda stepped into her worn slippers and shuffled away. Not long after she'd hopped back into bed, she drifted off to sleep, her hand inside my mother's.

Suddenly, she opened her dark eyes wide and squeezed my mother's fingers. '*Tengo miedo*,' she whispered.

'I am afraid.'

Her eyes closed again. A drop of blood bloomed on the corner of her pale lips, like Sleeping Beauty pricked by the poisoned spindle, and trickled in a thread down her chin. My mother screamed for the adults. But Yolanda was gone.

What nobody knew that day, though it would soon emerge, was that Yolanda had leukaemia. She'd been diagnosed some months before and the outlook was dire. It seems outrageous, but in keeping with the protocol of the times, Yolanda's parents had been 'spared' the news, and only a couple of the child's elder relatives had been informed. Says my mother: 'There were certain things that were not to be spoken of.'

That Yolanda had been unwell and spent a couple of days in hospital was the extent of my mother's understanding of her situation. There was no way she could have known of the seriousness of her illness, let alone that the little girl's death was imminent. So what force propelled her to the bedside of her dying cousin, where she was able to hold her hand in her final minutes? It's an experience with all the hallmarks of precognition – knowledge of a future event through extrasensory means – and as you'll read below, I've heard from many women with similar stories to tell.

'Precognitive ESP experiences do not usually cover the grand sweeps of time – decades or centuries – often involved in traditional prophecy. Many are fulfilled within minutes, hours or days,' says Louisa Rhine in her book *Hidden Channels of the Mind*. Last century, Louisa and her husband, J.B. Rhine, often referred to as the father of parapsychology, studied this type of phenomena from the 1920s to the 1970s. Their groundbreaking experiments under strict scientific conditions at Duke University in the US appeared to vouch for the existence of psychic abilities such as telepathy, clairvoyance and precognition (but were widely ignored by the scientific fraternity).

Louisa Rhine's book demonstrates that ordinary people, not heaven-ordained leaders, can foresee the future.

And for some, it happens time and again. 'These things have become an almost everyday event,' says Sydney grandmother Judy Mott, whose deeply moving dream led to some life-changing final moments with her estranged mother.

'My mother was in a nursing home and I hadn't been to see her for some time. Then one night I had a dream that my mum was standing near a gate and my dad behind her. I went up to them and my mother put her arm around me and kissed me. I had never been touched, let alone kissed, by my mum or my dad. It is a long story, but my dad always said I wasn't his. This dream made me feel like I belonged for the first time in my life.

'I had this dream three nights in a row, so on the fourth day, I told my daughter, "I must go and see Mum. I think this must be a message from God." On the morning I was going to leave, my two sisters happened to ring (which was also amazing, as we weren't close). They said they were going to see Mum and did I want to go with them? I said I wanted to go alone and would they wait till I saw her first? They agreed.

'When I got there, my mother was curled up like a little baby and weighed hardly an ounce. It was the most terrible sight I had ever seen. I burst into tears and went outside asking, "Where is my mother?" because this couldn't be her, I didn't recognise her at all. I went back in and pulled the blankets off her as she was sweating and dehydrated. My tears fell on her face and woke her. She slowly looked up and smiled, then lifted her arm and put it around my neck and pulled me to her and kissed me.'

Judy's mum died three weeks later. She was ninety-three and had just given her middle child the first and last kiss of her life.

According to my interviews and correspondence, information received may concern tragedies close to home, as with Yolanda and Judy's mum, right through to global crises, like natural disasters or the death of a world leader.

French translator Micheline Ratcliffe knew a week before the rest of the world that JFK would die with a bullet to the brain. 'Strange things have happened to me during my life; whether they be attributed to psychic awareness, precognition or simply good old-fashioned gut feelings,' says the Queenslander. 'As a child, I would often "see," "feel" or "dream" of events before they happened. This was perfectly normal to me until I realised that not everybody had the same experiences, so I started to pull back and stifle these feelings.' Micheline was twenty and working as a nanny in London when she had an explicit dream foretelling President John F. Kennedy's assassination seven days later, on the twenty-second of November 1963.

'In my dream, President Kennedy and his wife were in a car and then he held his head with his hands and there was blood everywhere. I saw a lone man in army fatigues running away. He was carrying a type of machine gun,' recalls Micheline, who watched the scene play out from above in full colour. She will never forget, for instance, how clearly she could see Jackie Kennedy's pink pillbox hat. 'There was no sound in the dream, it was like watching a silent movie.' Disturbed, the young nanny shared the dream with her employers the next morning, and also related it in a letter to her mother.

'As my mother's birthday is on November twenty-second, I had a card ready to send her, but I felt so overwhelmed by the dream that I included a short note telling her about it. The card arrived in France, where she lived, on the morning of November twenty-two. With the time difference, the shattering news of Kennedy's assassination did not come on TV till that evening. My employers called me into their lounge and we all stood there, speechless. My mum wrote several days later telling me how eerie it had felt hearing the news bulletin after having received my card in the morning.'

'I have had many premonitions in my life, but the Kennedy experience was the most significant for me because I had actually spoken and written to people about it,' says Micheline. 'It's always easy, after the fact, to say, "I knew that," or "I dreamt this" . . .

sometimes I would even doubt myself. But this premonition had been shared and then validated.'

It's also apparent that dreams are often (but not always) the channel for tuning into the future.

'I had a very vivid dream about my mum five months before she died,' says South Australian mother of two, Joyce Hammond. 'She was walking down a dusty road with our old battered weekend suitcase. She looked very ill with purple circles under her eyes. I said, "You are off then, Mum?" "Yes," she said. I did not think any more of this until I returned to the UK suddenly at the news that she only had weeks to live due to leukaemia. I arrived at the hospice and was with her when she died two weeks later. The purple circles under her eyes were just like she had in the dream.'

A joyful outcome can also be glimpsed in dreams, as Queensland nurse and mother of eight Enya Rub learned. 'During the last school semester in 1989, my triplet sons were offered a place at a prestigious boys' school in Brisbane. We travelled from Bundaberg to Brisbane for an interview with the headmaster. After talking to my sons for a while, the headmaster sent them out to look around and he and I talked money. I told him that I was on a deserted wife's pension and could not afford any fees. He replied that the boys would be wards of the school and all meals, tuition, board and uniforms would be provided, "all found, no strings attached."

'At this, I burst into tears. You see, I had had a dream some time before all this. In the dream, I was at a small hotel in a small town and needed to get money from the ATM, but I couldn't find one. As I stood there in the hotel, I became aware of a "being", angel, man – I don't know – standing behind me and he said, "Don't worry, I will give you money, *all found, no strings attached*."'

Anne Lawler, forty-five, a Sydney customer service manager, met her child in a dream six years before she held her in her arms.

'At the time, I had been married for a few years. I was a career woman so having children was the furthest thing from my mind, but I did know it would happen one day. In my dream, I remember being in a unfamiliar room, standing in front of a little girl with long hair who was sitting on an old lounger and behind her was a big window with the sun shining through the fine lace curtains. Her face was a shadow, but I could see the outline and shape. In the dream I was talking to her but when I woke up, I had no idea who she was or where I was or what it meant.

'The dream really hit a nerve. It sat with me for a few days and left me feeling quite strange and wondering what it was about.

'Then, about six years or so later – I had two little girls – I ended up getting a divorce and moved back to Sydney when my girls were three and five. I ended up purchasing a little house with my settlement and this house was a cute little cottage and the living areas had large bay windows that let in lots of sun. One of my favourite rooms was the family room that in the morning captured the sun through the fine lace curtains. I'd sit here to have my morning cuppa on an old lounge someone had given to me and the girls would do their hair and finish getting ready for school and day-care. I was a single working mum.

'I remember crouching down in front of my five-year-old daughter and doing up her shoes; she was brushing her long hair. I was looking up at her with the sun behind her and we were talking about the day ahead. As I was doing up her shoes, I suddenly stopped and took a huge gasp. I'd suddenly remembered the dream that had been in the back of my memory all these years and just stood up staring at my daughter with the sun behind her. My daughter looked at me and said, "What is it, Mummy?" and I told her that I had dreamt this very moment many years ago. I remember feeling quite faint and very strange.

'It really blew me away and has confirmed to me that life must be set out for us. I never knew I would end up being divorced let alone in a house raising two little girls on my own, yet this was all in my dream.'

Belinda McKee is certain that a recurring nightmare saved her little girl's life. 'In 1986, I was attending TAFE, while my daughter had just started school. Her after-school routine was to my walk to my brother's house with her brother and cousins, and wait there for fifteen minutes until I arrived to pick them up.

'For a week, I had a recurring dream of my daughter being hit by a car outside my brother's house, while playing with her cousins on bikes. The dream would always wake me and I'd be in tears, night after night. One afternoon, on my way to collect the children, I needed to go to the shops. I was about to turn into the shops, when my dream hit me like a ton of bricks.

'Needless to say, I went straight to collect my children. I never had the dream again after that day. I believe if I had gone to the shops, my daughter would not be here with me today. I believe the thought saved her.'

Apart from dreams, precognition may manifest as a powerful feeling, a vision or a voice. Amelia Andersson has had all four – just one of the anonymous women in our midst who live with the stunning knack of peering into the future. Her dreams have foretold fiery plane crashes and the deaths of people she knows, while her visions have warned her of harm coming to loved ones. The seventy-two-year-old from South Australia chronicled 'a few of the incidents I can remember,' from the 1950s to the present, in a compelling point-form letter. 'I am one of a large Scottish family. Many of us are psychic, or fey, as it is called in Scotland,' she wrote. 'I see and hear incidents, both when I am awake and asleep.'

Scattered like petals across Amelia's memory are moments like these, all of which occurred while she was awake:

'My children were watching TV. I walked past and glanced at the screen. I saw a newsreader sitting at the news desk in the TV studio. A woman came running into the studio and stabbed the newsreader in his right side. My children did not see this, they were watching a cowboy film. When the film ended, the news came on. The first thing mentioned was the stabbing of the newsreader by his ex-girlfriend.'

And this: 'I saw my mother in a car crash. Her face had smashed into the windscreen. She was unconscious. Her legs had been smashed under the dashboard. She had multiple fractures. I could smell the smoke because the car was on fire. I saw this three months before it happened.'

And finally, in 1985, a snapshot of a teenager's doom: 'I was leaving a friend's house. I passed a large window. My friend's seventeen-year-old son was sitting at the other side of the window. He smiled and waved to me. I smiled and waved to him. At the same time, I could see five points of flame dancing and weaving above his head. I felt very sad. Two weeks later, he was in a car fire and died the next day in Royal Adelaide Hospital.'

'I have had no training of any kind,' says Amelia, whose pre-cognition is just one thread in the fabric of a long, full life. 'The incidents happen and are totally out of my control.'

Queensland public relations officer Julee Robinson was also awake and going about her day when she experienced precognition. The warning saved her life. The fifty-two-year-old felt a warm, firm hand pressed against her stomach, stopping her from stepping into the path of a reckless driver, as she relates:

'In 1996, I was working as a consultant for a weight-loss company, and it was my turn to buy milk for our coffee break. To get to the coffee shop, I had to cross a four-car lane without traffic lights, instead, there was a garden divider in the middle.

'I proceeded to the corner, which was always busy and waited for the cars to stop so I could cross. I had just passed the second car when, out of nowhere, a third car decided it would try overtaking the two cars that had stopped for me. I walked past the first car, and was just passing the second car when I felt this incredible warmth pressing against my stomach, which held me back from taking the next step. I didn't see the third car, only felt the breeze as it passed me by and heard the screech of the tyres breaking to a halt just past me.

'Unsure of what had just happened, and somewhat dazed, I continued to the middle of the divider and looked over at the driver of the third car, who had his head in his hands and was looking back at me, shaking his head. I bought the milk and heading back to work, the whole scenario was going over and over in my mind. *What just happened?* I asked myself. *Did I really feel that hand touch me? Why was I saved?*

'To this day, I can still remember how that loving hand felt, with its warmth and love. That day, divine love and intervention stepped in and saved my life, and I'm still here to tell this story.'

Maryanne Lindsay, sixty, a mother of three from Victoria, had an almost identical experience. 'On my way back from the shopping centre, I was standing at the intersection: the "Walk" sign turned green and I proceeded to step off the kerb – one foot on the road – when, at the last minute, a small white van made a right-hand turn on the red light, right in front of me! It was so close, I could have touched the doors. How it never drove over me still amazes me. But even more amazing was the feeling of some invisible force, or shield, that seemed to have been between me and that van.

'It drove off, as I hastily stepped back onto the kerb, then I took a deep breath and crossed the road. I remember the looks on the other drivers' faces. I don't even know how I managed to continue walking without crumbling, but I felt a bit euphoric. I like to imagine that it might have been one of my guardian angels or spirit guides who'd intervened.'

Karamia Masry would tell her it's so. She first met her spirit guide as a teenager. He saved her life one summer's night and has been by her side ever since.

GUIDING LIGHT

'I heard the voice, saw the face, and it saved our lives.'

The sun had just slid into the west, its burnt orange embers still licking the sky, one scalding Melbourne night in 1971. It was the summer when the blockbusters *Love Story*, *Airport* and *M*A*S*H* ruled the box office, and friends Karamia and Peta, both eighteen, were treating themselves to a flick at the local drive-in theatre. Peta's green Austin Lancer was among the first cars to pull into the Village Essendon complex, its P-plate rattling at the rear. As the friends whooped and giggled, Peta cut across the parking rows in the darkness instead of following the roadway. Adulthood, careers, travel and romance lay before them like reels of unfurled film. But it almost ended right there, before the show had even started.

Karamia Masry was in the passenger seat when a face appeared at her window with the order, 'Tell Peta to stop.' Her hair's-breadth hesitation made the face angry. 'TELL HER TO STOP!' it shouted, and now she obeyed. Her friend reacted to the alarm in her voice and slammed the brakes. 'Almost immediately, a car passed at high speed across the front of our car,' says Karamia. 'If we had not stopped, my side of the car would have taken the full impact.'

'I heard the voice, saw the face and it saved our lives,' says the now fifty-five-year-old telephone crisis counsellor, who lives in the Victorian regional city of Bendigo. She believes the male face and voice was that of her spirit guide. 'He looked to be in his thirties or forties. Clean face, no beard. It was a bit like looking in a pool of water, not overly clear but enough for me to see.'

The girls had stared at each other, all hopes of a fun night forgotten. Peta, especially, was a jumpy mess; the shock of what happened and what might have been was too much for her. With a trembling hand on the ignition, she said sorry, but they'd have to go straight home. 'She asked me over and over how I knew to cry out to her given that neither of us saw the other car *until* it had passed across the front of our vehicle,' recalls Karamia. 'Peta realised what a close shave we'd had and was stunned and very shaken, as she'd not experienced anything like that before, whereas I was not a stranger to this type of phenomenon. I had been experiencing it in various forms since my early teens, though not quite so dramatic as this . . .'

Karamia has precognition. Like many of the women in her family, she is psychic, as she's known since she was fourteen, growing up as one of six children in a Catholic family. In her sleep, she receives messages from spirits and her spirit guide, which she passes on to others only if she feels it's appropriate. Karamia tends to keep her abilities to herself. 'I'm not interested in earning money off this, or interested in doing it professionally, because I don't believe I can turn it on and off,' she says. 'It comes and goes at its own pace.'

Five years after she averted danger at the drive-in, Karamia had a baffling out-of-body experience – only two decades later would she finally understand it. 'I was hanging out the washing one day when I felt myself in the high country on an unsealed road at the scene of a truck accident. I didn't see myself, I was looking through my own eyes, it was like I was watching a film,' she explains. 'The truck had gone over the embankment and there were lots of people around, rescuers and police. I was standing across the road watching and was quite overwhelmed but not frightened. I had a good look around the site so if I came across it, I would know the spot.

'I knew that no one had been hurt, but could not understand why I was there,' says Karamia, who rushed to call family members, as some of them were truck drivers. But nobody had been in an accident.

More than twenty years later, Karamia met a cousin who'd been given up for adoption as a baby. She invited Brian to her home for Christmas lunch and the group was enjoying trading stories about their lives when the man made casual reference to an accident he'd survived in his youth. 'He told us about when he used to drive an army truck and had crashed over an embankment in the high country area of Victoria,' says Karamia. The comment sliced through the jovial chit-chat around the table.

Karamia broke the silence by asking him to elaborate: 'Was it around the early 1970s? Had it happened during the warmer months? Could he describe the scene?'

The details perfectly matched her long ago vision.

Karamia was left to wonder why she'd clairvoyantly witnessed Brian's accident all those years before. 'Perhaps it was just a connection,' she muses. 'I talked to him about this at the Christmas lunch and told him that perhaps it was a way of people on the other side showing us that he was a family member, even though we didn't know it yet.'

Occasionally, Karamia picks up information that serves a more urgent purpose. In 1990, her father Bob lay ill at his Bendigo nursing home. On the morning of his death, Karamia awoke convinced that day would be his last. 'I rang the nursing home and was told that he was fine, his condition was as it had been for months. But I've learned to listen to my inner voice.' She called her five siblings and suggested they meet at the nursing home, where the staff could not understand the panicked gathering.

At around 11 am, seventy-seven-year-old Bob's condition deteriorated dramatically. 'At around 6 pm that evening my father passed away,' she says. 'But the warning had given us all enough time to get to Bendigo to see him before he passed, and he knew we were all there as he was lucid until the last few minutes.'

In 1994, she received a precise alert in her sleep: she had *one week/seven days* left with her sister, Kate, who'd been diagnosed with cancer three years earlier. Though she had just returned from spending a week interstate with her ailing sibling, she did not hesitate to make the drive back to her. Karamia watched with a mixture of devastation and relief – that she'd returned – as Kate's condition worsened. 'Kate passed away on the Sunday – one week, seven days after I'd received the message.'

A few years later, when Karamia was in her late forties, she had another premonition of a loved one's imminent demise – with a twist. Asleep beside her de facto, Jed, Karamia stirred in the small hours to see her good friend, Billy, at the foot of her bed. 'He was floating towards me, just his head and shoulders,' she says. 'I sat up in bed and he came forward and kissed me on the lips. I said, "Billy, what are you doing?" because we didn't have that sort of friendship. We were friends – if ever, he would have kissed me on the cheek, but never on the lips!

'He said, "I've come to say a final goodbye."'

Karamia shook awake Jed, her partner of twenty-eight years (they have since separated, partly because he couldn't come to terms with her abilities). 'I said, "I think Billy is dead or going to die." Billy's farewell kiss came at around 3 am on a Thursday morning. Karamia spent the weekend waging an inner debate about whether or not to pick up the phone to call Billy. And then, there was no need. On Monday morning, Billy's daughter called with words Karamia expected, but never wanted to hear. Billy was dead. He'd had a massive heart attack around midday on Friday.

'In hindsight, I probably should have rung him and said, "G'day," but when you have experiences like this, it affects you significantly, and it's hard to have a normal conversation without showing emotion. If he were to have picked up that I was upset in some way, I wouldn't have been able to bear it.'

However, there was one powerful moment when Karamia had no foresight of an upcoming tragedy – but felt it in motion. In February 2004, her brother Tony collapsed of a fatal heart attack. Karamia was around twenty kilometres away, working outdoors with Jed on their hobby farm. 'I felt a huge pain in my chest, like being kicked,' she says. 'I could hardly breathe, and thought I was having a heart attack, although I was fit and well. I asked my partner to take me to our house – I could barely talk. As I staggered through the door, the phone was ringing.'

Karamia's sister was calling with dreadful news. Though ambulance officers were still working on Tony, they could not revive him. Hearing this, the physical pain in her upper body disappeared, to be replaced by the more savage ache of loss.

Though the death of someone close is never an easy matter to live through, Karamia is grateful for her gifts because they've blown wide her understanding of life and what's beyond it. 'I have no fear of death, and to be honest, view it as a homecoming, where I will be reunited with my family and all of my beloved pets,' she says. 'I truly feel sorry for those people who just do not believe that there is another dimension, plane, or whatever we call it. I have absolutely no doubt that such a spirit plane exists. I also have no doubt that we are watched, protected and guided along our way, and I feel privileged to be sensitive enough to experience actual contact at times of need or duress.'

Her spirit guide also helps her reach out to others. In an echo of her night at the drive-in, here is what happened to Karamia and her lucky friend, Samuel, in 2007. 'One night, I was in bed sound asleep, and at about 1 am, I woke up screaming his name: "Samuel! Samuel!" Something was terribly wrong. I grabbed my mobile and rang him. He said, "I'm out of the car. I just fell asleep at the wheel, something jolted me out of it at the last moment. I was so frightened." Driving home from a work meeting, he was within feet of going off the edge of the road when his eyes snapped open.'

Did Samuel somehow telepathically 'hear' his friend's voice calling his name? Or perhaps he heard the voice of his own spirit guide. 'I firmly believe each person is allocated a guide at the time of birth,' sums up Karamia. 'That guide is with us until the last breath.'

BRIDE IN BLACK

'For several days, I had this sense of foreboding and heaviness.'

'I have dreams which I know are warnings,' says Freda Grossman, who was holidaying in Italy in 2005 when her late parents appeared to her in a dream awash with blood. 'I knew this meant illness of some kind. They were trying to warn me to take care.' Two weeks later, her husband suffered a stroke. The seventy-six-year-old retiree from Melbourne has a lifetime of 'knowing' fluttering in her wake, like a ribbon held to the breeze. She relates some of her experiences below, beginning in 1950, and ending in 2008, when a gothic dream prophesied a monumental loss.

'We came to Australia [from England], leaving a much-loved grandfather behind. He gave me a ring before we left which I had made two sizes too small and pushed it on my finger (to this day, the ring cannot come off). I was at work, and suddenly the ring flew off my finger across the office. I went home and told my mother that something was wrong with Gramps, and the next day, a letter arrived telling us he was very ill.

'Ten months later, one Friday night, I dreamt that Gramps was with me and I was telling him he had to eat and to get well, as he had lost a lot of blood. I awakened to my mother crying. A telegram had arrived telling us of his passing.

'In 1988, my father-in-law gave me a beautiful Siamese cat. This cat and I were inseparable and on the same mental plane. He always knew when I was upset and would come up and stroke my face. One day, as I opened the door for him to go out, I looked at him and thought, *I won't see you again*. He was missing for ten days, and I tried everything to find him. One night, I dreamt I had found him under a bush in a garden. He was terribly injured and I only recognised him by his nametag. As I looked up, I saw a woman pushing a pram and a large tree.

'I told my husband, but he said it was just wishful thinking. Two days later, I met an old man in the street and showed him my cat's photo. He told me he had seen it and pointed to a house on the corner. I knocked on the door of the house and the woman who answered said I could look around their garden. Needless to say, Cammy was lying under a bush there and so badly hurt that I couldn't recognise him at first. I looked up, and there was a big tree and a woman pushing a pram. Unfortunately, Cammy died soon after.

'Around the time of my birthday, in July 2008, I dreamt I was a bride, but dressed in a black dress with a white Peter Pan collar.

'I looked to my side and saw people looking at me through a doorway. I did not recognise the faces, but my deceased mother was getting me ready. In front of me, a small distance away, was a crowd of people seemingly waiting. I looked down and said to my mother, "I am a bride and have no flowers." She immediately said, "I will get you flowers from the ceremony area." She came back and gave me a small bunch of white flowers.

'I cannot possibly tell you the amount of dread I woke to, knowing dreaming of a wedding means a death, and for several days I had this sense of foreboding and heaviness.'

Freda's husband, who was diabetic and had kidney disease, was hospitalised on 1st August and shortly moved to intensive care, where he spent eight days.

'I phoned the hospital on the Monday,' Freda continued, 'and they told me he had responded so well to the dialysis that they were putting him back in the ward. I saw him that night, which incidentally was the fifty-ninth anniversary of the day we had met. He put his hand out to me, smiled and squeezed my hand. I now realise he was saying goodbye.

'He complained his right arm was aching, and that he couldn't hold the spoon for his meal and I fed him, but he was alert and lucid. He was even cracking jokes.

'I spoke to him on the phone at 9.30 am the next day, and he said he'd had a bad night. At 11.30 am, the cardiologist phoned and asked me to come to the hospital as he'd had a bad turn. When I arrived, the light of my life, my whole world, and the only person I ever needed or loved was gone, just four days before our fifty-fifth wedding anniversary.

'So you see, again my mother was warning me of disaster coming.'

CATCHING UP WITH NICOLA

'I thought you were dead?'

Tasmanian mum of two, Deb Cashion, thirty-eight, has always leaned towards the notion of a world beyond our own. She describes herself as an 'empath' who began reading tarot cards in her teens. Though she has always had a 'sense' of knowing what was to come, she says she'd never experienced anything of note, until one night when a curiously detailed dream preceded some shocking tidings, as she wrote to me in May 2008.

'When I was in high school, I had a very in-your-face girlfriend, Nicola. She had many ups and downs, especially with a violent partner, and after high school, she and I partied a lot. I last saw her when I was in my early twenties and we lost contact soon after. I had thought of her over the years but could not get in contact with her.

'In 2008, on the night of the 18th February, I had a dream in which I was wearing a very eighties-style business suit – black short skirt, white shirt, black jacket – with my hair tied back, and I was waiting with others to go into a large, nondescript grey building. There were about 100 of us waiting and I felt nervous. I had the sensation that I was waiting for an interview. Just then, someone tapped me on the shoulder and I turned around. It was Nicola wearing the exact same suit as me and with her hair tied back. She touched me on the shoulder and said, "It's so nice to see a friendly face, I was scared but now I'm ready to go in," and then the door opened and we all moved in.

'We sat apart and I was about two rows ahead of her. A man appeared. He was tall, with greyish-red shaggy hair and a three-day growth. He was wearing rumpled beach-wear (tropical shirt, linen trousers, shoes with no socks) and he started to speak. Well, he spoke to me in my head, because his mouth never moved. His speech was slurred, similar to the voice of a deaf person, but I understood him and he was saying, "I need you to give 100 per cent if you are going to work for me, I need commitment. People need the truth and I need you to deliver it," and as he was talking, he pointed to people in the audience. One of them was Nicola and she got up quietly and left the room via a door on the right.

'The man sitting next to me shook his head and said to me, "I can't understand a word he's saying," and then he got up and left via the left-hand door where we'd come in.

'The meeting finished and those of us he hadn't pointed to left the way we came.

'*Very strange*, I thought, when I woke up, remarking to my husband that I had dreamt about a person I had not seen for years. We got up and went to work.

'That morning, I received an email from a friend reporting Nicola's death on the 16th February. I was shocked.

'Last week, I dreamt about her again. In my dream, I was visiting a house and I rang the doorbell and Nicola answered. She had hair longer and curlier than I remember and I recall pushing her hair back off her head and seeing a scar on one side of her forehead. She was standing there patting a bulldog. "I thought you were dead?" I said and she answered, "Are you sure I'm not?" and motioned for me to come in.

'When I walked in there were children crawling around on the floor and Nicola pointed to them and said, "I regret not having those two now." Then she asked, "Would you like to go get a drink?" Okay, I said, and got in a white car with her and reminded her to put on her seatbelt. We ended up at a wine bar where she talked to me over a glass of white. "I didn't mean to do it," she said, "but he made me angry and I drove angry. My problem has always been to blow things out of proportion but I didn't mean it." And the dream ended.

'Yesterday, after speaking to Nicola's sister, I found out that she died in a car accident after leaving her house early one morning to search for her fiancé. She'd injured her forehead. She was not wearing a seatbelt and she was angry. She had a fight with him over going out for a drink (he wanted to and she didn't). To top this all off, she had a favourite bulldog she'd lost a few years earlier and lost two children before they were born. A final "Oh, wow," came when the sister sent me a photograph of Nicola just before she died. She had longer, curlier hair.

'I do believe in life after death and think that spirits need to fulfil things sometimes before going on to the next world or life.'

THE VIEW FROM THERE

'Her voice was neither a command, nor a request. She simply said, "Come."'

Writing *Spirit Sisters*, I've been fortunate enough to meet women with the most astounding life stories to share. Even setting aside the paranormal element, I have heard from women whose histories merit fat biographies and films starring Meryl Streep. Queenslander Sandra James, fifty-four, is a prime example. At the age of twenty-nine, she survived a gruesome car accident that killed her husband, Ray, forty, and left her with three children, two step-children, a piggery and a dairy farm to run. While you're processing that, consider that in the seconds before the accident, she left her body and travelled to an achingly beautiful afterlife, which she recalls in brilliant detail. Sandra's wonderful story sits in this chapter because precognition is an everyday part of her world – and because a celestial being's warning saved her life on a narrow wooden bridge in the country, on a day when Christmas filled the air.

Sandra set the scene for me: 'I have always been aware of having "episodes" which other people do not share, and once I understood that I was the one who was different, I kept things to myself. My experiences are usually only for my own benefit, and the warning only comes at the last minute, when I can do nothing but act on pure instinct. Once or twice, I have "known" about someone else. It always begins by hearing someone call my name. It does sound so much like a "person" calling, that I have to look to make sure it is not, but it has saved my life time and time again.

'My husband and I were dairy farmers . . . we were heading home from town, a long drive at the best of times, but this day my husband had been cleared by our doctor to go back to work. The kids and I had been doing all the work, and Ray had to stay home for a whole week – to a workaholic it is a lifetime – and it felt that way to me too. I was not happy that Ray had decided to have a facial skin cancer removed for an upcoming family wedding, because no farmer in their right mind has surgery at such a busy time of year, and we not only had cows to milk, we also had a large piggery, with an upcoming contract with Woolworths, which was harder to get than a chook with teeth.

'I had a strong feeling for almost a year that I could not understand. I had heard the voice, as usual, but the message was like nothing I'd had before. On the one hand, I believed it foretold of my impending death and that I should, and did, get my affairs in order, but Ray did not believe in such things, and I would not have told him anyway. Being left alone with the kids would have scared him to death. I did what I could without Ray knowing, to get things in order.

'On that Wednesday, we had to pick up all the meat we'd sent to be "dressed" for the large extended family that Ray had, and the kids' Christmas gifts that we'd kept on lay-by.

'The station wagon was full. I was so tired, but happy too, because Ray had kept two of the older kids home from school to help him, while I was to rest, then sort out the meat and wrap and store the presents. We passed through the ticket gates at Mallanganee as we always did. We spent a few minutes talking to Digger (we always called him "Digger", I doubt I ever knew his real name) as we always did on the way home, but something was not the same. I had just realised that Ray had not turned the radio back on, but was talking instead, he was so happy to be going back to his animals, and I do admit to wishing he'd be quiet for a while. I had never felt so tired.

'Then it happened, only this time it was a shout, not the usual call, but despite the terror I felt, I just could not move.

I had been resting with my head against the car door, and I was still in this position when I heard the voice. It was neither male nor female, but because it sounds so gentle and kind, I believe this is why people, especially children, refer to it as she. I can also see why we think of them as guardians, or angels or both, and it's because they are not on the ground, and while they may not have wings, we see it that way to explain their ability to "hover". She was outside my window, a silhouette of a form, and her voice was neither a command, nor a request, she simply said, "Come."

'It's the most compelling word I have ever heard, but my need to warn Ray that something was very wrong was stronger. I realised then that the voice had always been in my head, and that now there was no need for words, she knew what I wanted to do but would not allow it, and she said once more, "Come with me," and reached out her hand. I went.

'I still wanted to look back and while my body did not move, I could indeed see. I saw myself and Ray and the car, now a few feet away; every detail was clear, but nothing moved, time stood still.

'When I took the next step I was filled with the greatest joy I have ever known. My form filled with a light I knew would burn my eyes if I were still physical, and then I took the fourth and final step, and this life and every memory of its existence was gone. It was to be the most profound experience of my life, and over time I have come to understand some of it, the significance of it. The whole sky was of the brilliant light. At first I thought it was coming from God, but little by little I realised it *was* God, his being. It is a contradiction, for everywhere there were people. The sounds of so many should have been deafening, it should have been crowded, but it was all of these things at the same time, and yet it was totally empty. I was a part of the whole, myself, yet a part of everyone, and they a part of me.

'Then, when I looked at one particular spot, it became a park of sorts, the grass was so green, and there were so many children, laughing, playing, and as I looked from one place to the next, I could see other things, or another part of the "place" (is as good a description as I can manage), but it was the tiny children. Surely some could not have even been born, they were so tiny, but all of them were crawling over this huge lion, in intensified colours and their behaviour was so *normal*.

'The lion allowed the children to climb, to ride, pull themselves upon him by his mane, and he yawned and licked his paws as if it were his own babies playing with him. In all my time there, the lion was the only one to be identified by gender (because of his mane). When I looked up, people were walking and talking with each other, some on the ground but most above it, and I could join them if I wanted to with a thought, but I could also be alone and see any wonder I chose. Then I was with some people in a park, at the top of a hill, and I was put into a bubble of some kind, and as the light came in it was tinted gold, but it was the feeling of complete trust, joy and contentment that has been the everlasting impression.

Then I was rolling in this bubble, down the hill, and as I started to wake inside the car, I heard myself laughing. I don't know how long I was 'away' or how long it took to realise I was back.

'The after effects of the journey were not easily pushed aside, but slowly, this life came into being again. I still could not move for some reason, but out of the corner of my eye I saw Ray sitting as he had been, both hands on the steering wheel, and I saw a little movement, but I was still stunned, and believed he had had the same experience as I had. I said, "Can you believe what just happened?" but when he didn't reply I wasn't worried; I was still getting used to being back, too.

'Finally, of course, I had to move, and I didn't understand why the creek should be in front of me when it should have been on my left. Then I realised we were on the little wooden bridge that ran over the creek, and it was the *car* that was facing the wrong way. Again I tried to move and felt pain that woke me up quickly. I still didn't understand, but I knew something was wrong. At first I thought the bridge had fallen into the creek because I was wet, but I soon saw it was blood.

'I undid my seatbelt after pushing stuff off my lap, and opened the car door. I couldn't move my legs for all the Christmas meat and broken glass on top of them. And then I saw Ray's side of the car and there was not one item on him or near him. I couldn't believe it and let him know it. It finally got through to me that there was something odd about him and when I really looked at him I knew he was dead. I knew it, but I couldn't believe it.

'The movement I saw was the blood running down his shirt that made it look like a heartbeat.

'While from my view he'd looked completely normal . . . I knew I'd have to go to his side of the car to be sure. What if I could help him?

'But I couldn't have. I must have wandered away after going back time after time to make sure that what I saw was real, and I really could do nothing. Because the car was across the bridge, effectively cutting it in two, I was on the Bonalbo side of it when the ambulances came and Ray was on the Casino side. Even this seemingly random event was to have huge consequences. Bonalbo is a very small town, the hospital did not even have an x-ray machine and because I had walked away from the accident, it was assumed I was okay, and when asked I said I felt nothing much, even though there was a lot of blood everywhere.

'Ray, on the other hand, was taken to Casino, and the first one to see his body was the doctor who'd treated him a few hours earlier. He'd had no idea that it was Ray, someone he'd seen only a few hours ago, and it was quite a shock to him. As I said, viewing Ray from his left side . . . he looked perfectly normal, but the whole right side of his head and face was missing. A piece of wood from the bridge had broken off in the impact of the car hitting it and bouncing around it like a pingpong ball. It was a million to one chance that everything would conspire for that exact thing to happen at that exact time.

'The police later told me that if I had turned my head, even slightly, to the front or the right, I would have died too.

'It was a very difficult talk with the police, because I couldn't answer their questions without saying I didn't know if there were animals or other cars on the road that may have contributed to the accident, because I wasn't there – technically – so I had to say I'd been asleep and could not help them. They put it together in the end, but none of us will ever know exactly what happened. The doctor said Ray could have blacked out for a minute due to all the excitement he felt; maybe he just lost concentration for a second. It doesn't really matter, because I had known all along that something was going to happen, and while it turned out not to be *my* death I'd felt all that year, I was in fact close to death in another way.

'But I have no doubt that his death, that day, in that place, was exactly the way it was supposed to be. I was not meant to warn him or die myself, although I do admit that, during that first very hard year I did envy him, being the one who got to stay, and I had to come back and do all the hard work, and I still do envy him, to some extent. But I also know that when I get back there, it will seem like only a second after Ray has got there. There is no time there and one other thing you get to know, almost the very second you've taken that fourth step, [and that] is the knowledge of *why*, to everything that ever was and ever will be. I know I still have that knowledge, I just don't remember what it is. And no one will ever convince me that the place I was taken to was not heaven, and if it's not, then it will do me just fine.'

There were some wonderful accounts I had to leave out of this chapter, for lack of space. Dreaming or sensing the future, or receiving a warning, appears to be something many of us have experienced at least once, while for others, like Amelia Andersson, it happens so often that it's just another part of life.

Dreams seem the most common vehicle for information about the future (or a past we should have had no knowledge of, such as Deb Cashion dreaming the details of her school friend's final moments) and some of these fulfil an important purpose. Judy Mott's dream allowed her the opportunity to make peace, of sorts, with her mother on her deathbed; Belinda McKee is certain that a recurring nightmare of her daughter's accident prevented it from playing out in life and Freda Grossman's gloomy dream of being a bride in black primed her for her husband's hospitalisation and passing.

Other precognitive dreams are merely bite-sized pieces of the future, displayed to us for who knows what reason? There was no way Micheline Ratcliffe could have prevented JFK's assassination, yet she watched it unfold a week before the reality. Anne Lawler's sunlit dream of her future daughter seems nothing but a preview of her future, a trailer for the film of her life.

The warnings speak a language of their own. Could they be an externalisation of the potent intuitive gifts inside us all? Even so, that they present so physically – 'I felt this incredible warmth pressing against my stomach,' says Julee Robinson, and 'Some invisible force, or shield, was between me and that van,' recalls Maryanne Lindsay – is intriguing. Stranger yet, the voices that portend calamity, as heard by Karamia Masry and Sandra James, who both also caught glimpses of the guides or guardians behind the words.

At the other side of their encounters, these women emerged charged with life, touched by grace – in a sense, reborn.

THE FIERCEST LOSS

When a Child is Gone

'So has a daisy vanished
From the fields today
So tiptoed many a slipper
To Paradise away.'
EMILY DICKINSON

This is a tearstained chapter. For me, it was the hardest to write.

To do so, I had to open my mind to the unspoken terror that gnaws at every mother's heart. The mothers whose stories feature here all *confronted* that very fear, the horror of their child's death, and were prepared to pick anew at their wounds to tell me about it. All are walking lessons in courage and survival.

It is no exaggeration that my conversation with Kath Campbell one stormy autumn night upended my world. As she described her girls' deaths in a car accident, a profound understanding and appreciation unwrapped itself inside me. Just one room away, I could hear my children laughing and talking. That night, I fell to my knees at their bedsides, showering kisses on their velvet eyelids, humbled to be lucky enough to see them open again the next day.

But these stories are not without hope. Each woman has met the spirit of her lost child and basks in the comfort of knowing that he or she is okay, albeit no longer in physical form.

Louis E. LaGrand, grief counsellor and PhD, calls such experiences 'after-death communication' (ADC), a term first coined by US researchers Bill and Judy Guggenheim in 1988. ADCs come in many different forms, including visitation dreams, and share the same purpose: to help the bereaved heal. Diane Jakubans from Bendigo, in Victoria, waited three years for her son Paul to contact her. When he came, she was enveloped by a blissful sense of calm and warmth.

'In 1986, my seventeen-year-old son was tragically killed. He fell out of the open door of the Melbourne-Bendigo train. He had been drinking and fooling around with his mates on the way home from an AFL football match on a Saturday night.

'I have always believed I was a little bit psychic and really believed I would receive a sign from Paul, but after three years I was beginning to think it wasn't going to happen. While on a holiday, I had visited a psychic in the USA and she had said it would happen one day when I least expected it.

'I was asleep in bed one night, and at about 6 am, I felt like I was in a dream but it wasn't a dream. It was real. I was laying flat on my back, when all of a sudden, there was Paul, standing there looking into a mirror on the wall to my left and he was trying to do something with his hair! He had unruly, thick hair that he was always trying to tame when he was alive.

'He had long, jagged injuries all over the top of his head with stitches in them and his hair was growing between these injuries in tufts. (We were advised not to view him by the undertaker, although he'd said he had done the best he could with his injuries, so we didn't.) He seemed to be in ordinary clothes, like jeans.

'I seemed to be paralysed, I could not move, but could turn my head to the left to look at him. Then he came over to the bed and bobbed down so that we were face to face and with the most serene expression on his face, he apologised for the pain he had caused me and Dad, but not to worry anymore, he was fine.

'Then I kind of instantly woke up and experienced the warmest, tingly feeling all over, right down to my tippy toes. I lay there savouring the moment and could not share the experience with my husband until twenty-four hours later. I actually wasn't sure I wanted to share it with him, but felt I should. He wasn't happy about it and hasn't mentioned it since.

'I have been at peace ever since and rarely feel the need to go to his grave. The psychic John Edward has explained these dreams as visits from loved ones and I believe him.'

Naomi Kalogiros, whose experience of seeing a replay apparition has already been described, gave birth to a stillborn son, William, in the twentieth week of her pregnancy in 2003. Depleted after her ten-hour labour, she had this soothing dream.

'I stood, holding William, in a lovely dark forest with a gravel windy road, and my dad was walking down the pathway. My dad passed away in 2001. He said, "It is time for me to take him," and I said, "No, you are not taking him." He said, "I have to take him, he can't stay with you, he's coming with me." I handed him over and Dad walked away, stopped and waved goodbye and said, "I'll look after him for you."'

The dream was immensely comforting, says Naomi. 'I thought, "Okay, Dad has him, he's okay." In a poignant twist, she adds that for two years after her son's death, her father popped into her dreams, always in the lead-up to Christmas, always with her little son. 'He was showing me how he was growing.' (Many mediums believe that children continue to grow in the spirit world.) 'Since then, there has been nothing,' says Naomi, who last saw William as a toddler. 'I think that is because after two years I had finally released him, I had grieved, I had gotten on with my life.'

British medium Craig Hamilton-Parker, who regularly connects bereaved parents with their deceased children, says these are among the most difficult readings, often because the wall of grief around a parent is too thick to penetrate. Usually, he achieves communication, thanks to a more experienced spirit (such as a grandparent) helping the child come through. 'The medium Doris Stokes often spoke of these children as the lucky ones,' he writes. 'These children are well-developed souls who need only a short contact with the earth in order for them to spiritually progress. As Doris often said, "They are souls that kiss the earth."'

Like Naomi, Maryanne Lindsay, who we met in the previous chapter, also lost a child at twenty weeks, though she's certain she's still around:

'One day, I was out the back hanging washing on the line, when I heard a girlish voice say, "Mum," and at the same time, I felt a gentle tap on the shoulder. I presumed it was one of my girls who'd come home from school, but when I turned around, there was no one there. Very unnerving.

'It wasn't until I began attending clairvoyant readings that I was told I had a child "in spirit." I surmised that the little girl they mentioned could possibly be the baby I lost in 1973. I was told she has blonde, curly hair.

'In 2008, I had a reading and was informed I had four children, but one of these had passed over. She would be in her mid-thirties and has long, blonde, curly hair in ringlets.

'And she lives here, with me.'

Joslyn Roukos, a thirty-three-year-old mother of two from Sydney, is also convinced she met her lost baby in spirit in 2006.

'I was chatting on the phone whilst hanging out my washing outside. As I turned to look inside, I saw a little girl who looked about the age of two or three running towards my lounge room from the hallway. I got angry, thinking my daughter, who was almost two, was out of bed again. I went inside to tell her to go back to bed, but when I got in the house, she wasn't there.

'I thought she must have snuck back to her room. As I was calling out her name, I went looking for her in her room. The door was half open and there was who I thought was my daughter sitting in front of the mirror, playing. I started to tell her to go back to bed and all she did was smile and then disappear.

'I started to panic, but believe it or not, this whole time my daughter was fast asleep in the same room. My partner and I believe that the little girl is our stillborn daughter, Makayla.'

Tearstained this chapter may be, but it's also awash with love.

MISS BROADARMS

'She was fifteen-and-a-half, so alive, so beautiful!'

In the broken days following her daughter's funeral, Angela Wood received a blessing wrapped in the shell of a dream. In the dream, as she waited at a train station, her lovely girl approached her, smiling as she always used to. '"Ohhh!" I said, "Anna, Ohh!" I put my arms around her and I hugged her and I was sniffing at her, smelling her, I was filling up on all these beautiful smells that I recognised of hers. Real. Beautiful. Smells. And I'm running my hands through her hair, and I can remember saying, "Oh, darling! I'm so glad you've come to see me because I'm going to die if I don't see you." And she said, "Mummy, I'm fine, I'm fine, I'm *really* happy. I'm so happy. It's beautiful where I am, beautiful . . . "'

Anna Wood was only fifteen when she fell ill after taking ecstasy and stopped breathing in her father's arms on a spring morning in 1995. In death, she became one of the most familiar faces in Australia, the dimpled grin of the blonde schoolgirl beamed from the front page of every newspaper to remind parents that the worst can happen when your back is turned, that you can love, respect, educate and adore your children, but you can't always protect them. Her smiling blue eyes became code for This Could Happen to You.

'When Anna died it was like our whole world imploded. For all of us, for the whole family – you're never the same person again,' says her mother, Angela, buoyed by photos and oil paintings of her late daughter at her home in Sydney's northern beaches. Cheeky and witty, with an infectious love of life, Anna's big personality still sparkles in the apartment. Statuesque and elegant, but fragile following a debilitating fall down a flight of stairs in 2003, sixty-year-old Angela lives a quiet life with her husband, Tony, and her memories. Corroded by grief, she calls to mind the mother of missing Queensland boy Daniel Morcombe: their powder-blue eyes crystalline wells of sorrow. 'She was fifteen-and-a-half,' says Angela. 'She was so alive, so beautiful!'

On the twenty-first of October, 1995, the Year Ten student and her friends went to a dance party at a city venue, the Phoenician Club, where she took the drug. Her parents had no idea she was there; they thought she was at the nearby home of a friend. When Anna began to feel sick at around 4.30 am the next morning, the group left. Nervous and unsure of what to do, the kids thought they could look after Anna at her neighbour's house across the street. At 10 am, they finally alerted Anna's parents, who rushed over the road to find their daughter vomiting, incontinent and disoriented. Waiting for the ambulance, Angela says Tony 'felt' his daughter pass as he held her on the stairs, but paramedics resuscitated her and sped her to the Royal North Shore hospital. 'It was just awful,' says Angela. 'Every second is like a year.'

At Emergency, the waiting continued for Angela, Tony and their daughter Alice, then seventeen. An exchange student from Quebec, Julie, who lived with them, was also there. 'We were in the little "death room", that's what I call it,' says Angela. 'It's where people who have critically-injured family will sit and wait.' Cramped in their narrow cell, the family hoped for a miracle, and in a way, they got one. 'I saw my father, but my father was dead,' says Angela. 'I looked up and I saw his face and he was *smiling* at me. There was my dad and he wasn't saying anything, he was just beaming at me.'

'"Tony! Tony!"' She nudged her husband. "I can see my dad, can you see him too?" He said, "No, but I can see *my* dad." To this day, we know that they came to take Anna's spirit. I believe that,' says Angela. 'It was no accident, it wasn't imagination, because I said to my daughter Alice, "I can see Grandpa!" And she said, "So can I." Those two men were *there*.'

The uplifting experience was the first of its kind for Angela, but not the last. Seeing the grandfathers, Sid and Eddie, prepared her – prepared them all – for what would come all too soon, and the memory of their joyful, weathered faces will comfort them always. 'This young doctor who would have been not quite thirty, nice-looking boy, came into the room a second time and said, "I don't think I can save her,"' says Angela quietly. 'But by then, we'd seen the grandfathers . . .'

Their daughter was moved to intensive care, where she remained in a coma with a swollen brain for three days, while her family spoke to her and played tapes of *The Secret Garden*, her favourite book. When it was clear that there was no hope, Anna's life support was switched off and the teenager slipped away at 8 pm. Following their daughter's wishes, Angela and Tony donated her organs. 'You never think that you're going to have to make that decision, but that's what we did and we never regretted it.'

Hundreds of mourners, including students, teachers and media, crowded into Anna's funeral at North Shore Crematorium. Anna was dressed in an exquisite red linen cheongsam with black toggling. 'It was absolutely gorgeous,' says Angela. 'She was going to wear it to her Year Ten formal; instead, she was buried in it.'

At the end of the service, when it was time for Anna's white coffin strewn with white roses to slide behind the sheer curtains, the drapes wouldn't close. 'It was the first time that had ever happened in that chapel,' recalls Angela. The staff apologised, but she didn't mind. 'It was almost as if Anna didn't want to go behind the curtains.'

In the aftermath of the funeral, Angela was like a sleepwalker, shuffling through tear-stained days. 'You're numb. You're numb. I can remember I couldn't watch television, neither could Tony. We would sit in our living room sort of stunned, looking at each other.' Alice, whose HSC exams began the day after her sister's funeral, kept to her room and her books. It was on one of these nights, when each hour bled into the next, that Angela had the dream of Anna at the train station, a dream like none before or since. 'I'm not a big dreamer,' she says, 'I'm not the sort of person who always remembers my dreams, but this was *vivid, vivid*.'

In the dream, Anna wore her two school uniforms: the red-and-white striped skirt of Woy Woy South primary, and the green jumper of Forest High. She was radiant, shining with joy, telling her mother that her new home was beautiful, letting her know she was okay. Angela held her tight. 'I said, "Oh darling, it's so good to see you!" and she was saying, "I'm so happy Mummy, I just don't want you to worry . . . but I can't stay, Mummy, I've got to go, I can't stay here. I'm not supposed to be here."'

At that, Anna turned away. 'I said, "Darling, please promise me you'll come back and see me again," and she said, "Oh Mummy, you will see me, but not for *a long, long, long, long* time." Four longs; typical Anna! Anna was full of those words that *expressed* what she thought. And off she went.

'That was much more than a dream, wasn't it?' says Angela, her eyes gleaming. 'I mean, "dream" is the best way to describe it, because I was in bed and asleep . . . but it was very important, it was a landmark.' Whatever the label, it boosted the heart-broken mother, gave her strength to keep going. And she would need it, for in the months to come, Angela would take a very public stance against drugs. She quit her job at a book supplier, and spent four and a half years travelling to schools all over Australia, sharing her story in the hope of preventing another loss like hers. 'We were outspoken. We were parents of this dead girl and she was dead, because of drugs. We wanted to scream and shout that this could happen to anybody.'

One day, Angela was invited to address the audience at the speech day of a prestigious private girls' school in Sydney. Nervous at the thought of speaking in front of hundreds of people, she prepared palm cards, just as Anna and Alice, who'd both completed the Toastmasters public speaking course, had once done. 'My knees were knocking! I could feel them going,' she recalls. At the podium, she scanned all the expectant faces and thought, *What am I doing here? I can't do this. I'm going to fall over.* Then this: 'I felt a warm arm behind me, like that,' says Angela, her eyes moist as she pushes her palm out to show me. 'I always thought it was God; God put his arm around me and said, "It's going to be all right." I threw my palm cards away.'

Today, Angela is no longer a public figure, but she fills her life in other ways. In June, 2008, Alice, now thirty, and her husband welcomed their first child, Reg William. Though delighted with the new family member, recurrent ill health following that terrible fall in 2003 tempered the new grandmother's joy that winter. In August 2008, Angela – who has had a shunt in her brain since late 2007 – was hospitalised after suffering seizures, but later returned to her part-time job as a bank teller. Despite the setbacks, Angela remains positive.

Meanwhile, the months march by, and her youngest child is forever fifteen, though she finds ways to drift into her loved ones' lives.

Putting down her mug of tea, Angela makes her way over to one of her treasures, a photo of a thirteen-year-old Anna, fresh from the shower on a Saturday morning, wrapped in a towel, chattering away on the phone. She is grinning at the camera, focused on a life full of promise stretching for decades ahead of her. At her feet rests a single long, thin gum leaf. After Anna died, Angela would find those particular leaves everywhere – under rugs, on the kitchen floor, in the bedroom, even in the north of England, where Angela was born, and where the Woods operated a pub from 1987-91. She stores them all in a little gold box.

Anna Wood loved McDonald's and Havarti cheese. She was affectionate and tactile, enthusiastic and excitable, opinionated and sociable. She wanted to become a beauty therapist. She adored her parents and her sister. Are all these emotions, these building bricks of a life in progress, suddenly redundant because Anna is gone? Angela doesn't think so. 'It's not the end, there is more,' she says with a nod. 'My daughter's body is not here, but *she* is. Anna was larger than life as a human being, now she's a larger-than-life spirit.'

A year after Anna's death, her father, Tony, had a profound experience that made him change his way of thinking. Nothing like it has ever happened to him again. Lying in bed, very much awake, 'Anna came to me,' says Tony, who'd been waiting for this from the moment his wife had shared her own encounter with Anna at the train station. 'This was real, this wasn't a dream,' he stresses. 'Her lovely face was glowing. She was chatting to me; "Oh, I'm so busy, I'm *so so so so* busy! I've got so much to do, but I'm so happy, Daddy, so happy," she said. "They call me Cathy Broadarms."

'"I'm looking after all the little ones who come here too soon."'

THE SADDEST KNOWING

'Something's happened to Jamie.'

It was three o'clock on a June morning in 2007, and Shayne Wallace was sitting on the back verandah of her Perth home with her sister, Tuesday. As they talked, Shayne watched the tall and slender figure of her teenaged son, Jamie, stride up the driveway and stop by the pool fence. His handsome features were contorted in rage. His mouth stretched wide and he began to scream. '"Mum! What the hell is going on? Mum! Mum, what's happened?"' Sobbing, his mother begged him to come closer – she needed to talk to him. There was something she had to tell him.

Jamie had been killed in a motorcycle accident seven hours earlier.

Five days before his death, the sixteen-year-old had run away from the rehabilitation centre where he was being treated for marijuana and alcohol abuse. He was only one week away from finishing the program. In the last days of his life, Jamie didn't contact his family, friends or girlfriend. Hours before the accident, he broke into his aunt's garage and stole his cousin's motorbike. Riding off into the darkness, he ran a red light and collided with a car. The troubled boy with the winning smile died at the roadside in the arms of a woman who'd stopped to help.

Shayne can recall every beat of Jamie's final twenty-four hours, because from the minute she opened her eyes that morning, she knew death was tip-toeing her way. 'I woke up in a panic,' says Shayne, thirty-four. 'And as the morning progressed, I got more and more jittery.' Her thoughts were full of Jamie, swollen with Jamie. She blurted her fears to her younger son, Brayden, thirteen; wondered why Jamie hadn't called, fretted about where he might be

– over the last few days she'd spent hours driving around, searching, but always returned disappointed, her eyes empty of him.

'I have to go to the police station,' she worried, the seven words circling her thoughts, snapping at her peace of mind. That morning, she reported Jamie missing to the local police, handed them a snapshot of the eldest of her three children, the baby she'd had when she was only seventeen. Then she went about her day, trying everything to distract herself from the sense of dread that had settled over her like winter drizzle.

At 8.05 pm that night, an excruciating pain gripped the young mother's chest, convincing her that she was having a heart attack. At that moment, her partner Jeff came tearing up the hallway, yelling that their seven-year-old daughter, Chenae, had suddenly sat up in bed and begun to vomit. Ignoring her own pain, the feeling of icy hands wringing out her heart, Shayne rushed to her little girl.

Just after 9 pm, Shayne's sister called to say two things: that her son's motorbike had gone missing, and that she'd just driven past the scene of a major accident. Shayne's fears were finally taking shape, sucking energy from the atmosphere to manifest themselves life-sized and tangible. She advised Tuesday to report the missing bike. 'I'm pretty sure it's Jamie,' she said. 'Something's happened to Jamie.'

With a phone gripped in each hand – her mobile and the cordless – Shayne dragged herself to bed close to 11 pm. She didn't expect to rest. The mobile trilled at 2 am, slashing her fitful sleep. It was her sister, her voice solemn: '"I'm at the front door," she said. "Can you let me in?"'

The police were with her. The accident, Shayne learned, had happened at 8.05 pm, the very moment her heart cracked in her chest and her daughter had been ill all over her pink quilt. There was a subtle relief in knowing that now that the day had displayed its cards, the fear that had stalked Shayne for twenty-four hours would retreat. In its place stepped forward the stricken spirit of her son, raging in the moonlight.

When Chenae climbed out of bed that morning, some hours after Shayne and Tuesday had huddled together on the back verandah, numb from loss, she was acting oddly. The usually talkative third-grader avoided eye contact with her mum, kept quiet and walked away when Shayne tried to approach her. Eventually, as Chenae sat cross-legged on the living room floor, her mum broke the news of her brother's death. 'She burst into tears,' says Shayne, 'but a couple of hours after that, my niece, Cherry, who was twelve said, "Come and have a look at this, Aunty Shayne."'

Chenae was sitting on her bed, and she was having a chat. With Jamie.

'Don't be stupid, you're going to upset your mum,' chastised her cousin.

'Don't worry about it Cherry, he's okay,' said Chenae. 'He's talking to me.' And she smiled.

Shayne has always known that her fey daughter with the sea-green eyes has inherited her ability to see spirit. Occasionally she will approach the little girl's room, a basket of laundry balanced on her hip, and glimpse an unearthly child slipping out. Nights go by where Chenae complains of little sleep, because the restless ghosts of lost children crowd around, vying for her attention. 'We've sat down and had a really good talk to her,' says Shayne. 'She's been given strategies and tools to help them on their way.'

That was a crucial step for Shayne, who is determined to help Chenae understand what is happening to her so that she doesn't endure the same confusion she felt at her age. As a child living in a 1930s-era home in the Western Australia goldfields city of Kalgoorlie-Boulder, Shayne was startled by the strange 'people' who frequently appeared at her bedside, including a 'smartly dressed' elderly couple: the white-haired lady in her woollen suit and her dapper beau. 'For a long time, I thought I was crazy, so I blocked a lot out,' says Shayne, who attended Catholic primary and high school. 'I suppose I felt guilty a lot of the time when I was at school, seeing the things I'd see or sometimes hearing random things. I'd think, *If I'm hearing these things and not going crazy, then I must be evil*. It was quite hard and I guess that's why I made the decision to shut it out.'

It didn't always stop them. Shayne says her closest childhood friend was a five-year-old ghost named Sarah, who first came to play around the time that Shayne's dad died, when she was three. All of Shayne's children have made independent reference to a tiny girl called Sarah trailing them. Shayne believes Sarah – with her blonde hair swinging around her shoulders and 'giggly' demeanour – 'attached' herself to her family, and would still be with them today had a psychic friend not 'crossed her over' in 2006.

Shayne, who keeps the books for her partner Jeff, a mines mechanic, says barely a day goes by without a psychic experience of some sort. 'Sometimes, I can see someone just standing there, plain as you and I, and then I glance away and look again and they're gone. Or I'm in bed late at night and I hear the front door slam shut, so I get up, knowing I'm going to find it shut and locked. Sometimes, there will be tapping, or knocking on the front door; sometimes I can be sitting outside having a coffee and there is someone standing in the garden. And then they are gone.'

In November of 2007, famed psychic John Edward toured Perth. As he paced the stage, from left to right and back again, expelling his trademark rocket-fast messages from the afterlife, Shayne sat mesmerised in the audience. Edward was not alone. Hundreds upon hundreds of people surrounded him, all of them crammed onto the stage like so many peak-hour commuters. 'Can you see them?' she whispered to her mother-in-law. A stage full of souls tilts the atmosphere: to Shayne, the entire room felt zapped by something like an electrical current.

There is a difference, Shayne says, between the energies she sees. 'When they've crossed and come back, there's a more loving energy surrounding our loved ones. When they are lost souls [who haven't crossed over] and I see them, there is confusion around them; I don't see them in bright-coloured clothing, I see them shrouded in grey or black. Sometimes they appear with lanky, almost greasy hair. It can take an awful lot to convince those ones to cross.'

While it was obvious that the first time she saw her son on that fatal night by the pool he hadn't crossed into the realm of light, Shayne is certain that he has since found his way. Today, she is also more accepting of her ability – she'd rather not call it a gift, since it's not always so – and its role in assuaging grief. 'A lot of experiences I've had in my life growing up have all led me to prepare for Jamie's passing; I can't explain it any other way.'

On the anniversary of the teenager's death, his family and friends scattered his ashes at his favourite spot, the dazzling Lesmurdie Falls, twenty kilometres east of Perth. 'It was a moment of great healing,' says his mother, 'and he appeared the night before to let us know he was happy and that we were doing the right thing. We all felt a release, that he is finally free.'

THE HOMECOMING

'They're all gone, love.'

Side by side, the girls floated down from the corner of the room. Their arms were wrapped so snugly around each other, they seemed fused as one. This was how they'd always been. They called out – '*Mum!*' – and the sound was cloud music, silken and unearthly. As she lay on her side, tears bled from their mother's eyes and pooled into her ear. Now, she could go on for another day.

On March 5, 2004, Kath Campbell was on a mini-holiday in Melbourne. At the last minute she'd decided to join her husband, Greg, on a business trip, leaving their two daughters in the care of their paternal grandmother. Kath had just bought Jessica, eight, and Rebecca, nine, new swimmers and was walking back to the hotel with her husband and his colleagues when one of the men, Steve, answered his mobile. He listened for a moment then fell to the ground.

That same day, Kath's father-in-law, Ash, was tinkering in his shed at his home near Taree in New South Wales. Then, his veins turned to ice and he heard the voice of his wife, Barbara, yelling, 'Ash! Ash! I need help!' He felt compelled to rush inside and turn on the radio. The first thing he heard was that there'd been a horrendous car crash on the Pacific Highway at nearby Bulahdelah. He jumped in his car and headed straight there.

Back in Melbourne, the collapsed man's wife rushed over to him to see what was wrong. Then, to Kath's rising horror, the woman also dropped onto the footpath. The pair then picked themselves up and made their way to Greg and Kath.

'They walked across the road to us absolutely howling, fallen to pieces. That was when they tried to speak to us,' recalls Kath. 'They said, "We need to get back to the hotel room because the police want to see you. There's been an accident." And I've just gone, "Oh no, *oh no you don't* . . . Is it Barb? Is it Jessy? Is it Becky? *Who is dead?*" They weren't allowed to tell us, and we were all bawling, walking down the main street in Melbourne, just all four of us screaming.'

At the hotel, the police still hadn't arrived and Kath and Greg were desperately ringing friends and family for any news. Then Greg dialled Bulahdelah Police. 'All of a sudden, he just drops the phone and it smashes on the glass table,' says Kath. 'His head just fell into his hands.' She snatched the phone up. 'It's Ash, love,' said her father-in-law, his voice splintering. 'They're all gone, love.'

The noise that erupted from Kath Campbell's throat was at odds with the quiet Melbourne hotel, at odds with the two brightly coloured swimming costumes folded neatly inside the shopping bag. It was guttural. It scraped and clawed at the walls, and pounded the ceiling. It was the sound of loss bellowing from a mother's womb.

And it didn't stop.

The girls, travelling inside their mum's sunny yellow Hyundai, and their grandmother, Barbara Cheadle, had perished instantly in a fireball, innocently caught in a massive crash involving a prime-mover and five cars on a perilous, two-lane stretch of the Pacific Highway. As the truck ploughed into the back of a car, it bucked up in the air and landed squarely on Kath's car, which burst into flames and skidded 100 metres into the bush, still underneath the truck. Six people were injured, but Barb and the girls were the only fatalities.

'The whole car was squashed flatter than a ream of paper,' says Kath angrily. 'With my family in it.'

Not for the first time during my conversation with Kath, I am struck dumb by her strength. It's a privilege to talk to this gutsy forty-one-year-old who has survived the very worst and, subsequently, has a finely-tuned radar for detecting bull. 'I can't suffer people who are just not genuine,' she says. 'After what's happened, it's painfully obvious. When you've had grown men fall at your feet who could fill a swimming pool with their tears . . . it's just outstanding to see how much people care.'

It was that kind of support – from friends, family, neighbours and colleagues – which propped up Kath and Greg in the weeks after the accident. The coroner held the bodies for two weeks. The day they were released to the family, they held the funerals for the delightful blue-eyed sisters everyone mistook for twins, and their devoted 'Nanny'. At the crematorium, hundreds of sparkly balloons wafted into the autumn sky, but Kath could barely lift her head to watch them float away. Two days later, they would return to collect the ashes. 'It was all I could do to get through the weekend to get the kids back,' says Kath. 'Albeit in a box.'

This is the Monday that would unhinge her. It began with a careless act from an employee at the funeral parlour – Kath suspects he was new to the job. 'He was just totally insensitive. He was going to place all these three boxes of ashes in a plastic bag, and to me, that was like putting a plastic bag over my child's head! I don't even know how to describe it. It horrified me.'

She ran screaming from the office, past the receptionist who stood up in alarm and all the people in the waiting room staring at her, out the front door. 'I swear to God if that building was closer to a main road, I would have stood in front of a truck. I truly couldn't deal with it anymore. So I just waited outside for Greg to come with my children and my mother-in-law and I just cried the whole way home, holding on to these boxes.

'That was the day I was going to end it. It was so hard trying to live life and breathe,' says Kath, who had eaten nothing since the accident except one cherry tomato, and even that made her retch. Their children were 'happy, healthy, well-behaved, awesome little kids,' says Kath, who was riven by sorrow, aching to hold them. 'I would beg Greg, every single night, I would beg him when we went to bed, "Please come with me. I want to be with the girls. We can be a family again."

'It was that night that they came to me.'

At first, Kath kept on waking up, falling back to sleep, then waking up again. She now recognises it as a sign of a visit. Next, she thought she heard her brother's voice, though he lives an hour away. Perhaps he'd turned up at 3 am because he couldn't sleep and wanted to be with them? But then there was nothing and she closed her eyes again. When she opened them the next time, she heard her children. 'It was the welcome home you get when you've been away and you come home and your kids yell, "Mum! Dad!" and run to you,' says Kath. 'It was *that* sort of joy.'

'"Mum!"' shouted the girls, 'and it was absolutely beautiful, just the way it echoed, "*Mu-u-m*!" I don't know, it was a sound I'd not heard before. I thought, *Oh my God, they're here!* And then the pair of them just floated across the room to me. And I could see plain as day, Becky, who was that little bit taller, on the left, and Jessy on the right. It seemed like they were cuddling, with their arms around each other, tight in close together.'

In their long, white gowns, the girls fluttered like snowflakes in the dark room.

'Whenever any of them visit me, my ears ring so loud, it's this screeching, ear-piercing *eeeeeeer* in my ears and I can't move, hardly even to swallow,' says Kath, who was lying on her side with one arm stretched out in front of her. 'And when they've come to me, I've instantly tried to jump up and cuddle them. I didn't care that that was their spirit, I just wanted to give them a cuddle. I was fighting with my arm, it was like a lead weight, I was trying to lift it, and the pair of them put their arms on my hand, the bit that was hanging out of the bed, just below the elbow.

'They both held my arm and I could feel this sensation coming up through my arm into my chest, I felt this pulse. I still don't know what that was for, whether they were trying to make me feel better. I was trying to speak to them, I was trying to ask all those questions that you would if you haven't seen your kids in two weeks . . . I realised I couldn't get the words out so I'm thinking the questions, wondering if they can understand: *Where are you? What are you doing? Who's looking after you? Where's Nanny?*

'I just lay there with the tears pouring out of my eyes, it was the only part of my body that could function. I'm thinking, *Don't blink, don't blink ever,* ever *again, just don't blink.* And then I blinked and surely enough they were gone.'

Kath says that while she has since seen the girls around a dozen times, none of these subsequent appearances have been as powerful as that first time, 'I think because I was at my absolute closest to being with them that night,' reflects Kath, who has also seen the form of Nanny, but less vividly, 'like the heat shimmering off the road.' The visit 'really picked me up and dusted me off . . . It made me feel so good.' Her husband of seventeen years is disappointed that he has never seen the girls, says Kath, but he has heard them. Twice, while staying at Ash's house, the couple has woken to the sounds of lightning-quick footsteps running up and down the hallway. The experience, says Kath, 'made him quietly happy'.

In the aftermath of the tragedy, Greg and Kath, who'd been together since they were teenagers, clung to each other. The turning point was Greg returning to his job as a maintenance coordinator two months later. Though it'd been around ten years since Kath had worked, the bosses encouraged her to join him, giving the former full-time mum filing and administrative tasks. Eventually, she became the personal assistant to two managers and the couple is ever grateful for their employers' gesture, which inched them towards a semblance of normality.

Healing is a work in progress. Often, either Greg or Kathy will sleep in one of their daughter's rooms, telling the other, '"I just need to be with the kids tonight."'

But there is a wonderful new reason to warm to life again.

In October 2008, Kath gave birth to their third child, Thomas Riley. Getting pregnant was a challenge: they spent two-and-a-half years having IVF treatment. After six early miscarriages, even when the home pregnancy test said 'Positive', Kath refused to hope until an ultrasound confirmed the pregnancy. Somehow, her neighbours found out and, beside themselves with excitement, begged to know when she was having the scan. On the day of the test, Kath rounded them up. 'I said, "Right. When I come home, if I beep once, don't bother me, you'll know what the problem is, but if I beep twice, it's okay."'

She beeped twice, and almost caused a riot. 'They were all spying through the windows, but you should have seen them come running out of their houses! One of them I saw jump out from behind the bushes . . . all these neighbours running across this gravelly road so fast, like they couldn't get here quick enough. I fell out of the car laughing. They're the people who have kept us going.'

Kath and Greg are bringing up Thomas so that he knows he's not an only child. His room, his life, his heart will burst with the vibrant presence of his big sisters: Becky, who loved dangly earrings and pink polish on her fingernails, and Jessy, the cheeky chatterbox. Two little girls only thirteen months apart who adored each other above all else. 'I don't think they could have survived,' says their mum, 'one without the other.'

In March 2008, Kath sent a photo of Becky and Jessy to Kelvin Cruickshank, the resident psychic at *New Idea* magazine, who published his impressions. These were his parting thoughts: 'These two are so excitable. They're in good hands, protected and well taken care of. [They are saying] "Side by side we will always be . . . We love you, we love you! Stop crying, Mum. We hear you."'

Kath hears her babies, too. 'I'm lucky,' she says. 'I've got a family here and a family up there. I'm really lucky.'

∽

Peace. That's what the stories in this chapter signify to the women who've lived them. Even as the years roll on, only subtly blunting the edges of their pain, they continue to draw strength from the understanding that their children live on in spirit. Their paranormal experiences served a dual purpose: for the child to communicate his or her wellbeing, and as a means of helping repair a parent's shattered heart.

Diane Jakubans' son materialised, wearing 'the most serene expression', to reassure his mother that he was 'fine'. In turn, Diane was bathed in 'the warmest, tingly feeling . . .' Anna Wood came to her mother, Angela, in an unprecedentedly vivid dream at the peak of Angela's pain, after Anna's funeral. 'Mummy, I'm fine,' she enthused, talkative as ever. 'It's beautiful where I am.' The dream 'was a landmark,' says Angela, who drew from it the fortitude to, not only rejoin the world, but step out as a high-profile anti-drugs campaigner.

For Kath Campbell, suicidal in the wake of her daughters' memorial service, seeing them again proved a literal lifeline. The visit 'picked me up and dusted me off,' she said. 'It made me feel so good.' Brief respite in the face of the enormity of what befell her, but respite nonetheless. To gaze once more on her adored children put Kath, and the other courageous mothers in this chapter, on the road to surviving, though perhaps never recovering from, the fiercest loss.

HAUNTED HOUSES, HAUNTED PEOPLE

The Terror Next Door

'The stranger at my fireside cannot see
The forms I see, nor hear the sounds I hear;
He but perceives what is; while unto me
All that has been is visible and clear.'
HENRY WADSWORTH LONGFELLOW

Here are two words like an arctic breeze on the back of your neck: haunted house.

For me, those words always conjure *The Amityville Horror*. I was eight in 1979 when the film based on the bestselling 'true story' by Jay Anson was released. Even without seeing it, somewhere on the playground at Eastlakes Primary School, the key plot points seeped into my psyche – a demon pig, walls oozing slime, swarms of flies and a massive house with windows like blazing eyes.

And there they've stayed.

Even after the deaths of Kathy and George Lutz (in 2004 and 2006, respectively), their story, forever steeped in controversy, still gets under my skin. The couple claimed that their family fell prey to a malevolent supernatural force that chased them from their dream house in Long Island, New York, after only three weeks, paving the way, critics say, for the book, film – and fame and fortune.

But is it so hard to believe there was negative energy in the house? A year before the Lutzes moved in, Ronald DeFeo Jr – who bore a freaky resemblance to George Lutz – methodically murdered his sleeping parents and four siblings in the house. Of these, the youngest was sweet-faced John Matthew, nine.

On Halloween night 2008, Anibal and I were watching a contemporary documentary about the Amityville house. In it, George Lutz, not long before his death, mentioned a famous photo taken on the second-floor landing by a team of paranormal investigators that clearly shows a small boy peeking out of a bedroom doorway. No child was present that night, Lutz insisted, and of the many frames taken of this particular spot, only one contains the boy.

When this image flashed up on screen, I yelped. Anibal swore in Spanish. He is so lifelike, this little boy in his 1970s striped t-shirt and wearing a side-swept blonde fringe. His expression seemed to mirror ours, watching him down the tunnel of time. He looks semi-petrified, like he's thinking, *Who are all these people in my house?*

Most terrible of all, his eyes are as empty as his stolen future.

A few seconds online unearthed a picture of the littlest doomed DeFeo, a heartbreaking match for the boy on the landing. If this image is authentic, it is among the most compelling evidence for ghostly phenomena I've come across.

Today, the three-storey house still stands, looking far friendlier since its facelift. It is telling that the Lutzes have been the only residents to report strange phenomena there. Christopher Quaratino, who was seven when he moved into the house with his mother Kathy and her new husband George Lutz, has stated that the haunting was not a hoax, but was greatly exaggerated. He blames his stepfather for dabbling in the occult and inviting the forces in. 'He points his finger at the house and says there's something evil there,' he told *The Seattle Times* in 2005, '[but] he's a perpetrator and an instigator.'

In the classic haunted house scenario, earthbound spirits have not made the transition to the afterlife because of a powerful emotional bond with the house. The ghosts are attached to the building, not the living folk inside it. Though sometimes it is a psychic imprint, rather than a confused ghost, that is behind a haunting.

Mary Ann Winkowski offers a long list of signs to help you decide if you're sharing your house with an uninvited guest. Among them, hearing footsteps, your name called, or a touch when no one is there, temperature fluctuations and electrical malfunctions, as well as physical symptoms, such as headaches, insomnia and fatigue. Children in a haunted house typically chat about their 'imaginary friend' and might suffer from respiratory infections and asthma.

Around the time that we hosted our ghostly friends, our son, Tabaré, was dogged by terrible asthma. It has since improved, but that's likely due to treatment and his strengthening immune system. Yet it's probably worth noting that I had arranged for a house-clearing at the time, and the medium walked in, headed straight to Taby's room, pointed to the window and said, 'Oh yes, there he is. The old man is standing by the window. He's right there.'

A phantom ice-cube slid down my spine.

'That's exactly where the toys have been falling,' I managed to answer, explaining how a pirate ship had tipped over twice of its own accord in that spot.

'I'm not surprised,' she said. 'As far as he's concerned, this is his space.'

Another common sign of a haunted house is when objects and personal items mysteriously disappear then reappear, usually after all hope of finding them has gone. There's a certain playful quality to these events, as Queenslander Denise Horchner found.

'I lost a good necklace that I'd received as a gift two years previous to this happening and had mourned over it. Although my husband and I had made the most thorough search possible, we could never find it. I finally purchased a cheaper version, but never really liked it.

'One day, I was checking myself in my dressing-table mirror and decided that my cheap necklace looked very good – what had I been thinking? Then a little voice (I often have them) said, "Look down, Denise," and there was my cheap necklace. Around my neck was the one I had lost.'

Denise has also heard ear-splitting auditory phenomena, including 'the tremendous sound of crashing china. I actually heard plates skidding across the tiled floor. Jumping up in alarm and dismay, I could find *nothing*.' And household appliances are always playing up. Denise's radio has inexplicably stopped playing her easy-listening station, instead blaring rap and rock. Finally, she discovered that the AM/FM lever, stiff from non-use, had shifted. This cheeky trick happened three times.

Despite the odd goings-on, Denise is not in the least afraid. 'I have never thought of our house as being haunted,' she says. 'I have always thought of "them" as friendly members of my family who have passed over.'

Nurse and mum of three Joanne Letherbarrow, twenty-seven, has also experienced that classic hallmark of a haunting – interference with electrics – in a timber cottage built in 1910 in the western Sydney suburb of Wentworthville. 'Mum's bedside light would always come on five minutes before she got home, even when she arrived at different times,' remembers Joanne, who was thirteen when the following took place:

'My mother, my sister and I were watching television, and I wasn't interested in the show, so I got up to leave the room. Straight away, the TV went snowstorm fuzzy. Laughing, I sat back down, and the show came back on. My mum and sister were laughing, saying that "someone" wanted me to stay, so to prove they were wrong, I got back up. Same thing. I fell back into the chair absolutely horrified, and the show resumed.

'Another time, soon after, it was night time and I was trying to get to sleep, when I heard that it was starting to rain. I love the sound and the smell of rain, so I got up and opened the window to let the air in. There was no rain. I could feel the breeze and hear what sounded like rain, but it wasn't coming from the window, it was coming from my pedestal fan, which was unplugged! I reached over to touch it and my stereo, which was on the other side of the room, turned on and changed stations all by itself. I ran from the room, and as memory serves, didn't sleep there for quite a few nights.'

Eventually, these events may become an everyday part of life, as common as the pop of the toaster or the whir of the fridge, says mother and writer Vicki-Jo Shelton, thirty-four.

'I grew up in a house in central Victoria where it was common for the lights to be on when no one had turned them on. Light globes coming unscrewed and landing on the floor, just missing the glass coffee table underneath. Or doors being open, even unlocked, when we knew they'd been closed. Footfalls in the hall at night, the weight of someone sitting on the edge of my bed, the feeling of being watched, were all part of daily life.

'As I got older, I sensed the presence more. I'd feel it standing in my bedroom doorway and sometimes I'd feel as if it was pulling up my sheet and quilt or tucking me in. It wasn't threatening. But I was still a bit scared. As a teenager, I began to think there were two ghosts because there were slight differences in actions – different personalities.

'One day, I was home alone during school holidays. It was winter and raining. I heard footsteps on the front porch. Creeping to the peephole, I peered out, finding nothing but wet footprints leading to the door and then stopping. There were none retreating, just heading for the screen door.'

Well, why would they want to leave? Home, sweet eternal home.

'Our last house had a ghost,' says Jacqi Foster, forty-one, describing a brick-veneer family home in the western Sydney suburb of Liverpool where she lived from 2001 to 2004. 'On the first night in our new house, I woke to the sound of all the drawers in our dining hutch being opened and closed as though we were being ransacked, only to find that there was no one there at all. We would hear a lot of unexplainable noises.

'One night, I woke to the sounds of footsteps in our tiled hallway. I thought my son was up and I went out to follow him to his room, but there was no one there; the footsteps led me to the room where the door was shut to our dining/second lounge room and the footsteps disappeared through the closed door. French doors divided our kitchen and lounge. They would open completely by themselves. This happened to my husband a few times and scared him to death. He admitted this even though he is a complete non-believer of the paranormal.

'Another night, I woke up and saw the light on in my ensuite bathroom and the sliding door to the bathroom was slightly open. No one in my family was in there. My son was asleep next to me in bed and my husband was away on work. I could not move my head off the pillow, my entire body was pinned to the bed! All I could do was peer from my pillow towards the bathroom. I thought to myself, *If that bathroom door is still open in the morning, then*

I will know I was not dreaming. The next morning, that door was still open, but the light was no longer on. Something was definitely not right that night.'

Jacqi mentioned the weird events to her friend, whose parents had sold them the 1960 home six months earlier. She learned that the former owners would spot ghostly figures lined up on the front patio 'as though they were waiting on something,' says Jacqi. 'I never did see them, fortunately!' She also uncovered some of the home's history: 'The owners prior to my friends' parents had told them that their departed father was still in the house! He had died in one of the front bedrooms and never moved on.'

Certain circumstances may spark a haunting or exacerbate one, from home renovations to a turbulent family life, a common denominator in my interviews. 'In most [haunted] houses there is a trigger event in the life of someone in the family that makes them more sensitive to the spirit world,' writes British psychic Mia Dolan. 'Extreme loss, sadness or stress make people more susceptible to an awareness of the paranormal.'

And the presence of a teenager is usually a given where poltergeist activity – movement and throwing of objects, knocks, et cetera – is a feature of a haunting. Though poltergeist is the German word for 'noisy ghost', some parapsychologists theorise that psychokinesis (PK) – the mind-influencing matter – is to blame for these often violent episodes, not a hooligan from the spirit world.

Sometimes, people deliberately lay out the welcome mat for the unknown. 'Young people mess with ouija boards and they open up and say, 'Is anyone there?' and absolutely *anyone*, every dead head in the universe is invited in!' marvels investigator Robb Tilley. 'So you end up with problems.'

Since Amityville's 'problems' were summonsed by George Lutz, according to his stepson, I'd be curious to know whether Lutz ever used a ouija board, for all the experts I've consulted are unanimous on this point: it is a very dangerous tool. Especially in the hands of an inexperienced person with a powerful untapped psychic gift. Tilley believes it could even lead to mental illness. 'It's a bit of a game, but you're picking up the lower entities,' says psychic-medium Debbie Malone. 'You just don't play with that stuff.'

Caroline Laurence learnt this the hard way; her childhood obsession with the ouija board culminated in a showdown with a poltergeist that scarred her forever and wrenched her family apart. A teenager's repressed psychic power on the rampage? Or was the ouija a doorway to an evil force in her home? Perhaps it was a combination of both? You be the judge.

As with Caroline, who found, to her dismay, that frightening phenomena followed her around, and Simone, whose isolating experience of a force that wreaked havoc on her life can be read in the upcoming pages, the line between haunted house and haunted person is not always clear. Small-businesswoman Danielle Olver represents another case where mystery surrounds exactly *what* zeroed in on her. But whatever it was, it got personal.

'In the winter of 2005, I moved in with my best friend. She had recently lost her husband and I moved in with her to help her grieve,' says Danielle, twenty-six, a member of Victoria's Hide and Seek Paranormal Research group.

'Not long after, we started to experience poltergeist activity, such as objects being moved about the house. TV remotes would show up weeks later in sealed boxes that I had stored from my previous move from Ballarat. We would hear footsteps up and down the wooden stairs at night. We both put the phenomena down to my friend's late husband letting us know he was around.

'However, the phenomena continued, and with more frequency in the coming weeks. The spirit would present itself in all rooms of the two-storey house, but mostly on the bottom level, where my bedroom was. My friend and I both agreed that the energy was a male, which we named George, and was intimidating and dominating and we became very frightened. Neither of us would stay in the house alone, and I certainly would not sleep in my room alone.

'At night, I could hear George's heavy footsteps on the floorboards. They would walk out of our bathroom, past my bedroom door and continue on into the kitchen. On some occasions, I would hear the fridge door open; it had a recognisable squeak. At night when I lay awake, terrified, I could hear the floorboards beside my bed creak as though someone was standing, watching over me.

'George would follow me to work, where I worked graveyard shifts at a service station. He would overturn twenty-litre drums of oil and activate security doors that could only open with a key.

'George would travel with me in the car and on one occasion, would cause my brakes to fail, narrowly avoiding an accident. George would also come to my boyfriend's house and present himself as ice cold spots in the house.

'The last straw for me was the morning I woke with a bruise, perfectly hand-shaped, that appeared on my thigh. The hand shape was too large and didn't match my boyfriend's. That afternoon, we sat in the kitchen and discussed calling in a psychic we knew for help in cleansing the house. At that point I felt my voice box tighten and I could not speak. I ran out of the house and my voice returned. We figured that George didn't want us to get rid of him.

'The psychic came, and on *two* occasions, couldn't clear the house of George. The medium told me that George was attached to me and would travel to different locations. It wasn't the house that needed to be cleansed, it was me!

'After a long search on the internet, someone told me to see a kinesiologist, who does marvellous things with clearing spirits. I made an appointment and visited the kinesiologist who worked on me for half an hour, and I walked out his office like the weight of the world was lifted off my shoulders. I don't believe that George was an earthbound spirit, I think he was a result of the negative energies created as a result of the circumstances at the time. We never heard from him again, thank God!

'I have had many, many other experiences since that winter with the ghost-hunting crew, but with the help of the resident psychic mediums, I know better how to deal with these events.'

Haunted women. Haunted houses. Haunted hospitals? I have come across stories of patients who are seen gliding by the rooms where they took their last breaths, and of psychic nurses who feel honoured to see the spirits of long-dead loved ones waiting by the bedside of a dying patient. These next three experiences are all set in hospitals, buildings that buzz with death, suffering, survival and extreme emotional highs and lows.

'In hospital, when my first daughter was born in 1970, I experienced some sort of phenomena, like someone or something was trying to undo my sheet and this feeling of extreme coldness and heaviness was trying to lift the bed sheets and get to me,' says South Australian mother of two Gina Britto.

'I am a religious person and I felt so frightened by this that I reached for my rosary beads and prayed like I never have before. After a period of time, which felt like an eternity, it left me alone. About four days later, I mentioned this to one of the nurses. She informed me that my bed had been used by another patient a while back. The mother had picked up her baby and hurled herself and the little one over the balcony of the hospital and died.'

Sydney promotions coordinator Maria Fazo, twenty-three, says she will 'never, never' return to a particular hospital where her grandfather spent his final two weeks. Visiting him in 1997, Maria, who has been experiencing the paranormal since she was five years old, was trapped in a bathroom cubicle by an unknown force. 'I still do not know exactly what happened to me there, but something or some force locked me in the bathroom on the lower floor and

I could not get out,' says Maria, who also recalls 'feeling heavy' and how the temperature plunged. 'It took me several attempts and several screams of "Let me out!" for it to open. The funny thing was, the door was not locked.'

In October 2007, Queenslander Sandy Dearnley, fifty-eight, was admitted to hospital with a life-threatening throat abscess. After three days in intensive care, she was transferred to a room close to the nurses' station. Rest did not come easily.

'One night, I accepted a sleeping tablet, but woke about four hours later feeling incredibly cold, almost icy, and I could feel that there was someone else in the room. I turned on the light but there was no one there.

'The next night, I was dozing and felt as though I could not get out of the bedclothes and that someone was forcibly pushing me out of bed. I pressed the bell and a nurse came in and said, "How did you get like this?" I was wrapped tightly in my pyjama top and then wrapped tightly with the bed sheet.

'Another night I awoke and tried to turn over, but something was pushing heavily on my chest. I did not mention this to anyone at the time as my mother had been in the same hospital a year before and had her own experiences. I was scared if I told anyone while I was in there that something worse might happen.

'The previous year, the staff of the ward called a Buddhist monk in to do a clearing and blessing as there had been unexplained things happening. The staff said that clearing had helped considerably.'

However, there are many haunted places around the world where the flesh-and-blood owners live in a precarious harmony with their spectral housemates. The UK, for example, is swarming with haunted tourist attractions like Gloucestershire's Ancient Ram Inn, known as one of Britain's most haunted houses. 'They let you know who actually owns the building,' remarked owner John Humphries in 2006. 'I'm only a lodger.'

Australia has its own 'most haunted house': Monte Cristo Homestead, in Junee, New South Wales. Reg and Olive Ryan fell in love with the rundown mansion in 1963, moved in with their children and immediately set about restoring it to its former magnificence. Ever since, they've shared the nineteenth-century stately home with a plethora of earthbound spirits, an extra drawcard for many of the customers who visit for morning tea or stay for bed and breakfast. There'll be no house-clearings there.

Kiri Steele also learned to live in harmony with her ghost. The respite carer and mother of two from Armidale in New South Wales describes a caring spectre who took up residence in her 1970s-era red brick-veneer home in 2006. The man behaved very much like a concerned grandfather. The first time she saw him, 'I was in bed one night, not asleep, and I looked over and here is this person as if he was kneeling next to my bed. I just sat up and said, "Who are you? What do you want?"'

He was 'within arm's reach,' recalls Kiri, thirty-four, who felt 'petrified' at the sight of the man with the close-cropped hair. 'Initially you think, *There is some freak in the bedroom*, but then I thought, *Oh no, it's a ghost.*'

Her heart thudding, she tapped her husband awake. 'There is someone beside my bed, on my side,' she whispered. But as he started to roll over to see, the apparition vanished. Soon, their youngest son, Nick, then a toddler, began jumping into his parents' bed in the mornings and pointing to the corner of the room exclaiming, '"There is a man standing over there, Mum."'

What sealed the matter for Kiri, confirming to her that none of this was coincidence or scattered dreams, were the impressions of her psychic friend. Without breathing a word of the goings-on, Kiri invited the woman to step into the room. 'She sat there and said, "Oh, there is a man in the corner. He's got a weather-beaten face, teeth missing, looks like he's been working outdoors. We had started to call him Frank, and she said, "His name starts with F. Fred or Frank, or something like that."

'Sometimes I think he could sense when I was stressed, because he'd touch my ankle at the bottom of the bed. Also, he used to check on the boys. We had a long hallway, I could see his outline looking in their doorways. He was worried about us, he was moving from room to room, quite quick, and I'd especially see him at Nick's bedroom door.

'One night, I sat up and said, "Frank, everybody is okay. Go to sleep, or whatever it is that you do."'

That seemed to reassure him and Kiri hasn't seen Frank again.

Only two minor events preceded Frank's appearances and both occurred in the kitchen. Once, neatly stacked Tupperware containers tumbled for no discernible reason from a shelf, and twice, a family portrait fell from its hook on the kitchen wall. The latter takes on a poignant resonance when Kiri tells me that she and her husband separated two months prior to our interview.

Was the falling family portrait a hint of the turmoil to come? Was Frank's protective masculine presence meant to reassure Kiri that she and the boys would always be accompanied, no matter what? Kiri isn't certain. She only says, 'Maybe now the ghost will come back and keep me company.'

NIGHTMARE ON COBRA STREET

'I was up against something that wasn't human.'

Her email arrived like so many others.

Yet coiled within the small black print, a horror story to tempt Hollywood: 'All the lights in the house went out, I could feel it around me, *right behind me*, I was sixteen and trapped in my room with this thing behind me . . . that feeling of being trapped with it is the one driving fear I have carried with me to this day. It was complete helplessness, knowing that it had me where it wanted me . . .'

I sat up straighter in my chair. By the time I'd read to the end of Caroline Laurence's articulate, subdued email, detailing one night in 1988 of unimaginable terror inside a typical family home, I was standing up, heart racing, dialling her home in the central-western NSW town of Dubbo. A quiet, cultured voice answered. It would be no problem, said Caroline, for me to visit her and hear her story.

On Anzac Day 2008, as my train approached Dubbo station, I called Caroline, who'd arranged to meet me. 'I'm blonde, wearing black, and I'm with a tall man in a navy jumper,' she says, and it doesn't take long to spot her, with her towering partner, Michael, standing sentinel beside her. She smiles and stretches out her hand. She is petite, with smooth, long hair that gleams as if brushed with 100 strokes, swept off her face with black sunglasses. Her skin is light olive and her eyes are so startling, at first I mistake them for coloured contact lenses; the pupils tiny black buoys bobbing in a calm blue sea, and beneath, a thousand mysteries dart.

We hop into her car, the gallant Michael at the wheel. 'That's where it all happened,' says Caroline, pointing to a nondescript Californian bungalow along the main road of Cobra Street where she, her brother, sister, mother and stepfather had lived more than two decades ago. With its handsome 'period features' – the classic balcony at the front, thick white pillars, big sash windows – it looks more a renovator's dream than a hub of nightmares. The three-bedroom cottage is only a short drive from their neat little villa where we are headed to demolish a family block of chocolate while Caroline unravels her story. As we leave this street in our wake, she mutters: 'I hope there are no children in that front bedroom.'

It was a Friday night in 1984 and the thriller *Gorky Park* was on TV. Huddled around a homemade ouija board with the lights dimmed, Caroline was only twelve when she, her sister, Tracy, thirteen, and their mother, Vera, unwittingly invited something awful inside. At first, it looked like adventure. School friends soon joined in, the teenagers marvelling at 'the messages' rushing in, at the flimsy veil between our world and theirs. Imagine, that all you need is a wine glass and the letters of the alphabet scrawled on scraps of paper to rouse the dead?

Every day after school, Caroline, who would soon begin reading tarot cards, startling her family and friends with her accurate readings, would head home to the séance. 'I did hundreds and hundreds,' says Caroline, perched on the end of her couch, two black-and-white kittens running loops around us. 'I was doing two séances a day. I was so fascinated in chatting to the spirits.' More than fascinated, Caroline was obsessed: the séances were consuming her young life. While most children of the 1980s can match their youth to the pop beats of Duran Duran or Cold Chisel's rock anthems, the soundtrack of Caroline's high school years is the screech of a wine glass labouring across the ouija board.

As a child, the pretty, bookish little girl had never felt completely at home in her skin; at school in Dubbo, the kids nicknamed her 'Posh', intimidated by her precocious smarts and her big words. One girl even called her a witch. 'I had a lot of friends, I just didn't like them,' says Caroline, who also stood out from her family – she didn't look like them, her hunger for knowledge and experience didn't tally with theirs. But shuffling the tarot cards or holding a séance, a different world opened up for Caroline, a world of possibilities that spread far wider than anything Dubbo could ever offer her. One night, when a spirit came through with a mystery to solve, it strengthened her resolve. She was doing something important for this lost soul, a murder victim whose name, Jenny

Black, was writ large over the newspapers and TV news in the mid-80s. The group was like the Famous Five, bursting with a sense of purpose as the wine glass spelled out clues the spirit insisted the police had missed.

'Jenny would always start off in a friendly way,' recalls Caroline. 'My friends would come over and I would get them to ask questions, but Jenny would always interrupt; she would masquerade as other spirits and then eventually reveal herself.'

Caroline says she now realises it wasn't actually the spirit of the murder victim, rather a pretender 'attempting to make itself familiar to us,' which is thought to be a common hazard of playing with a ouija board: mischievous spirits purporting to be a loved one or a famous name. As the so-called Jenny became more demanding – barging in and commandeering the glass, silencing the other voices – strange things started happening at Cobra Street.

'We had two doors leading off the main lounge-room. On a regular basis, the first door would open slowly all the way and then close, then after a ten-second or so pause, the second door across it would also open and then close. It was as if something had walked down the hall, through the lounge and into the dining room,' remembers Caroline. 'My family joked about it, we called it Harold. It was more like a pet.'

Slowly, subtly, the activity increased: a clock would slide across the mantelpiece, items in Caroline's bedroom at the front of the house would shift themselves overnight. It became obvious to the child that whatever this was, it was narrowing in on her. She would be poked and jabbed in the back by unseen hands. After waking up in the morning to find her possessions moved around, she would walk into the bathroom and see that the stand which always sat underneath the window was now bang in the middle of the room. 'Often, I would wake up cold in the middle of the night to find that my bedroom window was suddenly wide open.

'The first time I became aware that something bigger was beginning was when the temperature in my bedroom changed. One minute it would be a normal bedroom, nice and warm, then there would be a sudden drop in temperature to the point where the windows would fog up.' This happened even in the merciless heat of a Dubbo summer. 'It was like living in *The Exorcist*.'

Truly frightened by this development, the schoolgirl finally called an end to the séances. Besides, they were taking up too much of her time; she was finishing up Year Ten, had a part-time job in a dog parlour to see to, and Jenny was now the only spirit that would, or could, come through. When the wine glass they'd used for the séances bounced and exploded in mid-air, 'I knew I'd brought something nasty across,' she remembers. 'I didn't understand what, but I knew that I was no longer in the room alone.'

There is something ethereal about the adult Caroline. She seems to float above everyday life, not amidst it. Though she formerly worked in IT recruitment, it has been years since she's been able to stomach an office environment. 'I absorb everyone's emotional bullshit,' she says in her quiet voice. Its low, steady timbre has a lulling effect and I start to feel a bit dazed. Caroline watches me shrewdly, and I regret not having collected my thoughts in the hotel before starting the interview. 'I'd hear my name called: "Caroline"' she mimics huskily, and it feels like someone has walked over my grave. 'Or I would hear distant yelling, like someone across the road calling out my name. That went on for quite a while.'

Instead of the unknown force disappearing with the last of the séances, as she'd hoped, matters worsened and were soon to come to a head. On Easter Sunday, 1988, Caroline accepted a friend's invitation to attend her church, a born-again Christian denomination. 'I'm not religious, I just thought it might be interesting,' she says with a shrug. 'It was the following Sunday everything went crazy.'

Happy after knocking off from her weekend job, the sixteen-year-old unlocked the front door and realised she was home alone. Her brother, Anthony, five years her senior, had long ago moved out; her sister, Tracy, was out with her boyfriend, and her mum and step-dad were at the horse trots.

She walked towards her room.

It was as cold as the tomb.

Next, she noticed the noise: 'The stereo was screaming.' With her hands clapped over her hears to block out the grating screech, she quickly walked over to it – a 'boom box', as most teens then owned – and tried to turn the volume down, and the power off, but the noise persisted. 'Then I went to pull the cord out and it wasn't plugged in. When I realised that, the sound stopped. Bang. You can imagine me, as a kid . . .'

Alone.

'At that point, I looked in my mirror and there was this fancy italic writing spelling "Help Jenny". The writing was backwards, as though written from inside the mirror in a thick, black substance. I ran out of there, straight to my friend's house and he came back with me. By the time we got there, it was like there was electricity in the air, a static charge, you could feel it in your hair. I could hear the cutlery shaking around in the drawer, too, but the static, to me, was the weirdest thing: it felt like it was really penetrating, kicking in, almost moving through you and around you.'

Together, she and Craig tried their best to wipe the frightening words off the mirror with tissues. 'It was thick and gluggy, tar-like and sticky,' remembers Caroline. 'It left a big smear and didn't come off easily.' While they worked, the house kept up its own hellish fun. 'The pictures on my wall started to rock, and we ran out of the room. We took some time, got curious and went back in.'

What they saw, says Caroline, was this: The word PLEASE written backwards, capitalised this time, in the same bizarre black goo. 'A part of you is terrified,' says Caroline, 'but you are also excited.' The cutlery continued to rattle, the electrical 'hissing' filled the air, the paintings were spinning on their hooks, toys and books leapt off Caroline's shelves, and into this pandemonium walked Tracy and her boyfriend. 'Evil house, that one,' shudders Tracy Finlay, now a thirty-seven-year-old mother of two, who's joined us at Caroline's house, along with her impish four-year-old son, Jay.

Her sister steers us back to 1988. 'As Tracy approached my bedroom door, Craig had walked out of my bedroom and I went to walk behind him and the door slammed shut. All the lights in the house went out, there was a lot of noise, like something whooshing. I'm in the room, my door doesn't lock but the bloody thing wouldn't open. They are on the other side of the door. I am screaming my head off, screaming because the bloody thing was all around me, everywhere, I'm screaming and screaming.

'The banging of the door behind me was the most frightening moment. I knew, if this thing kills me, it's taking me somewhere dark and horrible forever, a place far worse than anything you can imagine. I was up against something that wasn't human, as a child, it is the most helpless, vulnerable feeling you can experience because this is so much bigger than what you are.'

The memory of raw panic sharpens her words, makes them shrill. Resurrected fear swims in her veins, pumping blood to her cheeks, igniting her doll eyes.

'They were trying to get me out of the room, all I'm thinking is *Get me out, get me out, they are going to get me*, then suddenly the door popped open, the lights went back on and I ran out.' In that terrifying interim, many of Caroline's possessions had been rearranged, including her dolls, which now hung in a macabre puppet show from the light fitting. 'I had brass and glass stands I'd bought from CopperArt and everything had been moved around. It happened in a few seconds.'

Tracy's memories of the night are not as detailed as Caroline's, but she supports that it happened and acknowledges its role in destroying any semblance of a relationship with Caroline, who fled Dubbo for Sydney within a month of that night. Only in the last four years have they begun to reconnect. 'Caroline was hysterical. I can remember the writing in the mirror, that freaked me right out, scared the crap out of me,' says the straight-talking housewife, herself the survivor of delicate brain surgery when she was a teenager. 'The organ was playing on its own, just going off its nut. And the doors were banging. But the thing that freaked me out the most was the perfect hangman's noose that we found out the back.'

Now, sometime before 8pm, the girls' mother, Vera, arrived home.

Here was her house in chaos. Here was her youngest daughter bawling in fear and determined to sleep in her friend's caravan. A flawless hangman's noose danced in the evening breeze from her backyard pergola, but that surprise still awaited her. Tracy was nowhere to be found – yelling and shoving her sister out of the way, she'd stormed off to spend the night at her boyfriend's. 'There was no way I was going to stay in that house,' she shakes her head, 'but they brought me home.' When their mother suggested the girls sleep together in her room, Tracy scoffed.

Her exact words: 'I don't want that evil bitch in my room.'

Sitting in the converted garage-study where we've all drifted, Caroline doesn't flinch. 'Did you realise that was one of the big reasons I left Dubbo?' she asks Tracy. 'Because I wasn't allowed in your room?'

In her friend Sally's caravan, where girls sometimes gathered for giggly sleepovers, the night was just beginning. 'We'd fallen asleep at about 10 pm,' resumes Caroline. 'When we woke up in the middle of the night, every single window, door and cupboard in the caravan was wide open, and the static was back. For me, it was just unbelievable that it had followed me. My friend was scared and I was sent home.'

Back at Cobra Street, the reception wasn't much warmer. By then, it was almost dawn and Vera had discovered the noose. 'Mum didn't really understand what was going on, it was too much for her,' says Caroline, who slept with her parents until her move to Sydney a month later. She says she felt no choice but to leave home. 'I had to run, I didn't feel safe. Nobody felt particularly safe around me.' Her bedroom, which remained 'like a chiller,' says Tracy, was locked up and never used.

On the phone to Vera Laurence some weeks later, she sighs down the line. 'My memory's not what it was,' says the sixty-four-year-old. 'I knew there were problems in the house because we'd been having séances, which can be a bad thing, you know – my girls were at that age. I know I had a very frightened daughter on my hands.'

'My only recollection of Cobra Street is that when I got up in the morning and opened the back door there was a big noose outside, and it looked like brand new rope, brand new and really thick and done up in a perfect noose with the round bit at the bottom. I walked straight into it, and rang the police and asked them to come and take it away. I said, "If this is someone's idea of a joke, it's not funny."'

What about the activity that preceded that April night, the doors opening and closing? The knick-knacks moving? 'Oh, I didn't experience any of that, though her stepfather did,' chirps Vera, and Tracy's words play in my head: 'Mum doesn't want to remember Cobra Street,' she'd said, sitting back in an office chair in her sister's study-garage. 'She doesn't want to remember that Cobra Street tore our family apart.'

On cue, Vera presents scrubbed snapshots of a normal family home where the windows were opened by human hands to let in fresh air and sunshine. 'I was often home on my own, I used to clean like mad on my day off, they used to love coming home and the house would smell of Mr. Sheen. They loved it when I had a day off. I personally didn't have any problem with that house until the noose appeared.'

Growing up, Caroline was 'beautiful, a real sweet, happy, normal little kid,' says British-born Vera, who separated from the children's biological father in 1973. 'The girls were only a year and a day apart, but two entirely different kids. Tracy was more of a tomboy. Caroline was quieter. I had three jobs going at one stage to keep us alive. So we struggled, but she had a happy life.' It was Vera who helped find her daughter a job in desktop publishing in Sydney, where Caroline lived for 18 years, and had a daughter, Brianna, now fourteen, before she was diagnosed with a degenerative spinal disease and forced to return to Dubbo in 2004, into the care of her sister.

Before we hang up, Vera says, 'Do you want me to tell you what happened to me in England?'

When she was a single woman in her early twenties and staying in a friend's spare room, Vera had turned in for the night and was alarmed to hear the sound of footsteps climbing the stairs towards her, then her doorknob rattling. 'I turned and faced the wall, I thought it was this woman's husband . . . all of a sudden, the room was freezing, like Siberia, *I could see the steam*, and I knew someone was standing at the door. Minutes later, the door closed, the stair creaked, and the temperature returned to normal.'

'*Freezing . . . I could see the steam . . .*' Vera, who says her own mother had once bid good day to a newly dead neighbour, had an experience which would mirror Caroline's decades later. Tracy too has psychic gifts, including prophetic dreams, which she has most likely passed on to tiny Jay, who reports being tickled by his late granddad, Poppy.

I think of tiny Jay studying me during the interview at his aunt's house. With blue eyes shining, he'd looked up at me and said, 'I have these dreams . . .'

And so it continues.

I put down the phone thinking that Caroline's vast, complicated tale is a layered, ever-shifting thing, and it is still evolving. Though the phenomena followed her to Sydney, where in many of the rooms she lived Caroline would wake in the night, shivering, to find the windows gaping wide, today she lives a much more settled life, back where it all began. She is rebuilding her relationships with her mother and sister, and lives peacefully with law student Michael, her boyfriend of two years, and his little son. For friends and family, she performs psychometry – the art of picking up psychic impressions from photographs and personal items – never charging a cent, though she might spend four hours on a reading. She calls it 'spiritual counselling', and shuns terms like psychic and medium. Medicine and science intrigue her – she'd love to study nursing, and dreams of working in palliative care, 'to help people who are in the process of crossing over, and are afraid.'

As for her own healing, that is still a work in progress, much like her drawers bursting with unfinished novels, paintings and ideas. Venting her creativity has become a big part of Caroline's recovery; writing, art and designing have also helped her come through the other side of six years in an emotionally abusive relationship when she was in her twenties. She has been depressed and, like Tracy, cannot sleep with any part of her body uncovered. She even sleeps with a pillow on her head. It's a lot of fall-out from an event a psychiatrist once summed up as 'a grand delusion'.

'To be honest, the experience was that full on for me that if I had to go through that level of activity again, I would rather just kill myself and be done with it. There is no way I could survive that,' says Caroline, whose story has certain parallels with one of the most well-documented cases of a poltergeist haunting ever recorded. The 'Enfield Poltergeist' shook the lives of an English family – Peggy Hodgson and her four children, including Janet, eleven, and Margaret, twelve – in Enfield, North London, in 1977.

In 2007, Janet, who was the focus of the haunting, was interviewed for a TV documentary about the case. Trembling slightly, as if barely stifling a wail, her gaunt, lined face framed by long, bleached hair, her eyes fixed and brimming, she described a heavy chest of drawers sliding across the floorboards and how the voice of a gruff old man had spilled from her throat. There was much, much more. The phenomena – which happened over 11 months and was investigated by journalists, police and the eminent Society for Psychical Research – also included the spontaneous disappearance and re-appearance of objects, and was witnessed by over thirty independent people.

In Cobra Street in 1988, there were fewer players and no fanfare, but there is a whisper of Janet's fragility in Caroline. She is not the only one who carries the scars. As Tracy says: 'None of us have ever got over it.'

How could they? When just around the corner, the house stands strong, ever ready for its endless turnover of tenants, in sturdy double brick. A renovator's dream.

'Every time I walk by my old house in Cobra Street, part of me wants to go in and ask, "Is everything alright in there?" I'm at a level now where I could probably get rid of it, but what if I can't?' muses Caroline as I'm getting up to leave, clutching one of her artworks, an exquisite painting of a sunset she generously insists I have.

'This thing is a real trouble-maker, it is angry and violent and thrives on your fear. Sometimes, when I walk past, I think, *Is it going to get me?*'

A TRAVELLER'S TALE

"Twas not I that put the noose about his neck.'

No doubt you have snuggled beneath a blanket, as fat drops of rain pelted your window, and read a story that goes something like this.

But this story is not make believe.

Ruby Lang was driving in a downpour. Her boyfriend, Ted, yawned in the passenger seat and outside the swollen sky had darkened to the shade of a crow's wing. Tired, hungry and itching to stretch their legs, the travellers perked up when they spotted the warm lights of a bed and breakfast up ahead. Just south of Cooma, near the Snowy Mountains of New South Wales, the restored 1880s coach house proved too tempting, with its cosy face and the promise of a comfortable bed.

'It was a lovely little place,' remembers Ruby, thirty-six, the paranormal journalist behind the popular website strangenation.com.au. 'We thought to ourselves, *Wow, this is a real gem!* The owners led them to their suite, adjoining a lounge where a well-built fire leapt. They were alone in the hotel, except for a couple in the honeymoon suite upstairs. 'We had a really nice big roast dinner, a few wines, then retired to the lounge and had Baileys in front of the fire.'

It was as if, with its fine hospitality and the blaze to colour their cheeks, the house was lulling them to sleep, inviting them to fall into the antique brass bed and dream like the dead. The couple acquiesced. But two hours later, Ruby felt eyes burning her face and woke up with a start. Ted was watching her closely. There was something edgy in his stare. If she didn't know better, she'd have called it naked fear.

'What the hell were you saying?' asked Ted, his features shifting in the faint glow of the night light.

'What are you talking about?' she croaked.

'I can't *believe* what you were saying just then,' he muttered, raking a slightly trembling hand through his hair.

Like a zombie springing to life in a vintage horror film, Ruby had bolted upright and trilled in an unknown voice, *''Twas not I that put the noose about his neck.'*

She then dropped straight back onto the pillow, said Ted, instantly asleep. To Ruby, it felt like a family of baby spiders just scurried along her neck. What could this mean? She was known to mumble in her sleep, but this . . . ?

The room didn't give them much of a chance to absorb it. Moments later, the couple, silent and tense, could hear footsteps pacing in the lounge next door and something that sounded like the rustling of the *Canberra Times* newspaper they'd left on a corner of the sofa. Despite what happens in the movies – or perhaps, because of it – neither was keen to investigate. 'We were both big chickens so we refused to have a look!' says Ruby with a giggle.

Over breakfast, the pair debriefed, chasing their tails with questions that had no answers. Ruby is always on the hunt for scientific evidence, so this midnight episode was especially frustrating. Whose neck? What noose? *Whose voice?*

'Oh, are you talking about the ghost?' interjected the manager. 'The lady running the inn was really cute,' recalls Ruby. 'She dressed up in traditional mop hat and apron – daggy, but sweet – she must have overheard us talking. We asked, "Is it supposed to be haunted?"'

'Yes, we've had lots of strange things happening here,' nodded the woman, explaining how a week earlier a couple from Sydney had booked their room, putting their daughter to sleep in the bedroom adjoining the lounge. In the black of night, the father awoke to see the little girl framed in the doorway. 'Sarah, go back to sleep,' he scolded. The child didn't move. She stood as stiff as a model in an oil painting.

'Sarah, go back to bed before you wake up Mummy.'

But Mummy did wake up. She lifted her head and said, 'That's not Sarah.'

When the couple glanced at the doorway again, the figure was gone. Rushing to Sarah, they found her peacefully asleep in bed where they'd tucked her in. The stories flowed, says Ruby. Staff with arms stacked with linen would shuffle, crab-like, up the stairs, because if they ascended in the normal way, invisible hands would push against their lower backs. Doors that were locked tight when darkness fell would be gaping wide in the morning. In one room on the second floor, it was common to hear the din of a terrible argument: screaming, yelling and crockery crashing. Once, the racket in the dining room was so loud that the owners' daughter and her boyfriend called the police, convinced that thugs were trashing the exquisite period home. But the police found not so much as a napkin out of place.

'It turns out that the man who originally built the inn had some sort of fatal row with his wife,' says Ruby. He'd hurled her down the stairs and hung for the crime.

Gooseflesh bloomed on Ruby as she listened to the story. Last night's uncanny words seemed scribbled all over her skin. *'Twas not I that put the noose about his neck . . .*

Years later, Ruby roped friends into bunking down at the old coach house. 'I put my hand up to stay in the room nearest to where you could supposedly hear the row,' she says. 'That weekend, there were two couples who were involved in a car rally and they were leaving the next morning,' she tells. 'I woke up early and I could hear them fighting. I was thinking, *Rude people! Making so much noise!* This is not a word of a lie! This is me thinking, *He's having a row with his wife.*'

In a huff, Ruby pulled on some clothes, ready to march down and bemoan her broken night's sleep to the manager, 'but just loud enough so that the couple outside might hear,' she adds with a grin. But as she reached reception, the car rally enthusiasts were driving away. 'They're leaving already?' she asked. The manager sighed, 'Yeah, they were a bit grumpy. They reckoned you and your boyfriend were having a set to so they decided to hit the road.'

Did she catch any of the insults flung in this almighty screaming match? Ruby pauses, then shakes her head. 'No. You could just tell it was an argument: a man and a woman. It was the weirdest thing to be hearing something like that! It was just as if you were living in an apartment building and someone next door to you was having a row.'

What was behind the activity at the old coach house, I wonder, its rooms still crackling with centuries-old squabbles? A violent or traumatic event may 'imprint' itself on its environment, theorise parapsychologists, and Ruby believes that this may explain the haunted inn. 'Perhaps I picked up on the atmosphere of the place and was used as some sort of bio-tape machine, replaying past events,' reflects Ruby, who is wary of the notion that an agitated spirit used her as a mouthpiece.

'I'm quite sceptical of channelling, I've yet to see anything half-way convincing, and I've sat through a few sessions with various self-described "mediums",' she says. 'Most cases involve people airing parts of their subconscious. They like to believe they're giving voice to some discarnate entity, but in reality, they're just deceiving themselves and others – sometimes knowingly, sometimes not.'

On the other hand, 'I don't believe for one moment I have a murdered colonial wife living in some dark corner of my brain . . . the best explanation I can think of is I somehow tapped into the emotional atmosphere of the place, *well before* I heard that it was reputedly haunted.'

Whether the truth resides in the inn's time-worn walls, netting its inhabitants' sins and strife, or in the spirit of a wronged wife returning to have the last word, Ruby will never forget her stay in the bygone coach house.

'It was such a dark place, and so remote . . .'

IN THE BEDROOM

'He was slowly walking towards us, with his arms straight out in front of him.'

Kelly Hammond has never doubted the existence of a spirit world, or feared it, despite a bone-chilling early initiation. As a toddler, the twenty-nine-year-old from Tamworth, in country New South Wales, and her little brother, had a fright that still resonates almost three decades on. The former child protection officer, now a full-time mum, has never forgotten her ghastly visitor (neither has her sibling, though he has tried to). Here is Kelly's account of what happened one winter's night, in the bedroom.

'I have always believed in spirits and ghosts. In fact, I cannot ever remember a time when I didn't. I was brought up by my mother to believe in an afterlife and although my other family members tried to convince me otherwise, ghosts seemed to be a part of normal life for me. I don't ever recall my mother telling me about spirits until I was much older, but I do recall her saying that it was okay, and that she believed what I told her about seeing "people", and to not worry about what others thought.

'The most vivid recollection I have as a child seeing a spirit occurred when I was about three years old. I remember that I was this age as I still had blonde hair (that had turned brown by the time I was four). I lived in an old home with my mother and my brother who is ten months older than me. My grandparents had bought the home from the family of the elderly woman who had previously lived there and we had moved in not long after. My mother has told me that the previous occupant had been moved to an aged care facility in town as she could no longer live alone and had died shortly after moving.

'The house was built in the older section of town and still stands today. It has a white exterior and small windows. This particular night, my brother and I had been put to bed. We shared a room. I remember that our bunk beds were not together. They had been made into two separate beds for us. There was a window in our bedroom across from the bedroom door. I remember hating the window because there was a tree that sat just outside it that, in winter, had no leaves and it used to scare me. It was winter when this occurred and I know this because of the tree.

'I don't have a very detailed recollection of what happened, as I was so young. I do remember an elderly man suddenly being in our bedroom. He looked like he was around the age of my grandfather, which would be around sixty-five or seventy. He had grey hair. He was not balding like my grandfather but had thinning hair with a receding hairline. He was dressed in dark pants and what looked like a flannelette shirt. What I remember the most was the way he approached us. He was slowly walking towards us with his arms straight out in front of him.

'I remember looking at his face, absolutely terrified. It was as if he was looking straight at my brother and I, but he wasn't really seeing us. To this day the thought of his eyes sends a shiver down my spine. They were vacant. There was no sign of life in them whatsoever. The light did not reflect in his eyes, which were clouded over in a tone of bluey-grey that covered his entire eye. My brother and I were screaming and banging on the bedroom door for our mother to come and get us. We were absolutely terrified, and in our terror could not open the bedroom door to get out. Until about one year ago my brother denied all memory of this event. After our grandfather passed away, my brother finally admitted to me that he did remember seeing the old man in our room but did not want to believe it because it frightened him.

'I spoke to my mother not long ago and asked her about what she recalled about this incident. She told me that she remembers sitting in the lounge room and suddenly hearing my brother and I screaming and yelling. Mum told me that when she came to our bedroom and opened the door, both my brother and I jumped into her arms, crying, repeating over and over, "Mummy, there's a man in our room, there's a man in our room." After checking the room and being confident there was no one there, Mum then had to calm us down which took quite some time. Mum will say to this day that although she did not "feel" anything there that night, she did experience other unexplained things in the old home. We did not live there for long.

'I've always wondered if the older man was perhaps the husband of the previous occupant. I drove past the old house not long ago with my seven-year-old son in the car. I was looking for the number of the house to see if I could find anything out about it. I did not tell my son why I was looking at the home other than saying that I used to live there when I was a little girl. My son then told me that he thought the house was haunted. I asked him why he thought that and he just said that his head and his heart tells him it is. Make of that what you will. Strange coincidence? Or perhaps some kind of knowing? I don't think I'll ever know.'

THE FORCE

'I guess it was a kind of possession.'

Share houses can be hell, and Sydneysider Simone (who requested that surnames be omitted from this account) knows this better than most. What the IT consultant endured over six months in a typical terrace in inner-city Surry Hills tore her twenties to shreds and led her to the brink of a breakdown. A type of entity was making the twenty-six-year-old's life a misery at a time when it should have been bursting with promise. Though mourning the recent death of her father, she had just fallen in love with a wonderful man, Gus, a banker/musician, and her career was powering ahead. Even after she succeeded – with Gus's support – in ridding herself of whatever had sunk its hooks into her life, she had to dedicate years to healing and working through deep-rooted denial. For eight years, Simone and Gus, who are now married, didn't utter a word to each other about the events that engulfed Simone soon after she moved into the Surry Hills house. 'I wouldn't have survived it without him,' says Simone, now forty-one, who describes herself as 'intuitive' and has dabbled in divining – the sum of her paranormal experience prior to this. She has never played with a ouija board. The terror came completely out of the blue, as she tells below.

'It started in about 1993, my flatmate and I moved to a terrace house in Surry Hills with another friend. Gus had just begun staying over when things began to happen. Bad things. Violating things. Eventually over a few weeks, each of us living in the house was pinned down to our beds, paralysed and unable to open our eyes or defend ourselves. It didn't happen to Gus.

'The attacks in the house were dreadful, absolutely terrifying. It was like a blanket covering me, every inch of me. Each leg and arm was pinned to the bed. It seemed to come in through the window, but I was never certain, and quickly creep over me until I was completely covered. When I tried to move, I couldn't. When I tried to open my eyes, I couldn't. When I'd summon every ounce of strength I could to try to scream, a pathetic, gurgling noise came out. But it was enough, the sound made it go away.

'On one of the first nights we stayed in the house, a mate from the pub crashed in the lounge. When he woke up, he was spooked. He said there was something really strange in the house and he was never coming back. [The man did not specify exactly what took place.] I remember the day it happened to my flatmate. I got up really early, and he was already up and dressed, making tea. Then he told me it had happened to him, and since he slept on his stomach he'd been pushed face first into his pillow during the attack.

'It pretty much left the guys alone after that, but for me, things had just begun. The attacks were to become more intense, more frequent and more frightening, and not just confined to the house. I suppose I was more open. I'd been working with dowsing the previous year and was highly intuitive with day-to-day stuff. I was also an emotional mess, in the process of falling in love and having lost my father only a few months before.

'I remember being in my friend's kitchen and a terrible feeling coming over me. I felt really hot, and my attention kept being drawn to the knife on the bench which I told her to put away. I then started back out of the kitchen. All I could say was "I feel hot and bothered." She knew something was wrong. She got me into the shower. My ears were ringing, then all my jewellery began to vibrate. Unbelievable but undeniable, we could both see it and hear it! It was mad. We took all my jewellery off except a well-loved, favourite bangle that had been stuck on for a while. The vibrations wouldn't stop so we had to cut it off.

'I stayed in the shower until I came back. "Came back" is the only way to describe it; during these attacks, I was detached. My ears would ring until all other noises were consumed by the ringing. Sometimes I could see the lights on the stereo moving and people's mouths talking but I couldn't hear anything other than the ringing in my ears. I'd lose touch with reality.

'I guess it was a kind of possession. Whatever it was used to come and go, and Gus actually saw it once. He sensed it entering the room and then watched my body get pressed into the bed. He tried to talk me through it by telling me to listen to the birds.

'When attacks happened, within my mind I let "it" know exactly what I thought of it,' says Gus. 'On several occasions I saw what looked like ripples in the air above us – circling, waiting, threatening. The air did change, it became thicker, there was possibly a hissing sound – time seemed to go a little strange as well – it's very hard to explain.'

'Although I wasn't under attack twenty-four-seven, I couldn't control where or when it would happen. I used to carry a sage smudge stick in my bag, and if I felt an attack coming on I'd go to a park and burn and inhale the sage to try to keep it at bay.

'My friend was becoming involved with a Native American healer at the time and I'm not sure if the connection to her had any influence on the entity. It was her kitchen I'd had the attack in when all my jewellery had started to vibrate and she knew what to do, so I figured there was a connection. She understood that to get me into water and closer to nature was the best protection I could have. But I didn't have that Earthly spiritual connection that I needed and so I was constantly afraid.

'Also, she left the country just after the attacks started. So I was pretty alone. There was one woman here who I went to for treatments and I did leave there feeling pretty good, but it wasn't sustained. Whatever it was apparently had "hooks" in my aura and that was why I couldn't get rid of it. The Sydney healer then left the country too.

'So here I was, intermittently possessed by something I had no understanding of, with absolutely no one to turn to.

'The attacks started to come more frequently. I felt one coming on at work, in a conference, where I was supposed to be a respected technical consultant. My career fell apart. I fell apart. My world fell apart. I remember being at work one day. I'd been given the number of a healer in Brisbane: my only contact. My boss was away, I was in his office with the door closed, terrified, crying, and on the phone to some guy I didn't know, who was trying to calm me down. As if he could do anything from there.

'Between attacks, I had dogs stopping and growling at me in the street. One evening Gus and I decided to meet after work and walk through the Botanic Gardens. We were sitting quietly and I felt it coming on, I felt myself leaving. I always found it difficult to reveal to anyone that something was wrong, that I was under attack. I managed to tell Gus and asked him to tell me happy stories. The attack passed and we eventually moved off from our spot. As we walked out of the park, past the Art Gallery there were many people out walking their dogs. Gus looked around and said "Look at the dogs!" I muttered "yeah," almost paralysed with fear. "No, look! They're all looking at the same thing." He was right.

'Every single dog had stopped and started growling at me. Their owners were looking around to see what it was. There was no mistaking it, every dog in the park didn't like something about me. Stunned, we moved off as quickly as we could. There would be more incidents like this. Dogs would even stop on the footpath outside my house and growl at the house (I was in the front room).

'I ended up not being able to leave the house very often. I remember one day I thought I'd go around the corner and rent a video and there was a dog in the doorway and I had to come home. On another occasion, Gus thought it would do me good to get out of the house, so suggested we go to Glebe markets. I was terrified to leave the house, but desperate to get over this and be well. Being Glebe, there were lots of dogs. We sat down on the grass to have something to eat and no sooner had our bums hit the grass, all the dogs nearby moved over and started to circle us. In the same sort of pattern you'd see sharks circling a boat in a cartoon. We moved off quickly, deciding to walk and eat.

'I don't know how Gus put up with me, but thankfully he did. I was a fruit cake. I was terrified of everything, even sleeping. Exhausted and scared to go to sleep – not a great combination.

'Eventually, the Native American healer returned to Australia for another visit and, although he was fully booked, he was aware of my situation and made time to see us. He asked both of us a lot of questions and examined me, then performed a ritual to test for demonic possession, which ended with him asking my name. When I answered "Simone," the word had never sounded so sweet. He then got Gus to see if he could feel the breaks in my aura, which he was able to. Based on it not being demonic and Gus's sensing ability, he said that Gus would be able to do the work to "pull the hooks".

'He explained that this stuff happened to people that were open and intuitive, and that when it went, so too would my intuition. He said that trying to open up my intuition again would be like inviting it back in, and to discourage people from doing that he doubled his fee each time someone came back with the same problem. Then he explained in detail what we had to do to make it go.

'Our household had fallen apart by then. Both flatmates had moved out and we were in the house alone, soon to move ourselves. We followed the directions to the letter. The final step was for Gus to clap and when he did, the whole house shook.

'The ritual was successful, it was gone, although there were a handful of occasions in the following few years when I felt it trying to have a go. It actually tried with Gus once too, which it had never done while we were in the house.

'All my intuition had also gone (or I was too afraid to see if it was there). I deliberately lost touch with my friend because I felt she was somehow associated with it. I moved without giving her a forwarding address. I wouldn't even read her last letter in my house, I took it to the park to read.

'By this time, I was on long service leave from work, which I took at half pay to stretch it out as much as I could.

'For eight years from the day we left the house, Gus and I never really talked about what had happened. During those eight years I went back to work, got retrenched, had some consulting jobs and pretty much spent my time trying to drink and work myself to death. If I wasn't working a sixty-hour week, I was drunk.

'In 2000 we married. Strange that we'd been together so long yet the wedding had such a significant impact. The night before our wedding we asked each other if we expected anything to change and we both said no. We really just wanted to celebrate with our families how happy we were together. But surprisingly, after we married, I began to actually accept that many couples get to be really happy together, something I'd never acknowledged before. Prior to marrying, I'd spent most of our relationship in fear that it would end tragically at any given moment, and somehow this "ceremony" had helped to heal that in me, although it took a few years to realise this.

'After getting married I had planned to have a break from working for a few months but I found it really difficult to get a job, despite having been very employable for my whole career. During this time at home, I eventually realised that I needed to purge what had happened, or at least acknowledge it. For a few weeks, I sat at the computer and wrote about what had happened to me, how I'd hidden from it, how maybe now it was time to get well.

'I can't say it was all smooth sailing from then, but after more than 100 knockbacks, I got a job within about a week of writing it all out. I think on a spiritual level, I'd shifted at that stage and was ready to start healing, but my self-esteem was extremely low and I really didn't like myself. I was still drinking very heavily, and working sixty hours a week again – on a physical level it couldn't be maintained. I was an emotional wreck, I was pushing myself to my limits, and eventually my body gave way. I was diagnosed with carcinoma in situ – cancer waiting to happen – and I finally realised I was killing myself.

'Fortunately around this time I met a Sydney-based healer and spent the next four years working with him, learning traditional ways to heal myself and others, and techniques to help me move forward. He helped me to remember my connection to the Earth, and to know deep within me that everything will be alright and that it's OK to be happy. And finally, I was able to stop living in fear.

'So that's my story: an intense and terrifying experience, eight years of denial, and six years clawing my way back. As well as studying traditional healing, over the last five years I've studied iridology and nutrition and am just finishing off a degree in Health Science. I don't know where it will all lead. It started as a hobby to help me curb my drinking but it's been so much more. I've learned to set boundaries and to nurture myself. My intuition is coming back, my marriage is still happy and strong, and I feel I'm moving forward in many areas of my life, ready to share some of the knowledge.

'I know everything happens for a reason and it's healthy to forgive. I know forgiveness is for *you*, not the person or thing you forgive, but in relation to this experience I've found it pretty challenging. Especially never really knowing what I was forgiving.

'To this day, I don't fully know what it was all about.

Neither does her husband, but he knows exactly how he fought it.

'As simple as it sounds – love,' sums up Gus. 'That "it" never really had a go at me or that I was able to remove 'it' from Simone were both surprises to me, but I loved and still love Simone, so in a strange sort of way it was really that easy. That's not to say any of it was enjoyable or fun, that's not to say we didn't have things to learn, far from it. But we had an unbreakable bond – I'd found the person who I was meant to be with so I wasn't going anywhere, and I know "it" knew that as well.

'The funny thing is, that after such a hard start to our relationship – with nowhere to hide, being so alone together and having to trust so totally in each other – we had such a rock to build on, so as time has passed and so much good stuff has happened since, it only adds to that rock of strength that is our love for each other.'

A FORM OF FEAR

'There was evil in that house.'

'Did you have a good day?'

Perched on the end of a narrow single bed, storybook in hand, a mother might smile and ask this question before her child shuts her eyes on the night. Ghosts aren't usually so attentive, but many ghosts were mothers too, once.

One of Danii Ainsworth's earliest memories is of an elderly spirit lady who wanted nothing more than to have a natter before bed. Danii was a pre-schooler living in an old fibro house in the Melbourne suburb of Springvale with her mum, Kim, and her little brother Bob. Her dad, Brian, was a truck-driver and often out of town. Now a thirty-two-year-old married mother of two based in historic Tenterfield, New South Wales, where she is manager of the local paper, Danii can vividly recall the visits that heralded a powerful mediumship.

The first sign of her imminent visitor would be a 'queasy, sea-sick feeling' in her stomach. Next, her louvre window would open and 'she would glide through,' continues Danii, oblivious to the impact the scene evokes. It makes me wince, but as is almost always the case in these encounters, fear did not rule the moment. While conceding she was 'a little frightened, sometimes,' the real downer was exhaustion. This lady just wouldn't give it up – not unlike Great Aunt Molly trapping you in conversation at a family reunion.

The chatty chimera appeared to be at least seventy and sported a neat 'double bun' hairstyle and 'an old-fashioned dress that used to go right up to her chin with a collar around it,' recalls Danii. 'She looked solid, but you could see through her at the same time. Yet when she sat on the bed, you could see and feel the pressure. The right-hand side of my bed was against the wall, right next to the window, and she'd sit on the left side, facing me, around mid-way up the bed, where my knees were.'

Danii says she never touched the woman. What would she have felt, I wonder, if she'd stretched a small hand towards her dead friend? Icy air? Frigid flesh? Papery skin? Or nothingness?

'The lady was really nice, and very proper in the way she spoke. I think she was just lonely. She'd just want to sit on the end of the bed and talk all the time: "Did you have a good day? Did you have a nice dinner?" We would just talk, but sometimes I'd say I was tired and wanted to go to sleep and she'd want to wake me up. I'd go out and say, "Mum, she won't let me sleep. I can't sleep," and she'd say, "Don't be silly."'

'Sometimes, I'd run and say, "She's in the room, come and have a look," but by the time Mum got there, there would be no one. It got to the stage where it was happening nearly every single night and I started scaring Mum. It was frightening for her, you know, when your kids are dealing with something like that.'

'I was more frightened for Danii,' explains her mum, Kim. 'But *she* wasn't scared. She would just say she was cold, because "the old lady opens the windows in the middle of the night."' When a former resident came around to pick up her mail, Kim asked if she'd ever had any strange experiences at the house. She shook her head, but said she knew something of the home's history. Kim discovered that an old woman who'd lived there had moved into her sons' room (Danii's room, with its bed fixed to the floor) after her husband passed away. 'She died in Danii's bed.'

The family stayed there for a year, then travelled around the country. Baby Kylie arrived when Danii was seven. Moving constantly could be unsettling, but it was her parents' way of giving their three children 'life experience,' says Danii, who has some fond memories of her gypsy upbringing – 'fishing in Darwin, being in swamp water up to your knees and finding out there are crocodiles . . . Things like that you never forget.' But other flashbacks are less sunny. Though her mum and dad 'were like Romeo and Juliet,' domestic violence soured the romance, and the children and their mother occasionally sheltered in women's refuges.

When she was twelve, they moved from Darwin to Toowoomba, 130 kilometres west of Brisbane. One night, at the home of Danii's aunt Debbie – her mum's sister – and her uncle Mark, the little girl came face to face with another caring spirit. 'It was about eleven forty-five at night and I was sitting in the lounge room, which had a clear view up the hallway. Auntie Debbie went to check on her little ones.'

Satisfied that her children were sleeping soundly, Debbie returned to the kitchen where the adults sat chatting. 'Next minute, I see the light flick on in the baby's room and stay on for a couple of seconds. Then it turned off and this old lady walked out,' says Danii. 'She looked at me, smiled and walked into Debbie and Mark's room; their bedroom was straight across from the babies' room. I screamed and went running into the backyard.'

To Danii's relief, her aunt and uncle not only believed her, they confirmed the sighting, explaining that both of them had seen the 'harmless' spirit of a woman dressed, as Danii had seen her, in a floral nightie. Her routine was to switch on the light in the children's room, presumably to check the babies, and then return to the main bedroom. 'They never saw her anywhere else in the house. They said it was nothing to be frightened of.'

But the child's nascent abilities – combined with an occasionally fraught home life – were making her a sitting duck for paranormal activity, and the next encounter would not be so pleasant. Danii first told me about what occurred at a house in Crows Nest, just north of Toowoomba, in an email. Her closing line intrigued me: 'To this day, I believe those experiences have held a form of fear in me.'

The dread thrives inside her, as smug as a tyrant, casting a pall over her life.

The house – 'I wouldn't ever call it a home,' she scoffs – stood diagonally opposite a cemetery. 'I hated that house. There was evil in that house.'

Danii was just starting Year Eight when they moved in. In my second year of high school, my biggest problem was how to cram another Culture Club poster on my bedroom wall. Danii Ainsworth had much more to contend with. 'Mum had a party once. There were six adults and fifteen kids. A lot of the boys went into my brother's room. Some boys were in my room playing a game. Next minute, we heard a knocking at the window. We looked up and there was . . .'

She pauses, and her old fear of being ridiculed quivers between us. I wait.

'There was like a demon hand, cut off, knocking at the window.'

The children bolted from the room, howling like banshees. Danii insists it wasn't a practical joke – one of the boys brandishing a novelty arm to frighten the others – it was, she says, only one of many horrific memories she has from 'that house'. While the other parents told the kids they'd 'just imagined it,' her mother pulled her to one side, worry etched on her face. '"What was it, exactly?"' she quizzed, because by now she knew that her daughter was not like the other neighbourhood children.

But she was a lot like her.

In 1978, Kim lost her third child, Nathan, to SIDS. The two-month-old slipped away in his sleep, a sweet smile on his lips. Spent with grief, the young mother tried to rest, but stirred when she felt a presence in the room. Kim's late father-in-law stood at the end of her bed, transparent but unmistakable.

'It's okay,' he told her. 'It's alright. I'm looking after him.'

Kim is baffled by a sequence of dates that is always bobbing up in the sea of her life. Nathan was born on the sixteenth of June and died on the seventeenth of August. Four years later, her youngest child, Kylie, was born on the seventeenth of August, and would go on to have her own baby girl, on the sixteenth of June. Kim's brother died on her mother's birthday and his funeral was held on . . . the sixteenth of June.

'Even when things happen, you don't tell too many people, because a lot of people think you are crazy,' says Kim, who's seen a lot in her fifty-one years. In 1996, her husband, Brian, hung himself close to their Bundaberg home, where the family had long been tormented by the disembodied shouts of men fighting and the inexplicable crash of glass smashing. Within a day or two of his death, they moved out. 'My husband lost the plot in that house,' she says quietly.

Before he died, Danii's father – a staunch Catholic – gave his daughter a miniature bible, which she keeps tucked under her pillow. Like so many of the women I've interviewed, Danii's nights are turbulent – she catches most of her shut-eye between four and seven am. 'I haven't slept properly for a long time,' she says with a sigh. 'This sort of stuff, when I remember it, is the reason.'

She can't even bring herself to specify what she saw in the Crows Nest house two decades ago: she leans on terms like 'evil faces', 'horrible demonic things' and 'death and nasty things' to describe what she experienced in her short time there. She speculates that at some point before they moved in, some previous occupants may have drawn negative forces to the house and that her psychic sensitivity left her vulnerable to it. Says Danii: 'I'm hoping the house has burnt down.'

As for developing her abilities, it's unlikely. 'I am frightened of what might happen,' she says.

In 2006, the spirit of a tall man trailed her for two weeks. With help from a local psychic, Danii learnt how to cut ties with the spirit, who turned out to be her friend's dad. He'd been trying to reach his daughter through Danii.

Just as Danii feels she inherited her gift from her mother, so might Braydon, four, the younger of her two boys, be carrying it into the next generation. 'A week ago, we were lying in bed. My light came on three times; then the TV came on. Next minute, Braydon came running in, he'd been crying, and said, 'There is a man in my room.' Not long after that, Jake [his five-year-old brother] came running in saying, 'There is a man in Braydon's room.' This was the early hours of the morning. My husband, Chris, was asleep beside me. It was like an electric spark, you know, when you zap yourself. There was a static crackle in the air.'

'Could you feel or hear this crackle?' I wonder.

'Bit of both,' she answers. 'It was like a pulse, a feeling like some of the nightmares I have and the movies you see. I hid under the doona, telling the boys, "There is no one here."'

Did she get up and have a look?

She guffaws. 'No way!'

And the tyrant inside her laughs too.

THE ANSWER

'I jumped out of bed and chased it, but there was nothing there.'

To Rowena Gilbert, *Picnic at Hanging Rock* isn't just the name of a seminal Australian film. It is a crag in her memory – a landmark in her lifelong quest to untangle the enigma of ghosts and the spirit world.

When Rowena was seven, her parents, brother, aunt and grandparents all squeezed into the family car and headed to the ancient formation, also known as Mount Diogenes, seventy kilometres north-west of Melbourne. The location had become a must-see since the 1975 release of Peter Weir's haunting film, based on Joan Lindsay's bestseller about a group of schoolgirls who vanish on a day trip to the Rock on Valentine's Day in 1900.

During the road trip, Rowena's aunt recounted the story of the girls who were never to return from a summer's day outing. Rowena listened, wide-eyed, and something inside her ignited.

At Hanging Rock, she scrambled into the hills and bushes, drawn to, yet repelled by, the idea that she was treading in the doomed students' footsteps. She could almost see the posy of girls in alabaster dresses, ribbons streaming from their long hair and tied in bows at their waists. She could almost hear the sound of their laughter, like crystal tinkling at a polished dinner table, as they walked with parasols drawn into oblivion.

'Now I know that it was all made up,' says Rowena, in a singsong voice which makes her sound much younger than her forty years. 'But that story ran around in my head for years and years and years. I was *really* affected by it.' That fascination is evident in her Castle of Spirits website, one of the most respected and popular internet destinations for all matters paranormal. The Melburnian, who also established the off-shoot Australian Ghost Hunters Society (AGHS) in 1997, is a well-regarded name in the Australian paranormal community for her experience in investigating hauntings and her dogged, cool-headed search for evidence.

Her passion keeps her busy. In the weeks before we chat in January 2008, it's hard to pin her down; between her day job (as a medical secretary) and organising a weekend trip to Tasmania to film a potential TV series, Rowena was frantic. When I finally catch her on the last day of January 2008, she cheerfully settles in for a chat.

'I reckon ninety-nine per cent of the time, absolutely nothing happens on an investigation, except you might get a bit of a scare in the dark,' she says with a laugh. 'Bats might fly out at you! It's usually really, really boring, and it just takes a lot of patience. It's a lot of sitting around and talking.'

It's what happens in that remaining one per cent of the time that spurs her on – those fleeting moments when the camera or audio captures something uncanny. As an example, Rowena directs me to an EVP (Electronic Voice Phenomena) recorded at the Monte Cristo homestead, in New South Wales' Junee, reputedly the most haunted house in Australia.

Recorded by a male AGHS colleague at the gravesites of the home's original owners, the voice could be a little girl whispering something that sounds awfully like, 'Shoot me.' It is deeply unsettling. 'In reality, investigating ghosts is boring,' says Rowena, who had two favourite baby books as a toddler – one about dinosaurs, and one about ghosts. 'But if you do get that one little thing that happens, that's the whole world.'

Naturally, the queen of the Castle of Spirits, which brims with spooky encounters posted from around the globe, is not without her own ghost story.

For eight years, Rowena lived in a haunted apartment in the western Sydney suburb of Parramatta. 'Oh, I saw quite a few things that I couldn't imagine. Well, of course you could imagine them, but why would I?' The spacious penthouse apartment hosted an invisible presence that made itself at home in the spare room and regularly travelled the length of the hallway. 'I could almost put a timer to this: something would appear in the hallway and walk up, or just move up and down the hallway, at least once or twice a week. My little dog would always chase it.'

Rowena says that although the building only dated back to the 1980s, it was built on historic land behind the Old Government House. (Parramatta was the site of Australia's second settlement.) Yet she doesn't believe she was experiencing a classic haunting by an earthbound spirit. 'I got the feeling that it wasn't the ghost of a person. I think it was more of an energy. I think it was something that fed off the emotions of the apartment,' says Rowena, explaining that her relationship with her then-boyfriend was troubled.

The ghost-hunter experienced the gamut of frightening experiences at her former home. Not long after she moved in, she was alone in bed, while her partner was parked in the lounge, where he often stayed until the early hours, when she heard an unusual buzzing sound creeping along the darkened hallway. 'It was a noise that I'd never heard before. I can't reproduce it. The closest thing would be the sound a fridge makes, but *loud*. And I was thinking, *Why?*'

Behind the familiar symphony of her boyfriend opening beer cans at the other end of the hall, the buzz amplified. It was coming closer. 'I thought, *Oh, Jesus Christ!* I sat up in bed and I'm thinking, *What the hell is it*? And I'm in the dark and there's no bedside light to turn on, there's only the light switch in the doorway, which is where this noise is about to come down into, and I was just *staring* out into the pitch black darkness. I'm looking down this dark hallway for something to come and I don't know what!'

Though she was too frightened to yell out to her boyfriend, for some reason he got up and flicked on the light on at the end of the hall, 'and the noise was gone. Boom,' says Rowena. 'I screamed for him then, I went, "Aaargh! What was that noise? *What was that noise?*" I think that was the first time we said, "Yeah, there is something in the apartment."'

The second time she encountered something strange, Rowena was in bed reading, a low light illuminating the page. She looked up to see her partner walk out of the spare room and up the hallway.

Except that her partner lay by her side, asleep.

'When I saw it, I had to say to myself, "I saw that, I *saw* that." I didn't have a witness, I didn't have the camera, I didn't have anything, but I saw it. I was just sitting there thinking, *That was not my imagination, I* saw *it*. But this time, she felt no fear. 'I jumped out of bed and chased it, but there was nothing there.'

Stowaways from Rowena's ghost hunts also had cameos. 'Every time I came back from an investigation, I always had something happen to me – and I don't think it was the same presence [that was active] in the unit.' Falling asleep one night in bed, 'somebody ran their finger up the underneath of my foot,' she recalls. 'And I thought, *Oh, it's a bit of blanket*, because I would sleep with my feet out. Especially in Sydney, it's so hot, I used to sleep with my feet out of the blankets and on top of the bed all the time. I thought, *Oh, something's caught underneath*, and I moved my feet around and there was nothing there. Then something grabbed the top of my foot and wiggled it! I could actually feel the fingers grab it and I sat up and went, "Oh my God!" *That* scared me.'

As did the 'grey figure' who crouched at Rowena's bedside one awful night. 'I woke up in the middle of the night and there it was, with his hand in my face! I can tell you, *I hit the roof*. I leapt the full length of the bed and hit the wardrobe on the other side. I screamed the place down! It was an immediate reaction, but I wish now that I had stopped and gone, "Oh, hello."

'It looked to me like a squatting person, but not a solid person, he looked translucent. I can't say,' she says with a sigh. 'Maybe I imagined it? Maybe I was dreaming, but I certainly saw something that scared me.'

Like her childhood fascination with Hanging Rock, the paranormal is a puzzle that keeps Rowena on her toes; challenging her mind, stimulating her curiosity and offering plenty of food for thought to the thousands of fans who visit the Castle of Spirits site each month.

'Once you see something like that, you want to see it again. And you keep looking,' says Rowena. 'It's the excitement of trying to find out if these things really exist.'

Postscript: In April 2008, I was deeply saddened to find out that the lovely Rowena had passed away in hospital following an unspecified illness. My thoughts are with her family and friends. My hope is that she has found the answers she sought.

⤜✠⤏

Staring out of the passenger seat of our car, or daydreaming in the bus, I now find myself peering into the homes that streak by us, a seamless ribbon of black, red and brown brick. When we stop at traffic lights, I have a proper stickybeak. Who are the dead prowling those rooms, I wonder?

You see, I've heard – and now you have, too – a list of haunted-house tales as long as the obituaries column in the Saturday paper. I've learned that non-descript dwellings burst with ghosts and spirits, and dusty young soldiers seem especially likely to drop by, three popped up in my interviews. Might they still be trying to find their way home to their wives and families? I'm finally awake to the ease with which earthbound spirits, or free spirits, can claim a house.

The latter will never frighten the living, because they're loved ones visiting with an offering of hope. But earthbound spirits will be rude houseguests, just like the ghost who kicked at toys in my son's room. Which comes first, I've wondered, the haunted person or the haunted house? Does one give flight to the other? Maybe, in some cases. Someone with the unwrapped gift of a psychic-medium moving into a home harbouring an earthbound spirit – or an unspecific 'negative' force, as terrorised Danielle Olver, Simone and Rowena Gilbert – could be an incendiary mix, especially if you add emotional upheaval or a troubled home life to the brew. Could this have been the prelude to Caroline Laurence's horror story? If a less gifted tenant had lived at Cobra Street, someone more likely to pick up the remote control than a ouija board, would the haunting ever have taken place?

Others are never invited in, not even unwittingly. Kelly Hammond and her brother were innocent toddlers when an old man with eyes like holes in the dirt stalked into their lives, his arms stretched towards the abyss. Was he going to prod their warm flesh? Snatch them away? As sinister as he sounds, chances are he couldn't even see them. Earthbound spirits are known to be confused and disorientated.

While they will never know who he was or what he wanted, the siblings have never forgotten him. Now neither will we.

DOPPELGÄNGERS AND
OTHER MARVELS

Ordinary Women,
Extraordinary Encounters

'There are more things in heaven and earth, Horatio,
Than are dreamt of in your philosophy.'
WILLIAM SHAKESPEARE

While ghosts and spirits have ever captivated me, they are not
the only celestial mysteries that fire up my imagination. As a
kid, I spent many a Sunday afternoon glued to shows like *That's
Incredible!* and later, *Unsolved Mysteries*, and the possibilities they
presented (I loved their dramatic re-enactments!) made my head
spin. Though I knew that come Monday morning, I'd be zipping
up my red-and-white chequered Eastlakes Public uniform once
more, it was exciting to believe that beyond the secure routines
of the suburban bubble I lived in, the world held the potential for
inexplicable wonder and spooky surprises.

This chapter is my nod to those shows that made my heart skip
a beat. It's a home for all the wonderful tales of time slips, angels,

and even doppelgängers, that didn't belong in any other part of the book, but where the spine-tingle factor was just as high.

My conversation with Rhonda Rice refused to budge from my brain for weeks after we'd spoken. You'll understand why when you read 'Faith's Envoy'. As she told me, a childhood vision of an angelic being in her bedroom served the dual purpose of comforting her in the wake of a shocking accident she'd witnessed, and bolstering her ahead of the nervous and physical breakdown she would endure as a result of what she'd seen.

The word 'angel' derives from the Greek word for messenger, and indeed most accounts of angelic visits involve the communication of a message or guidance (this is implicit in 'The Winged Messenger', even though the being conveying the message looked nothing like the accepted idea of an angel). In Chapter Three, we explored the role guardian angels may play in warnings and preventing danger. Vera Coolidge of Western Australia believes she met her guardian angel on a gloomy country road as a small child, perhaps symbolising the important part he'd come to play in her life in future years. Reading her account, I wondered if he'd plucked her from the path of an impending catastrophe. Every detail of his resplendent appearance is branded in Vera's memory:

'When I was twelve, I was studying my catechism for my confirmation. At the time, I was living in the country and the roads are very dark. I was riding my bike and as I was approaching home, a beautiful person dressed in white was guiding me into the driveway. He was on the opposite side of the road, with one arm up as if to say stop and the other arm outstretched in the direction of the driveway. He had beautiful long hair (not a strand out of place), a white gown with a rope-style sash around the waist and roman sandals.

'Years later, I realised this beautiful person is my guardian angel and have seen him many times. I've since had many beautiful experiences with his help, seeing me through a very stormy marriage and divorce.'

Though he didn't resemble a traditional angel, Melburnian Janette, fifty, saw an apparition that she immediately understood signalled a positive omen of her labour that had just commenced. She had been meditating regularly during her pregnancy in preparation for natural childbirth.

'My waters broke at 4 am on the seventh of January 1995 and when I reached out to grab the beach towel I'd left beside the bed to tuck between my legs, I noticed there was a young man in a brown monk's habit sitting in the recliner chair in the corner of the room. I was totally awake and dealing with the flood and I could see him in the dim light of the street light outside the window as clearly as if he were flesh and blood.

'He sat very quietly with a kindly expression and just nodded slightly. I felt reassured that everything would go okay with the delivery and, after looking at him for a few moments, I drifted back to sleep for a couple more hours. Later, my husband couldn't believe how composed I'd been to just roll over and go back to sleep once my waters had broken.'

Janette, who adds that her aunt told of being attended through the night by a phantom nursing sister in nun's headgear following the delivery of her child in Brisbane in the 1960s, says that two years after her baby's birth, she had another profound spiritual experience.

'When my daughter was two-and-a-half, I separated from her father and went home to Mum for several months. Towards the end of this unhappy time, my niece was getting married and my estranged partner was due to fly in from Melbourne for the weekend to attend the wedding and see our daughter.

'I was very conflicted about whether or not to try to patch things up with him. The morning his plane was due I was sitting on the front verandah having a cuppa and watching a flock of native birds wheeling in the desert sky. While staring at them, the big question in my mind was *Should we get back together*.

'As I sat there, a second flock of birds flew into sight doing similar manoeuvres. To my utter amazement, the two flocks wheeled together and it formed the shape of a gigantic heart. My heart thumped with shock!

'In excitement, I shouted to my daughter to come out and see it too. We both stood watching the heart made of flying birds moving through the sky. The formation held that shape and the combined flock flew away towards the horizon.

'Needless to say, I took this to be a sign that yes, we should get back together, and happily we did.'

Janette's story appears to illustrate how when we decide to open our hearts and minds to spirituality, our increased awareness may allow us to recognise cosmic signposts that suggest we are just another part of a multi-layered, interconnected universe.

Occasionally, it's the other way around, and spontaneous glimpses of another reality lead to an awakening, or at least, a new curiosity about a spiritual or alternative realm. I can't remember whether *That's Incredible!* ever addressed this topic, but many years ago, I chanced upon the intriguing story of two tourists who visited the Palace of Versailles on an overcast day in August, 1901, and as they wandered the grounds, somehow stumbled upon a scene from the past. This paranormal event is known as a 'time slip', and what happened to Oxford academics Annie Moberly and Dr. Eleanor Jourdain is arguably the mother of all time slip encounters. The pair published their experiences, including the explosive claim that Moberly saw Marie Antoinette herself, under the pseudonyms Morison and Grant in 1911's *An Adventure*.

Critics have since poked holes in the women's accounts and controversy lingers, but I love this story for its promise that anybody might unwittingly side-step into another dimension if circumstances are right. My friend, teacher and historical fiction author Wendy J. Dunn, called to mind the Versailles story when she told me of her encounter with an exquisite voice from the past at Scotland's Edinburgh Castle in 1994:

'Fourteen years ago, I'm on a walking tour of the Castle when a woman sings right next to me,' says Wendy, fifty, a mother of four who lives in Victoria. 'I spend the first moments in disbelief. The tour guide is talking about the castle; how can someone be so rude by singing their heart out in a group of about twenty people? Why doesn't the guide growl at this person? Why is everyone so silent about it? I no longer hear the guide. All I hear is this beautiful voice singing foreign words. French, I wonder? It sounds like a ballad, a ballad that touches my heart and brings me to tears.

'I turn, wanting to see the person who has deeply moved me. It is as I turn my head that the voice peters away, as if pulled back behind a curtain. Beside me is a blonde woman, her eyes fixed on the guide, totally oblivious to my bewilderment. I feel like I have just stepped from one dimension back into my own. I suddenly think of Mary Queen of Scots. It strongly comes to me that the voice was that of one of her French attendants.'

While the combination of an intuitive person in an historical location might be said to spark a time slip, many of these incidents are also reported to occur on the road. Debra Jones, from Rockingham in Western Australia, may have tuned into the past as she drove the familiar ten-kilometre route back from her daughter's home, one typical day in 2005.

'As I approached the big two-laned roundabout, I looked up and saw a khaki-green plane. It was flying quite low and I was worried that he was going to crash. I saw the pilot's face quite clearly, that's how low he was flying! As I was driving on the inside lane, I couldn't get over as the traffic was heavy, but I thought, *Oh God, he's going to crash!* I looked at the other drivers and cars and they didn't look at all anxious like me.

'As I drove around the roundabout, I looked to my left, expecting to see the plane land in the fields there. I didn't see anything, so thought he must have managed to steer the plane over the houses and towards the sea. I rang my daughter when I got home to see if she'd heard anything. I also told my husband.

'Days went by and I heard nothing on the radio, news or TV. I did the same trip to my daughter's again, then something snapped into place. How was it possible for me to see the pilot's face as clearly as I had? He had smiled at me. He was flying very low – why didn't I see the overhead wiring? And why didn't anyone else see him?

'Then I realised he was flying happily in spirit. If I'd realised it that day, I probably would have crashed my car from excitement!'

At the library, Debra researched the type of plane she'd seen, and learned it was a World War II aircraft (she posted me a photocopied image of a similar-looking 1942 Supermarine Seafire model).

'His helmet was a khaki-green leather wrap-around,' recalls Debra, who subsequently learned that planes were known to fly over that precise area on their way to Garden Island, a sliver of land five kilometres off the Western Australian coast where gun batteries were stationed during World War II.

Did Debra see a spirit pilot, happily re-living a pleasant flight, did she tap into a psychic imprint – where the environment 'records' a long ago event – or was she momentarily flung back in time, like our Versailles ladies? The line between the three is not always clear. In fact, some in the paranormal field believe that ghost sightings may actually be a taste of time travel.

'It is possible that many experiences of ghosts are the result of the person's ability to view their surrounds at a different time to the one they exist in,' says Dr Hannah Jenkins, philosopher and president of the Australian Institute of Parapsychological Research.

'Perhaps there are atmospheric factors which make it more possible to obtain such information.'

'Science has not yet taken a fixed position on anything paranormal, including time travel or time slips,' says US author and investigator Marie D. Jones. 'I have experienced a major time slip, and I refer to it as a fugue. Many years ago, I lost about three hours of time driving in L.A. and almost ended up in Sacramento. To this day I have no idea what happened, and don't really care to find out!

'Time slips could quite literally be accessing time wormholes, or shortcuts in the space/time continuum that may occur right here on earth, like energy vortices where time passes in an entirely different manner than the linear time we normally perceive,' she suggests. 'They could also be our accessing the Zero Point Field, where time is a landscape rather than linear, and those who have time slips are simply interacting for a brief period with a point along that landscape, and coming out of it back into their own reality.'

Around the time that Versaille's time-travelling spinsters piqued my interest, I discovered the marvellous story of French teacher Emilie Sagée, whose doppelgänger – or double – was reportedly witnessed in 1845–46 by up to forty-two students in the exclusive Latvian girls' school where she taught. The double was said to mimic her movements, or act independently, and would materialise in broad daylight. After my first 'meeting' with Mademoiselle Sagée, I was hooked. I pictured myself in the classroom, jaw agape, as two Mademoiselle Sagées stood at the blackboard, two dainty wrists setting out the day's lessons. Only one held chalk in her fingers . . .

Collating stories for *Spirit Sisters*, I was hoping I'd come across a doppelgänger experience. I wasn't disappointed: Janette, who experienced a reassuring omen of childbirth in her vision of a kind-faced monk, has had two encounters with her double, as she shares in 'Seeing Double', and Perth nursing assistant Deborah Dalrymple, fifty-two, once met her younger self and did not feel in the least afraid:

'This happened towards the end of daylight saving in Perth, as it was about 8.15 pm or 8.30 pm at night and it was still light,' recalls Deborah. 'I was going to work the night shift and I backed out of my driveway onto the road and realised I had forgotten something, so I drove back into the drive up to the house and glanced across to the door. I was taken by surprise by what I saw.

'A young woman with blonde hair styled in a bob was coming out of the door of my home. She had a T-shirt on and longish shorts. She glanced across at me, then continued her way down the path and disappeared. When I looked at this girl's face, it was a younger version of me. She looked about late twenties or early thirties.

'The material of her shorts was sort of old-fashioned, not the kind of colour that I would normally wear. They were a drab cream and brown pattern. The top was a neutral colour, like cream, so the outfit was colour-coordinated. She was quite slim. It's been a long time since I was that slim, but that's how I was in my early years.

'I stayed in my car as I watched her for about two or three minutes. I was about six metres away from her. I did not feel frightened in any way, but it was like I couldn't move. I was gob-smacked! When I got out of the car, I looked down the path and couldn't see her, so I walked to the end of it, about fifteen metres, and nobody was there. She had gone.

'I wasn't frightened, just overwhelmed, but I was sorry that I didn't speak to her. I should have asked her if she wanted something. I should have said something to her.

'I don't remember having those clothes that she wore. She was like a real person, except it was like watching a hologram. I could see right through her.'

Unlike Deborah, Janette was terrified at the sight of her double standing just over a metre away from her in her bathroom. Not even the fact that this was her second brush with her twin could take the sting out of the encounter. The first time, though, she'd only heard of the sassy imposter who beat her home and gave her family cheek, as she tells next.

You'll never look in the mirror in the same way again.

SEEING DOUBLE

'The "other me" became known as Number Two.'

'After I turned fifty in October 2007, I started writing my own book about the various paranormal experiences I've had over the years, as much to make sense of them for myself as to provide a point of reference for other people who might have been as puzzled as I was by this type of thing,' says Melburnian Janette, who requested that her surname not to be published. 'These types of experiences don't come with a user's manual and, unlike TV shows, where the story unfolds within an evening's viewing, they could take years, even decades, to truly fathom.'

The former physiotherapist, now recovering from the serious illness Lupus, tells her amazing story below.

'In 1971, when I was living in Broken Hill in New South Wales, a doppelgänger of myself, aged thirteen, caught the school bus home, walked down the lane ahead of my older brother, walked up the backyard and into the kitchen past Mum and two of my sisters into my bedroom and shut the door. Two hours later, I arrived home on the shopper's bus (having missed the school bus, I had to walk up to the main street and wait for the only other bus service to our side of town).

'When I arrived home from school again there was considerable confusion. My family insisted I'd arrived home earlier and snuck off somewhere. They thought I must have climbed out my bedroom window and me thinking they were having a lend of me, for some reason.

'My brother said "she" was rude to him, and to my sister as well (whom she physically brushed past in the hallway going into my room), so she was quite solid and not a phantom image.

'My bedroom door was still shut and as we stood in the hallway bickering about it, Mum said, "Just look inside and see if the window is open." When we did, of course both windows – they were of the side-hinged type with a pull-down flyscreen that couldn't be opened from outside – were shut tight.

'We were perplexed, and it developed into a twisted sort of family joke. I was the eldest of five girls and as a reaction to the chaos that my younger sisters left behind them, I had become a bit obsessive about my own tidiness. For a time after this, my things seemed to disappear and then turn up again by themselves; despite knowing I had put them away carefully, I'd find things gone. When I made a fuss and accused someone of moving them, the family would laugh and say "it must have been that other you who moved it." The other me became known as Number Two and she got the blame for everything that went missing from then on. This lasted for a while and then just seemed to stop.

'As my family all experienced her to be me, she must have been identical in appearance and was wearing my school uniform and carrying my bag, et cetera. However, the way she behaved was not typical of me at all: at thirteen, like many teenagers, I was emotionally withdrawn and non-expressive. I was never rude to my mum in words, but tended to use the silent treatment. Looking back, I now wonder whether she may have been expressing some of the held-in irritation I was feeling at the same time while I was waiting at the bus stop in the main street of town.

'After this inexplicable and unsettling incident, I remember feeling afraid from time to time, of exactly what, I couldn't say. I began to avoid seeing my reflection in mirrors at night, because something about the eyes scared me. I did a lot of checking under my bed before I closed my bedroom door at night, and generally became a bit more anxious and highly-strung than I used to be.'

Unlike Mademoiselle Sagée, who apparently never met her double, Janette came face to face with a future version of herself twenty-two years later, when she was thirty-six and living in Adelaide.

'In 1993, I saw a doppelgänger of myself in the dead of night, in our later-to-be-renovated bathroom.

'I was sitting on the toilet, there was a glass shower screen to my left and bathtub to my right. I reached over for toilet paper from the dispenser next to the bathtub and as I straightened up, she was there in my peripheral vision on the left. This first glimpse really startled me. She was just suddenly there. As I was looking at her through the glass of the shower screen, I took a second to internally shake myself to check that I wasn't dreaming, or that she wasn't just a weird reflection of some sort.

'Once I was sure I was awake, I just stared at her, trying to figure out what was going on and who or what she was. She was standing between me and the bathroom door facing into the shower on my left, and approximately five feet [1.5 metres] away. Not close enough to touch me.

'She looked solid, yet slightly milky through the glass of the shower partition between us. She was wearing a long, white nightdress with a delicate navy-blue floral print, just like an old favourite of mine that had worn out and I'd thrown away. I was puzzled by the nightdress and by her hair, which was long and reminded me of how I'd worn it back at uni.

'I was glad that she wasn't actually looking in my direction, as that would have been terrifying. I felt like a rabbit mesmerised by oncoming headlights and instinctively kept very still so that she wouldn't notice me or turn in my direction.

'Her only movements were minor adjustments of her head as if she was examining herself in a mirror; and she seemed to have her hands held out at waist level as if doing something with them. It's hard to say how long she stood there – time seemed to be standing still as I was feeling afraid – I guess it was less than a minute and then she was gone as quickly as she'd appeared. No fading out or walking away.

'A year or more later, after the bathroom had been renovated, I was standing on the spot where she had stood, looking at myself in the new mirror and drying my hands at the new hand basin (where the old shower used to be). It was just after dinner and I was washing my hands, when the shock of it hit me. Out of the blue, I suddenly knew that, back then, I had really been looking at myself and a shiver went up my spine. I remembered how scared of her looking at me I had felt on the first night and I was very careful not to move suddenly or to look over in the direction of the toilet because it felt like this was the exact moment of connection between the two of us. I waited for the feeling to finish before I moved away.

'This experience seemed like a window I looked through at myself in the near future. She had been standing, washing her hands at a basin from the future wearing a nightdress from the past and with long hair as I'd worn it many years ago. The mixing of past and future elements got me thinking about the nature of space and time for many years after that.

'Much later, after reading Deepak Chopra's theories about the quantum dimension from which many possible physical realities can arise at any moment, I decided this experience may have had something to do with glimpsing the possibility of multiple simultaneous lives.'

FAITH'S ENVOY

'Although the room was very dark, the angel seemed illuminated.'

In a private hospital in Sydney, in the winter of 1969, mother-of-six Rhonda Rice, thirty-two, was in tears. She was being readied for a hysterectomy, a solution, promised her doctor, for 'all the wear and tear' on her uterus. But she had doubts. *Do I really want to do this?* thought the young mum. *What choices do I have?* Alone in her bed, she wept for two hours. As they wheeled Rhonda into surgery, she mourned the loss of her womb, the emptying of hope.

When she awoke in recovery, Rhonda knew instantly that something was wrong. 'I was aware of an awful heaviness on my whole body. My nose was blocked. I couldn't breathe. I tried to breathe through my mouth but was too weak. I couldn't even open my eyes. I could hear nurses nearby but couldn't attract their attention. I had always been terrified of suffocating, of that awful gasping for breath, and now here I was, in that dreaded situation,' recalls the now sixty-nine-year-old widow.

'But suddenly I realised I wasn't scared. In fact, I was overwhelmed with a feeling of calm and absolute peace. I remember thinking, *I'm not breathing, but what was I so scared of? I'm dying, but I feel so good.* I felt the awful heaviness leave me and I was so light that I could feel myself slowly floating upward and thinking how unbelievably happy I felt.'

Then a burst of voices pierced her bliss. 'I heard a nurse cry, "Quick, she's not breathing!" I kept thinking, *It's okay, don't worry, I'm alright, don't stop me.* But then I felt something cold and sharp pushed down my throat and a rush of air go into me.' She lost consciousness again. Eventually, the relieved nurses returned Rhonda to her room and she slept.

The next afternoon, Rhonda's mum Winifred popped in to visit her. It was only then, in talking to her mother, that Rhonda remembered her trip to the edge of death.

'What time did this happen?' asked Winifred, who was then living in a caravan in Liverpool, a few suburbs away from her daughter's hospital in Auburn.

'About 6 pm.'

'You mightn't believe this,' said her mum, a funny look on her face. 'But when I was sitting having my dinner at around that time, I looked up and there you were, standing at the door of my van. You had your normal clothes on. I said, "Hello darling, was your operation cancelled?" But you didn't reply. I said, "Come over love, and I'll put the jug on."'

But Rhonda stayed where she was, beaming the most beautiful smile Winifred had ever seen. As she got up to give her daughter a hug, she disappeared. Recalls Rhonda: 'She said she'd never seen me look so happy.'

Rhonda and her mum, who died in 1997, had always been particularly close, their bond sealed by a shared experience of unimaginable horror. In 1945, amidst those parched Sydney days heralding Christmas, Rhonda was nearing her ninth birthday. She lived with her parents, twelve-year-old brother, six-year-old sister, and baby Laurel, not yet two, in a rambling house with a tin roof in inner-western Petersham.

A blue-eyed toddler with a crown of flaxen curls perched in a timber high chair.

Three children at the kitchen table, waiting for their lunch.

An accidental splash of methylated spirits.

A flame.

Rhonda's voice fractures when she tells it.

'We had gas restrictions, it was around war-time. We had a little camp stove but it had to be lit with methylated spirits. Mum had the match lit and when she went to pour the metho into the stove, it sparked and she jumped back. The metho splashed onto my little sister and the flame fired. She caught fire.

'To make it worse, Mum couldn't get her out of the chair, it had a latch. She couldn't get her out and some of the fire was getting onto Mum. My brother got a dish of water and threw it over them.' Winifred finally wrenched Laurel out of the seat, the baby clad only in a singlet and nappy against the summer heat, and fled with her to a hospital two blocks away. She ran with Laurel in her arms, Rhonda close behind her. In an act of unfathomable cruelty, the hospital said it couldn't treat Laurel, as she wasn't a private patient, but offered to phone an ambulance. 'She was taken to a children's hospital,' says Rhonda. 'She died two days later. It was terrible.'

In the days following Laurel's death, the family shuffled through the debris of their lives, enveloped in grief as thick as the pungent smell that lingered in the shell of the kitchen. Back then, the bereaved were expected to mourn swiftly and with minimal fuss. But Rhonda was riven, consumed by the guilty memory of one of her last moments with her sister. 'One day, Mum asked me to mind her. I was cranky because I didn't want to mind her. I was sitting with her on my knees, bouncing her and she fell. She was crying, I was scared I'd hurt her. That is the main memory I have of her – I remember her catching fire, I can't remember playing with her or anything nice.'

One night soon after, Rhonda woke up thirsty from her sleep. She swung her legs over, so that she was now sitting on the edge of her bed, and reached for her glass on a small bedside table. 'Suddenly, I was aware of someone standing at the head of my bed, but I wasn't scared or even alarmed, strangely enough. I faced this lovely person who stood with arms in a protective semi-circle, head inclined a little to one side and with an expression of almost amusement.'

As a Catholic, Rhonda believed in guardian angels, but never did she dream that she would see one. This beautiful being, who stood bathed in its own soft light, was not distinctly male or female, though Rhonda refers to her as the latter. With her rosy cheeks and blue-sky eyes, she radiated an unearthly beauty that enchanted the child. She wore an ivory-coloured gown with a tie at the waist and long, gaping sleeves. Her feet, hovering about thirty centimetres off the floor, were bare. She had no wings.

'Although the room was very dark, the angel seemed illuminated somehow, but she was not at all transparent. I thought she would speak, and stood waiting patiently, enjoying the sense of happiness that flooded me. But she just stood there, smiling – not showing teeth, but a smile that looked as though she was going to start laughing.'

Rhonda's joy – the playful essence of childhood – had gone to the flames with Laurel, so this reminder of it was intoxicating. 'I wanted to hug her, so I moved towards her, but as I did, she moved slightly back. *She's playing*, I thought, and moved forward again, but she moved back, *gliding* actually. Eventually, I couldn't contain my curiosity and desire to touch her, so I rushed at her, and as I did, she moved behind the heavy curtain. I laughed. She was playing hidings! I quickly pulled the curtain back, but she was gone.'

Disappointed, Rhonda sat back on her bed, waiting for her angel to return, to no avail. Dawn was breaking before the excited fourth-grader lay down her head of chocolate ringlets. 'I told my parents, who believed me, because I was a religious child, and they thought I was being rewarded. I told the nun who taught us, and she thought my little sister might have visited me, but I said it wasn't her. I just had this inner certainty that it was my guardian angel. The nun then said something wonderful happened to me.'

Looking back, Rhonda feels this angel was a portent of hope, a sign that at the end of her suffering, she would emerge anew. But first, she would endure more pain. Rent by the tragedy, little Rhonda had a nervous breakdown, her nine-year-old self unequipped to endure what she had witnessed. She began to twitch and jerk involuntarily, every lurch a lament for her lost sister. Diagnosed with St. Vitus's Dance, a condition similar in symptoms to Tourette's, she was prescribed bed rest for a year. Here she read, played with plasticine and listened in envy to the sounds of the neighbourhood children playing in the street.

'I think I was allowed to see my angel *before* my breakdown, so I would know that I wasn't alone in the long days and sleepless nights that followed,' reflects Rhonda, today a writer, grandmother of twelve and a scripture teacher. She says she learned years ago to stop telling others her experience, for the pity that would cloud their faces. '"Oh that's nice, dear,' they would say, obviously thinking I had dreamt it all.'

She prefers to recreate the moment for her young charges. Perhaps in their wide eyes, their ready sense of wonder, she catches a glimmer of light, a flash of smiling blue eyes. 'Maybe the fact that I can share my tale is also part of the reason it happened to me,' says Rhonda. 'I have a feeling I'll see her again, one day.'

THE WINGED MESSENGER

'It was flapping its wings and looking at me.'

On a chilly May night in 2003, senior banking executive Forooz Normoyle awoke to an extraordinary sight. A creature standing 180 centimetres high was perched on the dainty ornamental balcony of her elegant terrace in Sydney's Paddington, balancing itself on her avocado tree and languidly flapping its enormous, transparent wings. Beyond their silvery luminescence, Forooz could make out the familiar details of her courtyard. It was barely three metres away and it didn't take its eyes off her. But the strangest part was that it wasn't alone ...

That year had proved a turning point for the Iranian-born career woman. At forty-three, she'd finally accepted that she'd never have children. After the loss of an ovary, four years and sixteen cycles of IVF, miscarriages and disappointments, Forooz had given up. She had little choice. 'Eventually, the doctors said "Don't come back,"' recalls Forooz, a statuesque beauty with the fluid limbs of a Modigliani muse. 'It was very hard.' She left her job of eighteen years with a major bank and poured herself into studying for her MBA, eventually securing a post with another bank, finding solace and distraction in the long hours and the interstate travel. Hers was a good life, she'd decided – she was blessed to have her job, her friends and David, her husband of eighteen years – it was time to finally forget her dream of motherhood.

Until that autumn night.

'I just woke up and in front of me was standing this *huge* human-like body but with pink skin, a big pointy face, long legs and two silver wings,' says Forooz, her voice deep and melodious. 'It looked like an alien of some sort, but it had these huge silver wings. It was balancing on this branch of a tree and flapping its wings and looking at me.' Then she noticed something else. Not far from the creature, a bundle lay nestled where the trunk met a branch. 'It was a little baby asleep, like a newborn child. I thought, *Am I dreaming?*'

She propped herself up against the bed's headboard and met its stare. Despite its grotesque appearance, she says she did not feel afraid, nor sense any menace. 'It felt extremely safe. I did think [Gasp] *What is this? Oh!* But it didn't feel like I had to scream or run away.'

Instead, she shook her husband awake.

'David, can you see this thing on the balcony?'

'What's going on?' he muttered, lifting his head and peering outside. 'I don't see anything.'

David flicked on the light and the being was gone, along with its tiny companion.

Forooz convinced herself that she'd had the most vivid and peculiar dream of her life, despite her rational banker's brain telling her that she'd sat up straight in bed and watched the visitor for three or four minutes.

Any doubts evaporated the next evening, when the moonlight offered up its midnight guests once more. 'The next night I woke up again and the *same thing* was on the balcony flapping its wings looking at me, with the *same* little baby asleep on the branch of the tree,' exclaims Forooz, who had suspected she had some psychic gifts but had never experienced a 'supernatural' encounter before.

Certainly never something like this. Its bizarre features are branded in her memory: the face recalled the elongated features of a whippet dog, its skin goose-pimply and pale bovine pink, the torso shaped 'like a teardrop,' explains Forooz, describing its small upper body, large belly and spindly legs. Most fantastic of all, the wings – massive and translucent, slicing the frigid air.

Again, she roused her husband. 'God, I wish you'd go to sleep,' he grumbled. 'Stop waking me up!' David couldn't see it, and Forooz was left to decipher the significance of what seemed like a scene from *The Twilight Zone* playing out in her Paddington courtyard two nights in a row – but it would be months before she truly understood it. In the thick of it, there wasn't much scope for rationalising. 'I didn't know what it was and I didn't know what it was trying to tell me,' she says softly. 'But he was there, he *really* was present.'

Could a higher power have been trying to deliver a message to Forooz? She now believes so. The creature never returned, and Forooz filed the experience away for safekeeping. She didn't have much time to dwell on it, what with socialising, work and a hectic schedule of business travel.

Five months later, Forooz began to feel off-colour and exhausted. Hardly surprising, since she'd been so busy, but her doctor suggested early menopause. 'I was really upset!' she recalls. 'I was going out and drinking jugs of Margaritas with my friends and feeling really sorry for myself, because at forty-three to be going through early menopause, it was terrible.'

Her pity party ended with a question from her husband that she'd long given up hope of hearing. 'What if you're pregnant?' asked David.

Forooz, cultured woman of the world and corporate high-flyer, said: 'Nah!'

Just in case, she fished a four-year-old home pregnancy test out of the bottom drawer. The double lines – positive! – glowed neon bright in her bathroom. After sighing and tut-tutting, 'Look, Forooz, why do you put yourself through all this?' her doctor looked as shocked as his patient felt when he confirmed that she was three-and-a-half months along. The expectant mum began to tentatively tell close friends about the 'presence' and the baby in the branch. 'People tried to be a bit polite,' she recalls. 'They'd think, *Oh my God, this is Forooz being a bit eccentric* or *God, she's just so happy about this pregnancy that she's trying to make it more than what it is.*'

There was one person who wasn't at all surprised, Forooz's mother in Iran, who has since passed away.

She said, 'This was your angel, you know that?'

'Angels are supposed to look pretty, with nice skin,' replied Forooz.

'They can be anything,' answered her mum.

Charlie arrived a month early in March 2004. 'A perfect boy,' coos Forooz, her voice soaked in love. 'I had less than one per cent chance of ever having a child and for me to have a normal, healthy baby was a miracle. Every day I look at him and think he's come to my life for a reason and somebody has helped him to be here.'

❧

Compiling this chapter, a grab bag of paranormal delights, it struck me that these experiences are among the most obscure in the book. However startling a ghost story, we have a cultural reference for it. Everybody knows what a ghost is. But what to make of Forooz's angel of fertility? Its grotesque form calls to mind a gargoyle, mythological creatures both evil and angelic. The latter were said to have been intentionally hideous, all the better to carry out their job of warding off demons and protecting humans. There's no shortage of theories about the origins of gargoyles, but I could find no similar report of a being such as Forooz describes appearing on such a precise errand. It's one of the strangest stories I've ever heard, more so for its stylish urban setting.

In these testimonies, the juxtaposition between the marvellous and the mundane is starkest. An angel with a perfect coif and roman sandals descends to light the way for a little girl on an unremarkable country road, a woman going into labour in the middle of the night is soothed by a young monk who materialises in her recliner chair, a mother driving a familiar route is stunned when a pilot from the past flies low enough to smile at her, a nurse on her way to work comes face to face with her mirror image . . .

Like Deborah Dalrymple's brief meeting with her younger self, Janette's encounter with her double is unforgettable. Einstein believed that the past, present and future are all occurring simultaneously, so perhaps Deborah and Janette simply accessed past and/or future versions of themselves? But what was the trigger? Why them, why then? It's interesting to note that both Deborah and Janette made subtle changes to their everyday routines, intentionally or not, in the moments before the experiences. Deborah forgot something as she was backing out of her driveway; it was as she drove back in that she confronted her younger self. In Janette's case, she missed the school bus. But her doppelgänger didn't. Such delicate tears in the fabric of time, but what vast possibilities we spy through them.

LIVING AMONG THE DEAD

The Adventures of an Average Medium

'An old world story appears before me,
It haunts me by night and by day.'
HEINRICH HEINE

Imagine glancing to the side while you're stopped at traffic lights and seeing a young ghost on the sidewalk, her mournful eyes pinned on you? Or, as you're washing your hair, to be startled by a sharp rap at the window, and know that a spirit wants to whisper in your ear?

Imagine what it would be like to have them seek you out, as eager as a crush of fans outside a stage door, at any time of the day or night . . .

The women in this chapter experience these things – and more – every day. Yet they rarely feel fear, which is less shocking when you accept that, for most of them, this has been a part of their lives since they were out of nappies. Rather, some feel frustration that they don't know how to help the ghost move on, others feel sadness for these souls trapped between two worlds, or curiosity, or a sense of privilege, but none want to turn and run. This isn't Hollywood.

According to my interviewees, there are spirits clamouring in homes all over our cities, suburbs and country towns – it's probably happening at your neighbour's place.

Or inside your own four walls.

For these unsung mediums in our midst, there is no such thing as a one-off encounter with something they can't explain – *life* itself is a ghost story, a weighty tome encompassing spirits alive and dead, husbands, children, tragedy, love and deepest loss.

And it's an old story. 'Mediumship appears to be at least as old as recorded history,' writes David Fontana, who says that the Classical Greek philosopher Socrates (469-399 BC) may himself have been one and 'made the first known attempt to explain the phenomenon.'

'Where does one start when telling about their life as a psychic? The only way is from the beginning.' So says Romayne Marjolin, who has always been surrounded by ghosts and spirits. 'My earliest memories were of always having other people around me who I could talk to; I must have been about seven years old before I understood they were not alive,' says Romayne, echoing some of the other women in this chapter. 'At that age, I still did not understand "alive" and "dead", so after many years receiving my mother's harsh discipline, I learned not to even mention who I talked to and could see. This was my secret.'

Romayne was nine when her mother's harsh discipline turned to fury that her daughter claimed to be communicating with the dead. 'I kept my friends strictly to myself after that,' she says. At the age of seventy-two, Romayne's secret is out in the open – she is now a practising psychic medium, doing readings at her home in Mornington, Victoria.

She offers a thought-provoking peek into what it's like to be the ghost whisperer next door: first, clients arrive and shuffle an old tried-and-trusted deck of tarot cards. 'While they play with the cards, all the information regarding their problems comes to my mind like tic-a-tape at a New York street parade. Like many psychics, I have sleepless nights. My mind is working like a computer – lots of information coming in I cannot place. I just store it in my filing cabinets in my head, and some days or weeks later, the right person arrives [for a reading] to receive it. How do I know this person? I don't, but the computer in my brain does. The filing cabinet opens and there is the information ready and waiting.

'Many psychics are dyslexic and many psychic mediums have severe health problems, which they deal with, without shouting it to the world,' adds Romayne, who nonetheless reaps joy from guiding people and reuniting them, albeit briefly, with loved ones who have passed. 'People come to me at the end of the line. Their family has failed them, the doctor as well, the priest has been of little help. These poor souls have landed on my doorstep and have left with a new vision in mind. They progress with their lives.'

But not all women who live among the dead are out and proud, or choose to make a career of it. Nurse and mum Bev Clayton is just one of the mediums I've met who live quietly and anonymously with their gifts. With one foot in this world and one in the next, they meld busy lives – full of family, friends, children and jobs – with their ability to foretell events and communicate with the spirit world. To these women, ghosts and spirits are not something to fear, they just are.

In *When Ghosts Speak*, Mary Ann Winkowski, who's been communicating with earthbound spirits since she was a baby, offers a fascinating insight into her world: 'Pretty much anyplace I go has a few earthbound spirits hanging around, but I've learned to ignore them . . . I've learned not to stare,' writes Mary Ann, who believes the dead have a window of three days to cross into the spirit world. If they don't, they'll remain as an earthbound spirit until someone, like herself, directs them to the light. 'Whether we're aware of them or not, ghosts have always been among us.'

Retired security officer Delise Moore, who first knew of her abilities when she saw the smiling spirit of her adored aunt as a thirteen-year-old, says that seeing them makes her feel privileged, as she tells below.

'I am of Aboriginal descent, but not raised in the cultural aspect. In the 1950s, on a sheep station in the Murchison district of WA, my grandfather, whom I was very close to, would pass certain stories to us grandchildren. I always felt close to nature.

'For the past thirty years I have been attending Spiritualism churches. About thirteen years ago, I was visiting my then-partner at the North Rockhampton Hotel. He was staying in a very old flat to the left of the hotel. He told me, "There is a spirit here, see what you feel about the place." From the moment I walked through the door on arriving, I felt I was being watched. About a week later my partner rang to say he was held up at work. I was sitting in front of the TV, when from the dark blue nylon carpet a mist started to rise. This was about two feet to the right of me. I was not afraid but in absolute awe as I watched as this mist became a swirling vortex reaching to about three feet [90 cm] in height. I moved slightly, and the mist slowly faded away to nothing. I sat feeling so very honoured to have witnessed what had happened.

'Two nights later, I was in the bathroom shaving my legs when I felt as if someone was watching me. At first I ignored the urge to look up. When I did, ten feet [3 metres] from me stood a young man in solid form. He was about twenty-two years of age, short fair hair, very fit-looking, dressed in a white T-shirt and jeans. We stared at each other, then he gave me a beautiful smile. I smiled back as he was so real.

'The thing that puzzled me was that he had no feet; the jeans stopped just below the calf muscles. I looked back to my leg-shaving. I thought, *What do I do now, he's still here!* so I looked up and smiled again. He returned the smile then slowly faded to nothing. I finished what I was doing then went to the room where my friend was and told him, "I've just met your spirit visitor, he's a beautiful, friendly young man."'

Tamara Warden, twenty-eight, comes from a long line of psychics on her father's side of the family – and could never forget it. Appliances and gadgets go haywire around the South Australian medium: battery-operated watches will blink date/time non-stop, TVs expire, lightbulbs smash and mobile phones have a shelf-life of eight months.

But her gift is as much a part of the fabric of her life as her love for her husband of seven years, Aaron, her children – Aanya, six, and Aramis, two – her scrapbooking and her beloved karaoke.

Tamara was three when she met her first spirit person, a tiny boy who matched her in age and height. 'I couldn't understand why Mum couldn't see him,' she says. 'The first night I saw him in my bedroom he sort of looked like moonlight; silvery and shimmery, but when I'd see him during the day he was more solid. He had blonde hair and wore a blue T-shirt. I remember his blue T-shirt; it was the same colour as his eyes.'

Ghosts are often just as shocked to see *us*, says Tamara, pinpointing a theme that winds through many of these stories. 'One night, I woke up and I could feel my daughter in front of me – well, I thought it was my daughter. I took a closer look and it wasn't. I put my hand out to touch this child and my hand went right through and she screamed! Then I screamed and my husband woke up and turned the light on.

'I know they are there before I open my eyes,' continues Tamara, who has had many of these night visitors. 'I feel the energy. The best way to describe it is, you know how you put your hand close to a TV and there is static electricity there? That's how it feels to me. I've gotten better at not screaming when I open my eyes. They are just standing there, waiting for me to wake up. They are generally very patient.'

It's not the easiest thing to live with, says Tamara, whose children have inherited her gifts. 'Growing up is confusing enough as it is, and knowing people do or don't like you isn't as exciting as it sounds. It can be more of a burden. You are growing up, you've got all these everyday issues to deal with but you can tell if one of your friends is lying, or kissed your boyfriend. And to top it off, you go to bed at night and wake up and there is someone beside you!'

It is also isolating. 'You can feel so alone,' says Tamara. 'I've got a daughter who is a lot like me but she's six, so I can't have conversations with her. It is so different to what a lot of people feel. Most folks don't have to worry that if you go to a funeral, you are going to have the deceased trying to get your attention.'

Now that she is doing readings for people, Tamara says the visits have dwindled off. 'It feels like I am doing the right thing now,' she says. 'When I'm introduced to friends, I'm not just Tamara, it's "This is Tamara and she's a psychic," and I'm okay with that now. I'm happy with that.'

Sydney singer Victoria, who asked that her surname be withheld, is also at ease and secure in the knowledge of what she sees, hears and knows about the future, though it's taken her some years to come to terms with it. 'I've only now realised that the people I saw in my bedroom as a child at night were spirits,' says the vivacious forty-six-year-old. 'I used to get really frightened at night and say, "People are in my bedroom!" and run into Mum and Dad's room and slide in between them.'

These days, there's little that fazes Victoria, who says the guiding spirit of her mum is always with her. 'About two months ago, someone was shaking the daylights out of my bed and as I sat up, my heart was pounding because, though it's always moved, it had never shaken so hard!'

Like Tamara and most of the mediums I've met, Victoria's presence interferes with electronics: 'I've broken two DVDs and the third one is playing up now,' she bemoans. 'They just stop working, and my new TV had to go back.' And, like the others, night-time drop-ins are commonplace. After belting out sixties, seventies, eighties, nineties and country tunes at gigs, she might find that a different audience awaits her at home. 'Once, I woke up and had three of them sitting on my bed, staring at me.'

When I ask her if she realises that that sounds like a horror movie, 'I do,' she answers breezily. 'I felt something was there but didn't realise there would be three of them. As I backed up, I understood they were spirits. One, a little girl with brownish curly hair, the woman beside her had jet-black hair and there was a man in a suit who was bald on top. And they were staring at me.'

My thoughts spring to Amy Shepherd, who met a ghostly family in Chapter One and used near-identical words to describe the moment. 'All in a row,' continues Victoria, 'the little girl, the woman and the man. They were sitting on the right side of my bed, looking at me really close to my face. Like if you go to visit someone in hospital and you sit on the edge of their bed? It was that sort of thing, and then they vanished. I blinked and they were gone.'

'Most nights, I hear old-fashioned music playing and I often hear chit-chat in the bedroom,' says Victoria, who also sees spirits in supermarkets and while she's driving. 'Some nights, I get quite annoyed and yell, "Oh, for God's sake!" I don't know why they are here, nine times out of ten if they wake me up, I just go back to sleep and when my bed moves, I don't even sit up anymore.'

Still worrying over the question of *why* some people are mediums, I turned to author and paranormal researcher Marie D. Jones. 'I think it all comes to down to the brain and consciousness. Some people seem more finely tuned to their own intuition, to the emotions of others, to subtle changes in the environment. It makes sense then, that some people would be more receptive to paranormal events, simply because their brain is wired a certain way,' she says. 'If information is coming to all of us from the other levels of reality, we could be like radios, each of us choosing which broadcast to tune into. Some of us get the right frequency to pick up on the information coming from "the other side", and some of us, for whatever reasons, just never do get the right station.'

The late famed Sydney psychic Margaret Dent, who had a two-year waiting list for a one-on-one reading, once revealed that as a budding medium bombarded by spirits, she simply asked them what they wanted. They told her. 'It's to let people know that they've survived the transition,' Margaret told *Who* magazine in 1999. 'If you have somebody who's killed in a car accident, for example, they want to give their side of what happened. If you have somebody who suicided, they want to get through their reasons. It's as varied as human nature.'

'I don't try to convince anybody, I do what I do and that's all I can do,' she summed up. 'It's never been a career choice. You either believe it or not. Truth is stranger than fiction.'

Tamara Warden agrees: 'There is still a stigma about this. Good doctors don't have to prove it, good cooks don't have to prove it, but if you are psychic, you are asked to prove it every day.' Nonetheless, she is grateful that high-profile mediums such as John Edward and Allison DuBois have demystified what they do, to a degree. 'The big ones have shown that we are people just like everybody else. You don't have to be frightened.'

THE RELUCTANT MEDIUM

'It's the look on their faces, a look of despair.'

His portrait hangs forever in her memory.

The young man sat in a chair by the side of a hospital bed where an elderly woman lay dying. He waited for hours, a cushion propped at his back, looking like a relic from a dog-eared family photo album. 'He had on light gabardine, flared trousers, with a chocolate-brown top, like a long-sleeved body-fitting T-shirt. His hair was slicked back. He had clunky shoes.' Nurse Bev Clayton describes him with affection, this incongruous visitor she paused to watch while on her rounds in 2007. She often sees spirit relatives at the bedside of sick patients, and it's her favourite part of the day. 'That's my biggest pleasure,' she sighs, joy flooding her voice. 'I absolutely love it when I see the family waiting for them. It's just really nice to know that a family member comes to pick you up when it's time.'

Bev has always been able to see the dead, but prefers not to discuss it, or share with friends and colleagues the way she 'just knows' about the intimate lives of strangers. 'I'm a nurse at a hospital in a country town,' she says with a choked laugh. 'They'd burn me at the stake.'

Growing up in the 1960s, she spent her primary school years alongside ghostly classmates only she could see. She just let them be, never wondering why no one else spotted the sad-eyed outsiders, never publicising that she could. 'I tried not to be noticed,' says Bev, whose scrawny frame made her a target for bullies. Only rarely did she drop her guard and mention the children to a friend.

'I feel sorry for that little girl over there,' she'd say.

'Which little girl?'

'The one over there, the one with the dirty clothes on.'

'I don't know what you mean,' shrugged her friend.

'Eventually, I stopped mentioning it to anybody.'

Today, Bev has three children of her own, and a husband whose credo is, 'What's black is black and what's white is white; unless you can see it, it doesn't happen.' The forty-six-year-old still lives in the same country town where she grew up, and still keeps her secret wound tightly inside herself.

Speaking at her home on a Saturday afternoon, Bev is uncomfortable at first. From her small, tense voice, it's clear that it's literally hard for her to expel the words. Apart from one or two trusted friends, few know that straight-shooting Bev can see *the people*, as she calls them. For Bev's spirits don't waft or glide or float, they walk with their feet on the ground and seem built of flesh and blood. But there is one way she can tell that they're not: 'It's usually the look on their faces,' she says. 'A look of despair.'

Like so many of the women I have spoken to, Bev can peer into a landscape that isn't quite this world, nor quite the next – it's a place where the dead tread the same earth as us, watch the world push past them in the supermarket, stand sentinel at the side of the road and take the empty seat in a classroom. Bev can't forget the lonely children she saw at school, though she never did get a sense of why they were there, or who they'd been in life. 'They all seemed to be not well-off,' she recalls. 'This little boy who used to sit in one classroom, he never had any lunch, he never ate. He would just sit in class and listen to everything.'

How did she know he wasn't alive? 'Because none of the other children could see him,' she says. 'I knew that if they'd seen him they would have been tormenting him.' She never approached the loners, because in that sense at least, she could be like the other kids. 'It was usually the ones who never ate lunch, I knew they weren't there [in body]. And nobody played with them. A lot of the time this little girl would be standing there, watching everybody else play, but sometimes she'd have a skipping rope and she'd be skipping by herself.'

For Bev, the memory is worn blunt by the years, but I find the image of the skipping girl hot and sharp, something to be held then swiftly released. Instead, she sticks fast. Arriving early to pick up my daughter from school one day, I can almost see the sepia girl in the empty playground, her skipping rope slapping the asphalt like a heartbeat.

The spirit school kids weren't the only 'people' Bev saw as a child. Between the ages of three and twelve, she had a 'spirit person friend' named Madge, an apparition who was 'solid; I wouldn't have known her any different from anybody else,' states Bev. 'She was a very old lady. She had grey hair with a little bun in the back, and she always wore a very faded brown dress with a creamy-coloured half-apron over the top. She would have been lucky to have been five-foot.'

From her style of dress, Bev thinks Madge lived in the Victorian era and that she was a spirit attached to their home, where Bev lived with her family – her mum, a nurse, her dad, who was a bookmaker and fruit delivery man, and her three siblings. After Bev let slip about Madge to her mum one day, she learned quick-smart never to do it again. 'My brother and sisters started teasing me about my imaginary friend. And I know that she wasn't imaginary, I've seen people like her all the time.'

Bev believed Madge was a living person until she had to go into hospital as a seven-year-old. 'She wasn't there! When I went back home I asked her where she'd been. She said she can't come and visit me, she can't leave [the house].' Looking back, Bev believes that Madge, the kindly old spirit nanny who 'looked like a wrinkled-up little apple' was assigned to her, that their coming together was no random event. She only stopped seeing her when the family moved homes. 'I think she was there because I needed her to be there,' reflects Bev, who would sit with Madge in the cubby house to play dolls, or make mud pies with her in the backyard. 'I think she was my guardian angel.'

Was Madge a ghost – an earthbound spirit who hadn't entered the light, as the theory goes – or a spirit who *had* crossed over and returned in visitation to guard Bev in her most vulnerable years? Either way, it is only in the last fifteen years that Bev says she has realised that not everyone had a version of Madge in their childhood.

Chatting with a friend at the park one day in the early 1990s, as their boys scrambled over the equipment, Bev mentioned in passing her recurring dreams, and the way she picks up 'feelings' from people as they walk past her. When her friend looked blank, 'that's when I started paying more attention,' says Bev. 'Before that, I thought everybody could see *the people*.'

Not only can Bev see ghosts, but she can identify remotely those who haunt strangers' homes. Hearing that an acquaintance was troubled by a presence in her home, she described the apparition – a woman with a long plait 'to her bottom' in a white linen nightie – to their mutual friend. The next day she learned that she had accurately drawn the spectre that'd stood at the end of the acquaintance's bed. 'I just *know*,' says Bev, when I press her to describe how this information comes to her. 'It's like you know that that's a tree in front of you, like you know what your name is, where you live. You just know it.'

Not everything is as simple in Bev's dealings with the spirit world. It troubles her, for instance, that she doesn't know how to assist the dead who flock to her. While some apparitions seem mere snapshots of the past – like the old man with the wood-churning machinery who would materialise by Bev's bed, waking her up with his noisy task – others expect more from her.

'I used to have one lady who would keep singing out for help: "Help me, help me, help me,"' says Bev, who couldn't see the woman, but could hear her as clearly as if she were in the next room.

Exasperated, she would yell, 'I don't know how to help you!' while her kids stared at her, wide-eyed. Eventually, the pleading ceased.

Similarly, four years ago, a boy in well-to-do turn-of-the-century dress began appearing to Bev at her former home. When the family left that house, he moved with them, and of all the spirits she has encountered, Bev, the reluctant medium, says this sweet lost boy affected her the most. Wearing breeches, his long hair in ringlets, the boy – aged around ten – would whimper the same stark refrain. 'I could be watching TV of a night and he'd be standing there, saying "Help me, help me." I could be in bed trying to go to sleep and he'd be standing there saying "Help me, help me." I could be cooking tea, I could be anywhere . . .'

Through gritted teeth, Bev could only throw out her standard retort – 'I don't know how to help you' – until one day, she knew he would never return. 'I'll never forget it. It was a Sunday afternoon and the three children were watching a movie. He appeared where the children were and he smiled. He looked so content. I smiled back at him, and he never came back. I just think that he found somebody who *could* help him.'

Other aspects of her gift are more of a burden, says Bev, who occasionally sees dark, shadowy entities – 'I call them bullies' – trailing troubled or drunken people in crowded places like the local club, or shopping malls. In 2004, she had a prophetic vision of her niece, who is like a daughter to her, being seriously injured in a car accident. Bev weeps while explaining that, sometimes, there are things she would rather not see, 'because I don't know exactly what I can do about it.'

Bev's thirteen-year-old son, Trent, has inherited her gift. One day, at the cricket, amidst the hubbub of Saturday sport, mother and son spotted a lone child, barefoot, perched on a camping chair following the game, unnoticed by anyone else. 'What's that little boy doing by himself all day?' Trent asked his mum. 'He's right, mate,' she replied.

On the street, in the shops, day or night, Bev can see them. 'They usually just stand there, looking at you, staring at you, as if to say, *You can see me!* And contrary to many popular shows and films, she says they are never standing stock-still in the middle of the road, shoulders slumped, dead eyes staring.

'I'll be heading in one direction and I'll sort of glance to my right, and there'll be one standing there. It's not like they want me. They're just *there*. They look like they could be waiting for a bus. I don't know what they're waiting for.' Just like the children in the schoolyard, they remain on the sideline, excluded from the action, not participating in life or death. Bev believes 'they're here because they haven't finished doing what they're supposed to have done.'

This everyday mum, from an everyday country town, feels blessed on the days she goes to work and witnesses proof that life survives death, that *love* survives death. 'Someone could tell you that and you'd have doubts. You'd think, *Is this what really happens?* But when you've seen it for yourself and you know that there really are family members sitting there waiting to take you when it's your time to go, I just think it's so beautiful for people to know that.

'And I know that I know that. Out of everything, that's probably peace, for me.'

GHOST GIRL

'Sometimes, they don't want anything. They just want to be remembered.'

Brenda Purden is a happily married twenty-nine-year-old living in the Victorian city of Bendigo with her husband and two cats.

Though she has been communicating with earthbound spirits since childhood, Brenda doesn't classify herself as a medium or psychic, or even openly discuss her abilities. In fact, much of her energy is spent dealing with the hearing fluctuations, severe pain and exhaustion that characterise the inner-ear disorder Ménière's disease, which she was diagnosed with at the age of twenty-two. This reminded me of Sydney psychic Debbie Malone, who suffers from tinnitus – it's common in mediums, she told me – and has struggled with ill health all her life. (Another psychic, Romayne Marjolin, added that many psychics are dogged by 'severe health problems'.) Despite the struggle of coping with her illness, Brenda is a candid and articulate young woman who may also happen to be one of the most gifted natural mediums I've encountered. 'At first, I honestly thought that I was going mad,' says Brenda, who tells her story below. 'Now I believe that if you are meant to see spirits, they will come to you if they want help.'

'My earliest memory with spirits was when I was about twelve. I lived in Victoria with my mum and stepdad. My aunty and uncle lived in Sydney with their three daughters. I didn't know it at the time but my aunty was suicidal and had attempted it several times. Only her husband knew of the emotional roller-coaster and eventually he had told his two sisters (including my mum). The week before my aunt's death I had various dreams about her. I was always close to her despite being so far away.

'I dreamt that my cousins (her three daughters) were coming to visit for a long weekend . . . And guess what, Mum told me that my cousins were coming. Over the next few nights I continued to have dreams about seeing my aunty, what I wanted to talk to her about and how she was feeling. She never told me she was unwell, but I knew something wasn't right. I was waking up at about 2.30 am every time I had a dream involving my aunty.

'My cousins came down and they stayed with my grandmother. My uncle also came, they told everyone that my aunty couldn't make it because she had too much work to do. I played with the girls like we always did but something felt different. Again that night I had a dream and woke up at about 2.30 am. The same thing happened the next night and while I was lying awake wondering why I kept waking up at this horrible hour, I could hear the phone ringing in the distance. I heard Mum getting up to answer it. I heard her crying. I got up to ask her what was wrong and she told me that my aunty had died and to go back to bed.

'I returned to my room to find a shadowy image at the foot of my bed. I climbed into bed, watching this image that had started to look a lot like my aunty, but it was still dark and hard to focus on. I did notice her curly hair and what looked like a dark green dress of some sort. I kept saying to myself, "Why did this happen?" I heard a voice and instantly recognised it as belonging to my aunty.

"My sweet niece Brenda. Please don't be sad for me. This was something I had to do. I wasn't well and didn't want my girls to see me like this. Please forgive me and know that I still do love my family." I didn't understand what she meant or what she was saying. How was this possible? I had so many questions I wanted to ask. Eventually, I fell asleep, and in the morning, we all got together at my grandmother's house, where we were told that she had committed suicide.

'For about three or four nights afterward, I continued to wake up at 2.30 am and kept hearing her voice. I desperately wanted to go to the funeral in Sydney, but I was told that I was too young. When things settled down a bit I visited the library to find out about angels and spirits. I believe that this was my first encounter with anything paranormal.

'In high school, my friends started getting into witchcraft-type stuff including ouija boards and spells. I didn't always agree with what we were doing because we'd all heard how this could come back at you threefold. While my friends were trying to cast spells to get a boy to like them, I was reading books on auras, ghosts and the afterlife. I started trying to read people by their aura colour and soon learned to recognise if someone had an injury or something similar because that part of them was a different colour. It is almost like running a thermal imaging scanner over someone!

'In Year Eleven, we were asked in English class to walk into town and just sit and observe four different people and write down different things about them, such as their emotions, what they might have been in town for, what they were wearing, their age et cetera. For me, this is where things got weird. I was sitting on a bench in the mall studying one particular gentleman who looked to be in his mid to late-forties. His clothing looked like something that my grandfather would wear. Neat grey dress pants, a white, striped long-sleeve shirt and a navy and green woollen vest with black shoes. He was also wearing what looked like an apron, but it was thicker, almost like leather, and glasses. He was tall and slender. His brown hair was neat, and parted on one side.

'He stood out to me because he was muttering to himself and looked rather confused. His clothes didn't look that out of date, but because it was a nice day, it seemed that he could have been too warm. He kept looking around and muttering about something not being right. No one near him seemed to take any notice or even look at him. I thought at first that maybe he was a loose cannon and should possibly have been on medication and in a hospital. I thought he was lonely and possibly lost.

'I wrote down everything I could about him and after about half an hour I decided that if no one was going to help this gentleman, then I would step in. As I approached him, he looked up and smiled at me. I asked if everything was okay and if there was something that I could do for him. He again smiled but with a slightly confused look on his face, and said, "I don't think I belong anymore. Everything has changed."

Now my mind was telling me that he belonged in a home but my heart felt sorry for him. He sat next to me and proceeded to tell me that his shop had changed and that the whole area was wrong. He also asked me why I was the only one that seemed to notice him and talk to him. Perhaps I was having this whole conversation on my own?

'The gentleman told me he was a shop owner named Bill. But the shop he was telling me about did not exist. He described a shop that fixed "time pieces". We were outside a cafe, music shop and newsagent. The nearest jewellery shop was too far away and not as described. I ended the conversation asking if I would see him tomorrow at the same time. "I'll be here Miss, I'm here every day."

'His voice was soothing and very well-mannered and his English was much better than how we speak it today. He didn't shorten words for example, and he used correct pronunciation.

'I left and went to the library to find out about the shops that were in Bendigo in the late 1800s and early 1900s. I managed to find a repair shop owned by a gentleman named William, which would have been located near where Bill and I had been talking. William had died of heart failure in the early 1900s. Up to this point, I thought he was mentally ill, but wanted to give him the benefit of the doubt, which is what made me go to the library in the first place.

'After finding information about the store – the fact that he worked in it was quite a shock – I then realised that he was telling the truth and that maybe I was talking to a spirit. I really didn't know what to do, whether to go back to the mall the next day or run and hide. My gut was telling me that curiosity would kill me and besides, what harm would it do?

'I went back into town the next day with a picture of what I thought was Bill's shop. I ran into Bill and asked if it were his. "Yes dear it is, can't you see the sign?" I really don't know what happened then, but I was becoming aware that I was either talking to myself or communicating with someone who wasn't there. I think what gave it away was the way that no one around me had noticed Bill or paid much attention to me. It was like Bill was invisible and I was in a bubble. I started to realise that I was communicating telepathically.

'I told Bill what year it was and who I thought he was. He looked at me again with his smile and said, "Oh dear, I'm so lost, what am I to do and why is it that you are able to communicate with me?" I didn't have all the answers, I still don't, but I told him what I could. He was very thankful and he started walking away from me and then somehow, in the blink of an eye, he seemed to have just disappeared into thin air. I didn't see him again.

'As for the English project, initially I had written down Bill's experience but after realising he was a spirit, I then sat and observed another person to write about.

'I shared my experiences with my "goth" friends, but after I finished school I kept it to myself a fair bit. I did have one friend that I revealed myself to, only because the spirit of her father kept appearing at the house. She was an older friend and she was religious. I asked her about the afterlife and if she believed in ghosts and guardian angels. She said yes, but also said that proof was hard to get. I explained what my thoughts and feelings were about her father and she burst into tears. I thought that I had hurt her feelings. Turns out I was spot on with information I couldn't have known. She has since helped me cope with different situations that have arisen.

'Since my first encounter with Bill, I have experienced a lot of paranormal things. I never assume that I am talking to a ghost or spirit unless I am 100 per cent sure. I do not always see, hear or feel the same thing each time. In Bill's case, I was able to see, hear and talk to him. Other times I only hear them. Sometimes I only see certain things, like clothing or tools. There are even times that all I have seen is an aura-type shape.

'I can also sense people who have perhaps lived in a building or who have passed away in that spot. I have been to a cemetery and seen a lot of spirits wanting help crossing over or who want to pass messages to others. I have been to houses where spirits dwell. I choose whether I want to help these people, but they also choose to be seen and heard. Sometimes they don't want anything, they just want to be remembered.

'When I was twenty-one, I had a life-changing experience. Unfortunately, my husband's grandfather fell ill and passed away, essentially of old age. He was eighty-seven and had fallen ill with a slight cold. The day we got the call to tell us that his condition had deteriorated and that today may be his last day, we arrived at the hospice at about 10 am. It was evident that he was not going to be around much longer. His breathing was shallow and he looked very pale. He also had a lot of trouble talking. The last words he spoke were to my husband. He wanted his daily shave to look good for when his wife arrived. Most of the family were at the hospice except for one of his daughters who lived two hours away and couldn't be reached. When she was finally told, she drove down as quickly as possible. Grandpa held on until she arrived and then passed away shortly after.

'Everyone was overcome by grief. During Grandpa's final moments, his aura changed colour several times and when he did finally exhale his last breath, what I saw was unexplainable. In movies they show that when someone dies, their spirit jumps out of their body and flies through the window. It didn't happen that way at all. Grandpa's spirit just appeared beside his own body, but instead of being in pyjamas, he was dressed in his favourite brown suit. He stood there watching everyone in the room and how they were reacting. He even looked at his own body, laying there on the bed. He saw that I was looking at him and telepathically we started talking.

'He told me that he tried his hardest to wait until his daughter arrived and was glad that she got the chance to say goodbye. He asked if my husband and I could keep an eye on the house for him and then asked where he was supposed to go. I couldn't really give him an answer, so I asked him, "What do you feel you should be doing?" He had a funny sense of humour. He scoffed, saying that without wings he couldn't fly anywhere, but that he would like to keep an eye on his wife to make sure she gets through this okay. His spirit then just sort of faded into the background.

'I was smiling, so my husband nudged me, a curious look on his face. Later, he asked me what I saw. My husband has always been aware of my gift but never encouraged or discouraged me from using it. I told him that Grandpa wanted to keep an eye on Grandma, so we were bound to see him one day . . . Strangely enough, since the day he passed away, the Grandfather clock in Grandpa's house never runs on time anymore. The clock has been in the same spot for years and is still serviced regularly, but for some reason, it slows down and loses time. I always tell my husband that it is Grandpa letting us know that he is still here.

'My life has changed a lot in the last six years. I was diagnosed with an inner ear disorder known as Ménière's disease. This illness affects my hearing, balance and more. I suffer from severe pain in my inner ears, loss of balance, tinnitus, noises in the ear, nausea, vomiting, and my hearing is like a volume button. It changes whenever it wants to and even leaves me completely deaf sometimes. The disease can leave me exhausted even if I haven't done anything, and I may end up spending days in bed just resting. It's unpredictable.

'I never take my gift for granted and now that I have hearing issues, I never tell people that I hear spirits, because there is a chance that it could be my ears causing the problem. I always ask a spirit for some other form of confirmation or proof.

'I think that everyone has a gift similar to mine but many people choose not to explore it, or it is not within their religious behaviour. There are also people who think maybe they will go mad if they see or hear things that are not "normal".

I do not class myself as a medium or anything else because I cannot confirm everything I see, hear or feel. There are no classes to take to see if you are real or fake. I do not share things unless I feel that someone has to know. I still enjoy dressing in black and wear black eyeliner and occasionally black lipstick, but not because I want to look different or scare people. I believe this is me. This is who I am.'

A DIFFERENT LANDSCAPE

'Clear as a bell, he said, "Ta-ta, bub".'

Leonie Evans has died three times.

As a newborn in 1963, she contracted the dangerous golden staph bacteria and was clinically dead for several minutes. When she was five, a car ran over her outside the family home in Guildford, in Western Sydney. The bottom of her ear was torn away and her eardrum burst, among other injuries. She can remember leaving her body and watching over a scene of mayhem. 'My mother was hysterical! All she'd seen was her baby with blood pouring from her head. Dad was not long home from Vietnam and was wearing his uniform. He was screaming at someone to "Get that filthy thing away from her!" because a neighbour was trying to stem the blood with a towel. I could see him trying to resuscitate me.'

Leonie, now forty-five, remembers the moment in high-definition detail. She says her late grandmothers and a third woman were with her as she calmly took in her little body in its school uniform lying motionless on the road, her long blonde hair streaked with blood fanned out beneath her.

'I didn't feel like I was floating, I felt like the ground was solid under my feet. My maternal grandmother had on the same dress she was wearing in a photo my Ma had up in our lounge room, and that's how I recognised her – she had passed twelve years before I was born. My paternal grandmother had only passed the year before my accident, so I knew her on sight. She was wearing her usual uniform of a knitted cardigan, high-necked blouse with a clasp at the neck and a skirt that ended just below her knees. I could see her stockings and her favourite brown shoes.'

The grandmothers stood two metres behind Leonie, who was 'aware of them; I could feel them and I could also see them very clearly and knew they were happy to see me. I didn't speak to them, but I did know that if I did, they would have replied.' Alongside Leonie was an unknown woman whose chestnut hair fell in loose waves around her 'kind' face. 'She was wearing a robe of sorts. She was draped in this soft, soft material – like nothing I've ever felt since. I don't remember a colour to her robe, but she was emitting a golden glow that encompassed both of us, and also reached and embraced my grandmothers.

'The woman was kneeling next to me with her arm around me, comforting me, although I'm not sure "comfort" is the right word. Maybe "guiding" would be more appropriate, but I don't want to insinuate that she was forcing me to make decisions I didn't want to make; I *knew* she wanted only the best for me. Though there were no words spoken, I knew what she was asking and saying, and I was replying the same way. She did ask me specifically if I wanted to go back and because I could see my parents were so upset, I asked what would happen if I wanted to stay with her. She told me my parents would eventually be okay, but they would miss me every day. I knew then I had to come back.'

The third time Leonie clinically died, she was fifteen years old. Run over again – ironically – at the same intersection where she'd been injured ten years earlier, the teenager was 'pretty messed up, physically' and prescribed medication including antibiotics and painkillers. When a school nurse administered an accidental overdose of the powerful prescription drugs, Leonie was rushed to hospital, and again felt herself lifted in the air, watching as paramedics worked on her body. She was kept in hospital for just under two weeks, but the nurses weren't the only ones keeping watch on Leonie. A spirit girl, who looked to be around the same age as her, was constantly by her side.

'There is this girl and she is hanging around me and it's driving me nuts,' Leonie told a nurse. 'I know she is my sister.' Leonie had no idea why she would say something that seemed so nonsensical – after all, she had three sisters and a brother safe and sound at home – but the knowledge that the inquisitive girl in the Lee jeans and plain white T-shirt was her sibling was absolute. 'I gave her a name, Jenny, and this girl hung around me the entire time I was in hospital. She would just watch. She was really interested when they were taking bloods. Sometimes, when I was off the drips and I was able to shower on my own, she'd be in there, waiting.'

Within a week of being discharged from the hospital, Leonie's eighty-six-year-old grandfather – her mother's father, whom she called Gogga – lay critically ill at his nursing home. During one of their last visits, Leonie and her family were gathered around his bed when he turned to her mum, Jean, and said, 'Baby Jenny says, "I miss you, Mum."' Her mother blanched, muttering, 'Oh, no . . .' Sensing her discomfort, Leonie didn't press her mother for an explanation. Only in 1997, when Leonie herself was grieving a miscarriage did her mother tell her about the baby she had miscarried in her second trimester nine years before Leonie was born. 'Apparently, Ma had named her Jenny in her own mind. She never mentioned that she'd named this baby to anyone, not even my father.'

I meet Leonie for lunch at Sydney's Hyde Park, close to where she works as a finance officer. She has blonde hair, smiling chocolate eyes and a lifetime of paranormal encounters behind her, which she reels off as city workers loosen their ties and snooze around us, their faces tipped to the sun. When my recorder suddenly stops working, and I have to scribble madly in my notebook to keep up with her, she's not surprised.

'I blow light bulbs at the rate of knots!' she says cheerfully. 'Now I use the energy bulbs, they seem to withstand me better.' If only she could find a solution for her television sets: 'My TVs have a habit of not only fading in and out, but also blowing up. I have three at the moment, and I like having three because one will blow, or the colours will go weird, or another might just stop working altogether.'

For Leonie, living side by side with the spirit world is the only life she knows. Her mother, Jean, too, was sensitive. 'When you've grown up with it, it becomes normal,' she says, shrugging. 'They've just always been around.' That's why she was nonplussed when her spirit sister paid her a visit in the hospital all those years ago.

'I definitely wasn't frightened! After all those years of seeing people, being frightened wasn't an option. The main thing that stays with me about Jenny was the sense of peace she gave me, that everything would be okay and work out how it was supposed to.'

By the time she met Jenny, Leonie had been seeing the 'people' for twelve years. She calls up a vivid picture of herself at age three, sitting at the kitchen table, colouring in, when someone began handing her the colours. Here, a blue texta. There, a green pencil. The toddler began to chatter, a honeyed sound that made her mother smile. Jean turned around from the sink, wondering what had sparked the babbling, but as she stood observing, her smile soon faded. Pencils were moving by themselves across the table. Her daughter was clearly in conversation, not merely talking to herself. But whose questions was she answering?

'Yes.' 'No.' 'Good,' said Leonie, her head bent over her work, where a burst of colour had exploded like a firecracker on the page. 'Who are you talking to, bub?' asked her mum, who had inched closer, fascinated. 'The lady,' said little Leonie. A few minutes later, her mum sat next to her, clutching a bundle of photographs. Together, they looked through them until Leonie pointed to a photo of her mother's mother, who'd died twelve years before. 'That's her.'

Two years later, after she'd been hit by the car and was recovering at home, five-year-old Leonie encountered some unexpected playmates to ease the boredom of the enforced separation from her kindergarten friends. It was a group of children, she says: four girls her own age, three boys, and an older girl who 'used to keep them in line. When it was time to go, she'd round them up and they would all wave at me.'

The group would play games with Leonie inside the little room she shared with her three sisters. Here's an inventory of an ordinary bedroom in a typical suburban home in an everyday Sydney suburb circa 1968: four bunk beds, a dressing table, a wardrobe, a tiny girl recovering from a head injury, and a gaggle of ghost children.

'They used to play peek-a-boo with me around the wardrobe door. Or, I used to play cubby-houses by pulling the blankets from the top bunk to the bottom so it was all dark. They'd pull the blankets across and have a look. Although I couldn't hear them, I could understand what they were saying.

'They were in their Sunday best; church-going clothes,' recalls Leonie, her sandwich half-eaten on the park bench beside her. She drags on a cigarette and squints into the March sky, as if searching for her friends in the clouds. 'Their hair was always done in plaits or ponytails with ribbons. The little boys were dressed neatly too: you could tell Mum had ironed the shirt, the shorts had creases. It was March, still warm. It's funny the things you remember . . .'

Leonie revels in the novelty of summoning her secret history, the parallel life she usually keeps to herself. Like a time traveller, she soars across her memory, revisiting particular events as the fancy takes her. Now, we zoom ahead to when she was a lanky Year Ten student full of dreams of being a teacher. Recovered from her stint in hospital, she was at a friend's house, a regular hang-out for her group. As the others smoked and gossiped, Leonie was quiet, 'watching out the door,' when she saw the most incongruous sight: her beloved Gogga, her grandfather, who'd lain ill in bed for two weeks, sauntered past.

'I've opened the screen door, torn out, and he looked and smiled.' Without a word to her friends, she ran home and found her mother in distress. With tears pouring down her face, she fled to her room and buried her head in her pillow. 'Dad came in and said, "Gogga has gone", but I knew. I'd seen him at the end of the drive. He had smiled, but I knew he was gone.'

After twenty-eight years of mourning his wife, her Gogga had died, says Leonie, of a broken heart. 'He was perfectly healthy. He just willed himself to die.'

Leonie recounts another experience with the newly passed-on spirit of a loved one – this time, her father – in 1995. At the age of seventy, World War II digger Rick Evans lost his long battle with emphysema, a side effect of being exposed to Agent Orange during two tours of Vietnam, says his daughter. With his family scattered around the country, many were left to say their goodbyes *after* he'd died in a Sydney nursing home. Two days after he'd passed, Leonie visited the funeral home with two of her sisters and her eldest niece.

The women gathered by Rick's side, before Leonie asked for a moment alone with her father. 'I was just standing there, talking to him and telling him I was pleased he wasn't struggling for breath anymore, that now he could rest. I was with him for a few minutes, chatting.

'As I turned to leave, I had to walk away from the coffin. I put my hand on the door handle and, clear as a bell, he said, "Ta-ta, bub." I walked back over to check he wasn't breathing. There was a little stitch on the corner of his mouth: I went and checked that that hadn't come away. It was *his* voice, it was him.'

For eighteen months after her father's death, Leonie would regularly smell him around her, the particular scent of 'cigarette smoke and testosterone' was unmistakably his. Five years later, when her mother passed following a stroke, she too made herself known to Leonie.

'I was sitting up in bed on a Sunday morning, having a cup of tea, and I watched this grey mist move across the mirror of my dressing table,' says Leonie. 'I was speechless. I was looking above and beyond it, but it wasn't going over, it was just *in* the mirror. It moved side to side for about a minute and a half. I knew instinctively that it was Mum.'

Her parents have reached from the grave to put comforting arms around their daughter more than once, especially during trying times. Death has always danced around Leonie; she has grieved the loss of many family members, including a newborn great-nephew, a brother-in-law, sister-in-law and mother-in-law. After her own mother's death in 2000 she began to see the apparitions of a small boy and a tall, thin man, hand-clasped, always at the threshold of her bedroom at her home on the New South Wales Central Coast. She is not sure how they are connected to her family, but she is certain her mother sent them her way.

'The first time I saw them, I was lying in bed, really upset. It wasn't long after Mum died, I was losing weight at the rate of knots, couldn't keep anything down, didn't want to eat, I was hysterical. Then I *felt* a smile and I knew something was there. I opened my eyes, all puffy and red, and I saw a little boy holding the hand of a tall man. The child looked at me and he smiled. It was his smile I'd felt.

'He was shimmery,' she recalls. 'It was like looking at a mirage, or when you are at the beach and everything gets hazy. It was like he was standing in that haze. I never sensed his name, and I think if I get his name, I'll lose him and it will be time for him to go and help somebody else.'

Back then, the sandy-haired boy was tiny, 'he looked about two,' and wore 'a little pair of blue shorts and a T-shirt with blue, white and green stripes, and sandals.' Amazingly, Leonie says his spirit has grown, so that now he presents as a ten-year-old. 'He doesn't hold the gentleman's hand any more; he's a big boy now.

'He has a cherub's face,' she says, her husky voice melting, as if speaking of an adored nephew. 'I've watched him grow up.' Knowing that she can see life go on, even in death, brings great peace to Leonie, and she feels that her calling is to help others achieve the same in their lives. 'My day job is just that; a way to pay the bills and keep a roof over my head. My *real* job, the one I'm most comfortable with, is helping people through the hurdles life throws at them, helping them through the hurt and the pain of loss, helping them come to terms with the fact that it's okay to be them.' Leonie is keen to commence part-time study to become a professional counsellor. 'I don't want to pass on to the next realm and have any regrets.'

To that end, she fills her leisure hours with activities that smack of joy. She loves fresh air and reading – S.E. Hinton's classic, *The Outsiders*, is her all-time favourite. She treasures her friends and loves when they pop over to listen to music and play board games or cards – 'anything to get conversation going and laughter ringing'. She is dating a younger man – 'Yeah, me!' She walks, often taking a book with her and stopping to breathe in the scenery.

'I have no fear of death, I know it will be somewhere like this,' she says, her brown eyes quiet as they pan our surrounds. 'A beautiful green park – but full of the people I love.'

THE NIGHT SHIFT

'I wake up very tired.'

'A lot of people die in my dreams. I feel their death.'

These words belong to Sandra Ruiz, a policewoman, and they sound wounded, as if something inside her throat has tried to cut them down before they reach her lips. Not many people know that Sandra's dreams swarm with murder and terror. The exhausted mother of two has no doubt that the dead reach out to her when she is asleep, so many cold cases trying to claw their way out of paper tombs built of yellowing snapshots and faded police notes.

'In one dream, a plain-clothes officer died. He was stabbed in the neck, and I wake up and feel the heat of the knife go down,' she says. 'Every night I go to sleep, I have these dying dreams. I wake up very tired.'

The thirty-eight-year-old, whose husband is also a police officer, believes she is witnessing events that have taken place in Australia, 'but I don't know who the people are,' she frets. 'In the last two years, it's become more connected to my job. Unfortunately, what I see is not all pleasant.'

Only a couple of Sandra's colleagues have an inkling of her abilities, and she must be very careful about communicating the messages she receives, which arrive intermingled with references from her own life so that she can pinpoint when a crime has occurred. For instance, Sandra witnessed a young woman being tortured and pack-raped in a dream. She knows her first name and can speculate that her murder occurred around the late 1970s to early 1980s, because 'I got a flash of the house I used to live in in the eighties, and that puts me in the time-frame.' How deeply she delves into the atrocity depends on the dead woman's powers of persuasion. 'If she really wants me to look at it, she will keep coming back and pushing it.'

Which is what happened with a certain missing persons case to which the policewoman was assigned. Sandra knew the man was dead, and where his body lay because his spirit 'would not leave me alone,' she says. The elderly man, Jim, would growl in her ear and punch the blinds in the lounge-room. Discreetly, she approached a colleague who was also working on the case. 'I said, "This is where you need to look." It just sort of happened at the same time that a fire ravaged the area and he was found exactly where I said he'd be.'

But even after his body was discovered, Jim's spirit lingered at Sandra's house.

Along with all the others.

'I call my house Grand Central Station sometimes. I have to shut down and literally say, "I need you all to leave tonight, I'm really tired."' Sandra says her home is a pit-stop for travelling spirits. 'It's like they are passing through, they seem comfortable doing that. I used to see a World War I soldier in my family room. He was only in his early twenties, with light blonde hair, little glasses, army pants and a stained singlet top. It was like he was resting, and then he'd go.

'I know they're in the house when I see a flash of light – it can be light or dark, depending on the spirit – and feel a *whoosh*, like a cold draft, blow against my cheek as they go past. Sometimes they'll tickle the back of my neck, or pull my hair lightly. My grandmother likes to tug on my shirt.'

Sandra receives her information courtesy of the dead. 'I'm not psychic, I just feel whatever they give me,' she explains. Describing herself as 'sensitive', Sandra can remember having her first experience when she was no more than eight years old – but the apparition belonged to a flesh-and-blood person; her mother.

'I was definitely awake, sitting up in bed, I couldn't sleep. I saw her enter the room and sit on the end of my bed and she was filing her nails. She had her dressing-gown on, like she normally did. The next day, I said to her, "Why did you come into my room last night and sit on my bed?" but she denied it.

'Looking back, there was some trauma around our lives back then. I think I saw a protective thing that she projected. I believe that's what it was.'

Then the nightmares began.

'In high school, my dad got me dream analysis books (God love him!) to help me try and figure it out.' All her life, she has carried the burden of the dreams, though she feels that her abilities became more powerful following a spate of deaths in the family. 'Household items were being moved around and the dreams became really intense,' she says. But as frightful as it can sometimes be, Sandra's nightscape is as much a part of her as her blue eyes and brown hair.

Sandra's nine-year-old son, Michael, has also inherited his mother's mediumship, which was clear to Sandra from the time he was a baby. The boy has reported seeing his late grandmother in the home, and was only four years old when he mentioned a dead relative popping in to 'say hello.'

Sandra is nonplussed: 'I told him, "That's fine, you talk to him." I've always been open, I don't want them to fear anything.'

She knows that's easier said than done. Inhabiting her shoes is a daily challenge; much harder than it's depicted on *Medium*, where the mystery is neatly resolved in under sixty minutes. After all, this is an ordinary woman, living in suburbia, juggling marriage, motherhood and a career, all the stuff that's hard enough to cram into a day without the complication of seeing – and *feeling* – strangers slain each night.

'Sometimes it's frightening, sometimes it can get you down,' she sighs. 'In my profession, you apply logic to everything, and this is an area where you can't do that.'

RIPPLES IN TIME

'They looked solid, corporeal; I had no idea that no one else could see them.'

Leonie Hitchenor, forty-four, is studying to be a counsellor and a celebrant, and lives on the New South Wales Central Coast. She has read tarot professionally and is considering doing so again, but 'I won't charge,' she insists. 'My readings have always been more like spiritual counselling than fortune-telling.' I was particularly intrigued by her natural knack for peering into the past as opposed to receiving communication from a spirit (which she also knows about). The story she shares below is a detailed and candid insight into what it's like to be 'one of them.'

'My mum always told a story about the Queen of the Australian Gypsies wanting to adopt her when she was two. Apparently, she saw Mum playing out the front of the house, then came and knocked and told my grandma that Mum was "one of them" and wanted to adopt her. Not surprisingly, Nan refused! I've sometimes wondered what life would have been like for Mum if she'd said yes.

'Anyway, seems there's something about the women in our part of the family. When I was not quite ten, we moved into a new home my parents had built in Townsville [in Northern Queensland]. It's still there, on the edge of the old river course in Hyde Park. Turns out it's built on the grounds of an old hospital and we had an unexpected resident. I think it was a nurse; light-coloured clothing and blonde hair was all you'd see and she was short in stature. Initially, you'd see glimpses in mirrors and out of the corner of your eye. My mum was very ill at that time and later she told me that the woman would sit next to her bed, watching over her when she was really bad.

'I had two definite sightings. The first was a large swirling pillar of smoke that came in our kitchen door, crossed slowly through the kitchen/dining area into the front entry and out through the main entry to the house. It took minutes and didn't dissipate. My nephew, who was about four at the time, watched it with me and still remembers. I was thirteen. We were eating a meal at the kitchen table together and the fluoro light was on, so it was very well lit. I got pretty scared and my older sister suggested I talk to "it" and say I was frightened.

'I did, and I didn't see "her" again until I was about eighteen. Dad and I were in the lounge watching telly, Mum was outside hosing and again, there were lights on everywhere. I saw a blonde figure in light clothes walk past the entry to the lounge and out the front door. I was seated directly opposite and she was directly in my field of vision. I thought it was my other sister's blonde son and got up to see if they'd arrived. Mum was right outside the front door. No one had arrived or walked past her. Mum wasn't surprised, as our nurse followed her round the house all the time.

'Shortly after that, I moved to Sydney and over the years I've lived in many old terraces in the [inner-city] Darlinghurst area. It was rare for them not to have something there. We had one old lady in one place who would appear as a golden photo negative apparition sitting on the internal stairs. She initially slammed windows and doors and made me feel quite ill. We moved in and painted and tidied the place. She liked that and settled down.

'I was in England from November 1988 to April 1990. My partner was an excellent horseman and we managed a hunt stable in West Sussex for a little while. It was a huge brick quadrangle stable on the edge of a hill and we lived in a cottage next to it. Our nearest neighbours were in a couple of houses about one kilometre down a dirt road round the edge of the hill.

'There was the spirit of a woman there that constantly sang and talked to my then two-year-old daughter, Bec. Mark and I both heard her and we'd hear Bec laughing and chatting back. I saw the woman once. I went round the corner of the kitchen door into the dining room and we were face to face for a few seconds. She whirled around away from me and vanished. She was about twenty-five to thirty and pretty, with long black hair and dark complexion – Spanish? – and had a woollen shawl round her shoulders and a long, full, dark skirt.

'There was [also] an old man there that scared the crap out of me in the veggie patch early one winter evening. It was just dark and I needed a few more greens for tea. I could feel someone watching me and when I turned, an old man in a shirt and waistcoat with wispy white hair was standing a few feet away, glaring at me. We stared at each other. I moved and he vanished. We found out he was an old gamekeeper, long deceased, who'd lived in our cottage.

'I also saw the head of a bay horse with a hogged [shaved] mane emerging from the wall of the stables one night when we did the last feed. The area was well lit. Initially, I thought one of the horses was loose and yelled to Mark, who was feeding in that section. As I did so, it vanished and I realised, firstly, our only horse with a hogged mane was in the section I was feeding, and secondly, it had been coming out of the wall not the door!

'The hill was scary, dogs were very easily spooked there, running off yelping for no apparent reason and when the wind blew, the trees in the nearby woods gave off a strange vibrational hum. My little daughter had a favourite tree at the edge of a field that she would sit in front of for hours if I let her. She told me it was singing to her.

'Lots of things happened when we moved back to London. Visits to the Tower of London were always interesting, but my favourite happened in the middle of Green Park near Buckingham Palace on a blustery autumn afternoon. Mark and I had taken Bec to the park and we'd been playing in the mounds of fallen leaves. We were all relaxed and happy. We were walking back and I saw two women riding sidesaddle on beautiful horses on the path ahead of us.

'The dark-coloured riding habits and top-hat style hats were Victorian. I got a good look at them as they rode along. At first sight, I thought maybe they were extras in a film or it was an historical group in a re-enactment. Mark and Bec didn't notice them and I said to Bec, "Look at the beautiful horses!" Mark said, "What horses?" They'd vanished! There was nowhere for them to go. They looked solid, corporeal; I had no idea no one else could see them. The people walking near us were looking at me rather oddly.

'They don't always come as visions. A friend of mine became very ill and died about fifteen years ago. I woke on the morning he died knowing it would be that day he passed and that I had to get to his place immediately. His favourite flowers were yellow roses.

That night I was sitting with friends at about 9.30 pm, when a wave of scent came through the window and rolled across the room. It was the heady smell of roses in full bloom, not perfume, the real thing. It was so strong it was almost overwhelming and we could all smell it. I was living opposite the train station in Townsville; there were no rose gardens anywhere for kilometres! Other friends of his also experienced the same thing that night.

'At his funeral many people, including his mother, felt he was there. I sat and watched a confused usher try to stop a very heavy wooden door blowing open through the service. He kept putting heavier and heavier things against the door to keep it shut. It actually became comical. My friend was quite theatrical and he wanted the church just right, I think. The wind made the cloth over his coffin flutter and the candles were all flickering. Very *Phantom of the Opera* and just what he would have liked.

'When I got up to give the eulogy, my friend saw a large light behind me seemingly touching my shoulder. To this day, I can't tell you what I said, but everyone told me it was beautiful and exactly what they felt he would have wanted. I'd gotten up with absolutely no idea of what to say and I did feel calm and guided as I spoke. I actually heard a voice say to me, "That's enough", and knew to stop speaking.

'I think that many people see spirits but don't realise it, as they're not always transparent shades. Either that, or for a brief moment time overlaps and we see things that have been. I think that the women in the park were either a ripple in time, or a replay of past events. There was no feeling of connection with them. Present spirits usually make themselves known with more than just a fleeting vision; there's more of a reaction.

'It is a wonderful thing to be able to see these things, but it can also be painful; not everything is pleasant to tune into. Violent events or very angry souls give me an instant headache and make me want to vomit. Sceptics can also make life frustrating. Some people are so good at this they have real control, but I can't perform like a trained seal and it often depends on what's happening in my life. If I'm ill or overloaded, it seems to shut down. A self-protection thing I think.

'It's strange to live with this. I've always been fascinated by science and am quite sceptical about many things, but as I'm not mentally ill, apart from the odd bout of stress or depression over the years (these days, who doesn't have that?), I've just had to accept this is real. I don't usually go out looking for this and it often happens when you least expect it and in broad daylight or in a well-lit room, too. The sightings I've mentioned weren't just corner of the eye glimpses. I've had too many of them to count over the years.'

MEMORY BOX

'The whole family used to see them, they just used to pass you in the hallway.'

The man slithered on his elbows along the floor.

He was dead, of course, but there was something else askew about him.

Lying stomach down on the wooden floorboards, he propped himself up on sinewy forearms and shuffled forward, dragging his flaccid bottom half. Closer he crept to Patricia Turnbull, who studied him without fear, but with some pity. He lifted his face to look at her, his mouth a mute slash, his black eyes howling. 'He was crawling towards me like he was paralysed from the waist down,' says Patricia. 'I decided to go to him and tell him it was okay to leave. I thought I'd try that. I went to the corner where this man was laying, in this house that had been handed down through generations, and said, "It's okay for you to go . . ."'

Patricia has a story to tell. It is a story of abandonment, hardship, of grief and tragedy, of love and loss, of life and death. It's a story that will pin itself to the walls of your skull. And naturally, it is a ghost story.

It was 2006 when she met the crawling spirit. At that point, Patricia was in deep mourning for the loss of her son and husband in heart-splitting succession, and had returned for nine months to the quaint weatherboard home in picturesque Battery Point, Tasmania, where she'd taken her first steps. If the sight of the maimed visitor didn't frighten her, it's because he was by no means the first. Ghosts of every variety populate her history, jostling for space with the living and the beloved dead in the memory box in her mind's eye.

And it all started in an old house by the sea.

Patricia's childhood home, where her brother still lives, was built around 1803, when convicts laid the first foundations in Tasmania. It is part of Arthur's Circus, the ring of historic cottages encircling a park in the heart of Battery Point, the former fishing village that is today one of Hobart's most prestigious addresses. Since it was one of the larger houses in the Circus, Church of England Sunday School was held on its verandah for the local children every week. With two bedrooms upstairs, and three on the bottom, the house was a tight squeeze for twelve children and their parents, but the family made do.

It was a time when life and death were housemates, and the sight of coffins being carried to and from the cottages in the Circus became a familiar sight to the neighbourhood kids. 'Loved ones should always be brought home to be properly farewelled,' was the lesson that burrowed into Patricia, the third youngest, whose mop of unruly curls made her stand out from her sleek-haired siblings. There was something else Patricia learned as a toddler: when a spirit approaches, it makes a sound like the crackling of autumn leaves.

'In the house as I was growing up, I used to see spirits, a lot of different sorts – some that were outlines and some that were "sparkly" – and when they come towards you they sound like a rustling of leaves,' says Patricia, fifty-six, who was three when she saw her first ghost, a 'white one' floating down the stairs.

'I've seen very tall spirits in white, like an outline, and spirits in my bedroom that look human, but are doll-like; they have no expression, and the room was always hot when they appeared. The whole family used to see them, they just used to pass you in the hallway.'

'Was anyone in the house frightened by this?' I venture.

'Oh, some of the children used to scream at night when 'they' made a loud entrance. Sometimes, the door would fly open; there was a crackling sound like a fire lighting up, then a rustling of leaves as though they were coming into the room. So some of them used to get scared, but as we got older, we tried to ignore it. We knew it was there and coming, but we wouldn't turn and look.'

Voices from the past also echoed in the halls. 'We'd hear the "*Heave-ho!*" of men in row boats, laughter, music . . . you had to learn how to sleep in that house.' Patricia's elder sister remembers it well: 'The convicts! We could hear them rowing and laughing,' says Margaret Kobylinski, sixty-two. 'It was very hard. I was shrewder than the rest of them. I knew there were things around, but I was on my guard.' Margaret stuns me with a detail that speaks volumes about the haunting's effect on their father, Ben: in the mid-fifties, not long after little Trisha saw her white spirit descending, he dismantled the stairway, forcing the family to cram into the ground floor. 'Entities would come down the stairs, and to stop that, Dad just thought he'd take them out,' recalls Margaret.

'They were beautiful stairs, but that's the only way he could handle it. Problem is, that didn't stop them.'

The strange happenings only intensified after a shattering event: 'When I was about nine, my mum left,' reports Patricia, who never saw her mother, Doris, in the flesh again. 'She just left the house.'

Patricia can only speculate as to why her mother would abandon her husband and twelve children, ten still living at home, the youngest only seven. 'I think the children were just too much,' she says quietly. 'We never had hot water, we could only have a bath once a week, we never had a stove or fridge. If we had fresh milk, we had to keep it in cold water. Our cooking was done on the fireplace, so it was pretty basic.'

For Ben, life became a struggle. 'It was very sad. We couldn't talk to our dad about certain things. There were eight girls, we weren't allowed to sit on his lap anymore, he put some distance between us, but he was very loving,' says Patricia, who was in and out of hospital with rheumatic fever, causing her to miss much of her primary schooling. 'That was probably why I never learned to read and write,' says the articulate, gently spoken grandmother.

Masking his devastation, the fisherman remained a steady, reassuring presence, tending his vegetable plot or polishing ten pairs of shoes by the hearth in the chill of the morning. He could not have known that another ghostly voice would soon be joining his household, and this time, it would belong to one of his own.

When Patricia was thirteen, her brother Jimmy, sixteen, was involved in an horrific car accident. Jimmy decided to join his sister Lyn and her boyfriend, who'd offered to pick up a young couple and their three-week old baby from hospital. The car slid in the rain and, in the days before mandatory seatbelts, the baby was thrown from the car and killed. Jimmy suffered terrible head injuries.

For three months, Jimmy lay in a coma, and yet the sounds of his wailing pummelled the cottage's whaling-board walls. As if that's not astonishing enough, Patricia says Jimmy wasn't alone: a baby's high-pitched cry accompanied him. 'We had the baby and my brother in that house,' she states. 'We'd hear them crying. We'd hear him yelling – it was very *loud*.

'*Very loud*! Loud enough for anyone to jump up and take off,' seconds Margaret, who believes her father and siblings were all psychic, which created a kind of energy trap in the house. 'The young ones suffered badly . . .' Then, when the boy died on November fourth, 1965, it was utter bedlam. His phantom voice would shriek, pleading for his sister Lyn, who'd survived the crash. Bright random flashes lit up the house, and music seemed to 'come from nowhere', says Patricia. The walls played his favourite song, 'Donna', the 1958 ballad. 'We'd all just stop and look at each other. And run.'

It reached the point where the siblings refused to be in the house after their father left for work. Instead, they'd line up on the path outside and wait for his return. They even stopped going to school. 'We were losing sleep,' says Patricia. Jimmy's pitiful cries of 'Where are you, I can't find you . . .' kept the clan awake at night and made them a jittery mess in the daylight hours. Finally, a group of neighbours reached out to the splintered family. 'They decided to come in and do the housework,' recalls Patricia, a tiny smile turning her lips. 'As he started to scream, those ladies were the first to leave. We turned around and they were gone. We ran out after them but they swore they'd never go back into that house.'

Ben didn't ever deny that his son was haunting the place, he'd seen and heard too much, but the stress consumed him. 'It was worrying the hell out of him; Dad went white overnight,' remembers Margaret. '*Completely* white.' He sought the help of a psychiatrist, who listened to each child's account individually, 'to make sure we weren't making anything up,' says Patricia. His verdict? 'He called us all in together and told my dad that my brother was actually trapped and all he needed to know was that Lyn was okay.' They were instructed to head home and calm Jimmy in their thoughts. 'We had to tell him that Lyn was okay, she was with us and it was okay for him to go. And he did.'

The house wiped its tears. Jimmy hushed.

A photo arrives of Patricia with eight of her brothers and sisters on the lawn outside their house. I easily spot my subject, aged around three, for her springy curls. She's exploring her shoe. Jimmy is at the rear: the sun spotlights his white-blonde hair and he wears the littlest of grins for the camera. The elder kids stare out of their eyes with ancient souls.

The grainy black-and-white snapshot enchants me. It reminds me of my own ancestors' big clans; my maternal grandmother – *mi abuela* – was one of nine, my grandfather, one of twelve, until time felled them, one by one. Over and over, I dig out Patricia's photo from underneath piles of interviews and clippings, just to pore over the children's expressions. Patricia also sends me 'then' and 'now' views of Arthur's Circus, and I think of the tourists who stroll the postcard-pretty area today, ignorant of the layers of life and death each charming façade conceals. Especially one.

Though somewhat hypnotised by the pictures of Arthur's Circus – its circular green is like a whirlpool I've fallen into – Patricia eventually left it behind, so I'm obliged to follow. As she told me when we first spoke, early in 2008, 'We grew up with ghosts, but that's not the story I want to tell you . . .' In 1974, she had her first child, Amy, with a volatile man who would belittle her for her illiteracy, so that when she met gentle, caring Wayne Turnbull, she was keen to start a new life with him. They moved to Queensland in 1980, and had their boys, Brett and Sam.

Wayne worked in the mines so the family moved around the country. Patricia was content tending to their quiet lives, setting up house where the work led them. The spirit world slept, her memories of growing up alongside ghosts faded. That is, until 1998, when Patricia realised for the first time that she would be warned when a loved one was about to die.

The first time it happened, she was sitting at the family's home in Darwin, watching television, when a large black shadow stalked in front of the set, the Venetian blinds rippling in its wake. 'I thought, "What the hell was that?" but I felt it was a warning so I marked it on the calendar and started ringing around, telling family members.' Then she forgot about it, until six weeks later, when a phone call brought the news that her eldest brother had died. 'He had fallen down the stairs and his ribs went through his heart,' she says. 'His name was Robbie.'

Sam inherited his mother's uncanny foresight. Not long after the sixteen-year-old casually mentioned 'a man standing behind' his mother, Patricia heard that her father, Ben, lay critically ill. She rushed home to Tasmania, to her Apple Isle house of the spirits, to say her farewells.

In the early hours of the morning, just before he passed, he came to Patricia as an explosion of light, 'like somebody putting a flashlight in my face,' she reports. Simultaneously, the television sprang to life. It was an old-fashioned set, where you had to pull a button to turn it on. That sent one of Patricia's sisters quaking to her doorway, but Patricia felt the opposite of fear. 'I felt so overwhelmed with love, that I felt like laughing,' she says. 'He'd never told me he loved me, but I think he came and gave me all the love he could in that flash.'

It had been six weeks since Sam's vision.

The next time it happened would sear Patricia with fright. In 2003, she and Wayne were living in Parkes, New South Wales. They lasted two days in the rented house before Patricia experienced the most terrifying event of her life. Sleeping alone in bed – Wayne was on night shift – Patricia's eyelids flicked open. 'There was this thing hovering a couple of inches above my face. It was like a big, black mass, it had streamers or ribbons floating, it was all uneven . . .

'All I could think of was that I wasn't meant to look at it, I should run. I ran to the lounge room and wouldn't go back into the bedroom.' Without hesitation, the pair moved out. Patricia didn't think to mark it on her calendar.

'A phone call came six weeks later,' she sighs. 'It was my sister; she was crying. My youngest brother, Peter, was dead. He had a Mini Minor. He went and put petrol in it and sat in it and lit a match.'

Patricia pauses. The bloated silence doesn't cushion the impact of the hideous image of her brother's suicide. My mind summons again the blanched family picture, where one of the big children cradles an infant like a doll in her arms. 'He was the baby of the family,' says Patricia, as if reading my thoughts.

To her dismay, in 2004, her own baby, Sam, accepted a post working with explosives in mines in the New South Wales city of Armidale. Patricia didn't want him to go and told him so. Every part of her lurched against the idea, but it was a good opportunity and Sam's mind was made up. In bed one night in the days before his departure, Patricia heard a calming male voice say, 'The Lord Giveth, the Lord Taketh. You are strong enough.' Instead of being afraid, Patricia was lulled to sleep by the soothing tones. 'Then, on our last meal together before he moved to Armidale, Wayne and Sam were having a joke that *they* were going to cook tea tonight,' she tells, lost in the sweet memory. 'They were making veggies and patties and having a really wonderful time together.'

'Every time I tried to go into the kitchen, they'd shoo me out. I found myself standing outside in the garden, watching them. I thought, *Is this what it feels like on the other side? Looking through a window at us?* Her musings sparked a memory of the voice. She wondered if it was a warning of her own impending death. The message had deemed her 'strong enough' and now, standing at the glass, she thought, *I'll be okay. I'll be able to come back and look at my boys.*'

The fuss-free dinner the boys served up would be their last family meal together.

Not long after Sam left, something began to stir in and around Patricia. She was packing up the Parkes house to move again; Wayne, who'd been feeling unwell, was heartened at the prospect of managing a mine in Tasmania. It should have been a sunny time in their lives, but the atmosphere around them seemed to crackle and spit, suggesting otherwise. 'Things in the house started to play up of a night: the video would turn on, the lights would flicker, the music would be playing – like violin or piano,' says Patricia. 'It was like somebody or something was trying to get my attention. I was jumping out of bed to turn the power off, the video was screaming, its insides were going but there was no tape inside it. I couldn't work out what was happening.'

Could it have been a warning? The spirits' brusque way of announcing that her world was somersaulting – that the careful life she'd built around 'her boys' was spinning out of control? As if to prove her suspicions correct, Wayne was diagnosed with bowel cancer and given only three months to live; their hopes dashed, the couple moved back to Western Australia to be closer to their daughter, Amy. 'He had to give up his dream job,' she whispers. 'When the surgeon told him, I couldn't see. He was a blur in front of me because the tears would drop.'

Amid the shock of Wayne's prognosis, the couple couldn't shake a nagging worry for their youngest son, who'd lost his licence in Armidale for drink driving. 'Sam was *always* telling us he was going to die on the bike,' recalls his mum. 'When Wayne recovered from his operation, we decided to fly over and drive back, bringing Sam and his motorcycle with us.'

They booked a flight to Armidale on Monday, the thirteenth of December, 2004.

'On the 10th of December, Sam called us up and said he was just letting us know he was going to be killed. He said, "I am definitely going to be killed on the bike."' His parents begged him to keep away from it, repeating that they'd be there on Monday. He had only to wait out the weekend. 'But he just kept insisting it was going to happen.'

The twenty-four-year-old was killed the next day. He'd been doubling friends on his bike around the block when he veered off course and slammed into a picket fence. His passenger was only mildly injured. When Patricia spied the two police officers approaching her door, a wave of ice and heat engulfed her. Her handsome boy, with his dancing hazel eyes and blonde curls, was gone.

From somewhere within her well of grief, Patricia found determination. After flying his body home to Perth, to lay at a funeral home in suburban Northbridge, Patricia felt her son was too far away. She asked Wayne and her eldest son, Brett, to do something she hadn't seen since her days at Arthur's Circus: 'I said, "You'll have to go and get Sam from the undertaker's. Sam is coming home for Christmas."' The men put Sam's coffin in the back of the ute, and with dead rapper Tupac Shakur blasting from the stereo, they brought their boy home, where Patricia waited with open arms. 'I put a bed beside Sam and I slept there the first night. Wayne got the courage to come in for the last two nights. I used to comb his hair and talk to him.'

For four days and three nights, the mother kept vigil by her son's body. Her family left her to her mourning, occasionally setting a cup of coffee beside her. Even though Sam had been embalmed, his body began to discolour and an odour of decay permeated the room, but Patricia didn't mind. 'Doing that showed how much I loved him,' she says. 'I never got to say goodbye to Jimmy, or to Peter, so I think I knew what I had to do. It was heartbreaking when they took him away.'

Eight months later, Wayne, with a secondary cancer on his liver, was drawing his last, ragged breaths. As she sat by her husband's bedside, he suddenly became lucid. 'He grabbed my arm and said, "Trisha, I want to tell you I love you." I started to cry. I looked at him and said, "Please don't leave me." He said, "Trisha, you don't realise how strong you are. Remember, I'll always be with you."'

The gentle miner with the lopsided grin died shortly after. He was fifty-one. Patricia's premonition at the kitchen window had come true: she was now an outsider to her boys' world – because her veins still throbbed with life.

As she did with Sam, Patricia laid out Wayne at home. In the whirlwind of those fractured days, she had a visitor from her past. 'One night, I was just laying with the light on in the bedroom. I had the feeling someone was standing behind me in a coat, hat, handbag, old shoes that laced up with heels, and old-fashioned stockings. I could see what she was wearing.'

Who is that? she wondered.

'The next night, I was asleep, and I woke up and I saw the same lady, but she was younger, in a spotted dress, combing her hair.' On the third night, the woman appeared '. . . sitting in a hospital chair. There were tanks beside her and she was trying to breathe. She had a mask over her. Somewhere in there, I realised it was my mother. I remember yelling out, "Mum! My God that's my mum!"'

Patricia believes that she was clairvoyantly shown select scenes from her absent mother's life, from her youth to her lonely death in hospital. I wonder, in her final days, did her mother reach out in her dreams to kiss a dozen forgotten cheeks?

Soon after she saw the final vision of her mother, Patricia woke to the sight of a young soldier squinting down at her, a bullet hole where his eye belonged. 'He wore an old uniform in heavy khaki with silver buttons, real old boots and a big hat. He was very young.' The boy digger was there, and then he wasn't, leaving Patricia to ponder if the trauma of losing her adored husband and son had somehow resurrected her ability to see dead people?

'I don't know how to explain it,' she says, shrugging. 'It's like, "Oh, who are you?" and then all of a sudden, they just disappear. I think I'm just trying to develop what I've got, but I've got no idea what I'm doing.'

Which is why, when she returned to Battery Point, to the old house by the sea in Arthur's Circus, she thought she would try to help the spirit of the paralysed man who squirmed towards her one night. She hopes it worked because he vanished. She hopes he's where he's supposed to be.

Today, Patricia is back in Western Australia. She has sold the home where she mourned her 'boys' and is living in a new house she had built forty-five minutes from her children Amy and Brett. 'I just know all these spirits are encouraging me to go forward,' she says. 'I've lost my two loved ones, but I've still got two children and my grandchildren. I'm going to a quiet life.'

In a new house, by the bush.

∽∞∾

Each of these mediums could fill an entire book of her own with the story of her life and the gift she struggles with. And it is ever a struggle, physically and emotionally. Like Romayne Marjolin whose mother cracked her skull because she dared mention her friendship with the dead, these ladies have learned to think carefully before revealing what they know or see, if they reveal it at all. Bev Clayton feared being branded a witch in her country town; Sandra Ruiz faces the daily challenge of balancing her investigations as a policewoman by day with the information that stains her dreams at night; and Leonie Hitchenor is irritated by the expectation that she constantly 'prove' what she can do.

It's draining, frightening, frustrating and may expose you to taunts and finger-pointing, but the gift of mediumship is not one that you can return or exchange. However, you can 'regift', as became apparent in my conversations and correspondence with these eloquent and open-hearted interviewees. Although passing the gift onto your children (or inheriting it from your parents, for that matter) is never a conscious decision, it was a common feature of the stories here and throughout *Spirit Sisters*. Leonie, whose mother was 'one of them', has heard her toddler talking to a spirit when they lived in a haunted house in the UK; Bev, Tamara and Sandra's children have their mothers' second sight, as did Patricia Turnbull's son, Sam, who announced his imminent death – and the manner of it – to his parents.

He was absolutely accurate, as the gentle-voiced Patricia told me. Yes, each of their stories could be the beating heart of a book, but in the place of happy endings, a reader would be wiser to expect only a courageous new beginning.

LOVE AFTER DEATH

An Embrace From Beyond

'Far off thou art, but never nigh;
I have thee still, and I rejoice;
I prosper, circled with thy voice;
I shall not lose thee though I die'

ALFRED, LORD TENNYSON

In the background, but constant, like a beating pulse, there is a message that lights up the shadows of this book: love survives death. And I am so relieved to know it.

Before beginning *Spirit Sisters*, I was afraid. Afraid of what I may hear. Afraid of horror stories waking me up at night and creeping out of my digital recorder to scrape and claw at me as I slept. What I feared the most was that all this talking about spirits – so much discussion and energy dedicated to them – would send them my way. For twelve months the book floated in my head, a complete idea waiting to exhale, but I delayed acting on it because I feared that to do so would summon ghosts to our house once more.

I didn't want the toys to start imploding again in the dead of night in Taby's room.

Or for the atmosphere in the house to swell once more and turn thick as soup.

For phantom children to tip-toe anew on our floorboards.

I remembered some sage advice after the house-clearing shooed away our spirit squatters: 'Do not speak of them again. If you do, they will return.'

There are echoes of this idea in the Japanese game, 100 Candles. Players light a hundred wicks, gather in a circle around them and start telling spooky stories, blowing one out as each tale concludes. Supposedly, when the 100 candles are extinguished, spirits will swarm in the darkened room.

I wondered, would my book, so crammed with stories, entice fearsome ghosts to my side?

I needn't have worried. As the interviews progressed, I was delighted to hear of so many experiences celebrating the sweet, subtle and astonishing ways our loved ones make themselves known to us, and how these visits fill the bereaved with a sense of fulfilment and peace. Not even death can erode the bonds between a mother and a child, siblings, a husband and wife, grandparent and grandchild. Our beloved dead drift in on the scent of vintage perfume or cigarette smoke, stand guard over our slumbering babies, hold us tight in our dreams, whisper in our ears, or swirl at our bedsides in a misty dance. To a select few, they stand before us wearing their prettiest dress or favourite suit.

Louis E. LaGrand calls such spontaneous events ADCs (after-death communications) and lists the many different types in *Messages and Miracles*, including auditory, visual, tactile, olfactory and dreams. He also describes symbolic ADCs, which involve natural or manmade objects acting as a bridge between the living and the dead, as you'll read of in 'Butterfly Kisses'.

'An ADC is an important healing tool because the departed is loving [the bereaved] back through symbol, sign or apparition,' he writes. 'Peace ensues. Love is eternal and seems to shine through the anguish of loss, but so too does the awareness that the bond of love is reciprocal.'

He might categorise Jill's sensing of her father, below, as a tactile ADC.

'My father passed away on the twenty-sixth of July, 1998. He was my inspiration and I felt as if he took with him a piece of my heart,' says South Australian grandmother Jill Sikorski, who's experienced ADC from both her parents. 'The night of his passing, after everyone had left my home, I felt fingers very gently running through my hair. I realised this was Dad's way of letting me know that he was okay. I asked if it was him and started to laugh, as it tickled. I asked him to stop and he did. To this day, I feel my dad run his fingers ever so gently through my hair, and I know he is around me most of the time.'

Six years later, Jill's mother died of a massive stroke, but she too found her way back to her daughter. 'I used to be able to smell my mum's favourite perfume, 4711, for a long time after she'd died. But on the night of my daughter's engagement it was very strong, and all the guests commented on it. But once the engagement party was over, the perfume smell had gone, never to return. I think it was Mum wanting to be there for my daughter's big day.'

In February 1983, after the funeral for her adoptive mother, Queenslander Fran Baas says she appeared to her as a swirl of mist. 'At about 3 am that morning, I awoke to the feeling that someone was looking at me, and as I sat bolt up in bed I saw what appeared to be a circle of mist just in front of our wardrobe. As I watched it, it moved across the room, out the door and down the hallway,' recalls Fran, fifty-six, a support worker for people with disabilities. 'I feel it was my mum come to say goodbye and checking up on us, as she was always a sticky beak!'

Melburnian Anna Marie Holden asked her bedridden mother, Marcia, to return to her after she'd gone. 'We made this deal probably a year before she died. I told her that I didn't want her to leave me and she said, "I will never leave you." I said, "Mum, when you die, will you talk to me?" and she said, "I will try my hardest, Anna Marie," and I think she did.'

Anna Marie, whose husband is the Australian entertainer Mark Holden, had flown to LA with their eighteen-month-old daughter, Katie, to take care of Marcia, who suffered from emphysema, among other ailments. Anna Marie held her seventy-one-year-old mother's hand as she slipped away in a Los Angeles hospital on the twenty-first of January 1999. The next day, as she lay down to rest at her mother's home where she was staying, she had a conversation with her.

'I said, "Mum, where are you?"'

'"I can't talk to you now," she replied, telepathically. '"I don't know where I am. I'm spinning, it's all going really fast. I'm flying."'

A day or two later, she tried again. 'The voice was in my mind, not a sound in the room, but it was *her* voice, it wasn't my own,' explains Anna Marie. 'It was the middle of the day, and I am a completely sane and sober person.'

In her personal organiser, Anna Marie jotted down, word for word, her mother's message: *You think about you and that baby. For the rest of your life you can talk to me. I'm okay now and I'm with God. He's gonna take care of me and he'll take care of you, too.*

'I really believe it was her talking to me to make me at ease,' says Anna Marie, who says it doesn't worry her that subsequent communications have never been as clear as that day's, because her mother came when she needed her the most. 'I think there are miracles and magic in the world. I don't believe that a soul just disappears.'

'Our souls definitely live on once we die and our loved ones can still communicate with us,' agrees New South Wales mother of four Sharon Eckhardt, thirty-four, whose tragic loss of her sixteen-year-old sister Mandy to a sudden asthma attack in 1995 set her on a spiritual quest. 'I just couldn't accept the fact that she was here one day, dead the next. I needed to find out what happens to us once we die.'

At first, Mandy came through indirectly, says Sharon. 'A friend told me about a detailed dream she had about my sister, where Mandy had told her that she was too young to die, but it was her time to go.' In the dream, Mandy showed the friend her headstone and when the friend described it to Sharon, it was a perfect match; Sharon even took her to the cemetery to show her. 'My friend couldn't believe it, because it was exactly the same. This definitely started me thinking that Mandy was still able to communicate and that we live on, somehow.'

Then it was Sharon's turn to dream of her lovely blue-eyed sister with the long brown hair. 'We were going to her funeral. In the dream, it was an open viewing and once we (the family) arrived to the church we got to take her to a room where we could say our last goodbyes before the funeral. As I went over to her coffin and gave her a kiss on the forehead, she sat up and got out. I was really shocked to think that she was alive again. She acted like nothing had ever happened and we were chatting and giving her cuddles. Then I remember looking at my watch and saying, 'You had better get back in your coffin as your funeral is about to start. I then woke up!

'I couldn't believe how real this dream was and I thought to myself, *Mandy has come back to say goodbye to me*. None of us *did* get to say goodbye as she died so suddenly. To me, this wasn't a normal dream. It was so real and it made me feel great inside.'

Later, Mandy returned in other ways. She would turn on the touch lamps on her nieces' bedside tables and once whispered, 'Good night!' loudly in Sharon's ear. One evening, she actually showed herself. 'I was leaving a friend's place late one night. I had placed my two young daughters in their car seats and was sitting in the driver's seat, waiting for my husband to finish saying goodbye,' says Sharon. 'When I turned around to look back at my children, I could see my sister's apparition in the back window. I thought to myself, *No, I am seeing things*, so I turned back to the front and then turned back to have another look. Sure enough, she was still there.

'I had never experienced anything like this before, but I wasn't scared. I felt very privileged. I'm very grateful for all of my experiences after the loss of my sister.'

I've heard it said many times that the love of a grandparent for their grandchild has no comparison, and my interviews appear to confirm this. As with Cherie Frazer's story of her grandmother taking on the role of spirit babysitter in the following pages, Deaneen Webster also knows what it's like to see an adored grandparent return to watch over her child.

With her youngest child, Harry, asleep upstairs, the Sydney mum linked a baby monitor to her computer, so that she could keep an eye on the two-month-old as she grabbed a quick bite for lunch downstairs. 'All of a sudden, a flash of light made me look at the screen, and I saw my baby's blinds whoosh open, as if a wind blew through,' says the thirty-seven-year-old mother of three. 'I thought, *That's a bit odd*, and then I saw a silhouette, like a "negative" of a man standing over the crib, looking down on my son. I watched it for about three or four seconds, though it seemed like an eternity.'

Deaneen immediately recognised her paternal grandfather, Thomas, who'd died five years earlier. 'I could make out his trousers, shirt and glasses. He had a smile on his face. He was looking down, but I could see his short grey hair on the back of his head. I was really, really happy. He was checking out the newest addition to the family.'

Growing up, Tamara Warden enjoyed a close and loving relationship with her grandmother, Shirley, and her great-grandmother, 'Nanna' Elsie. 'They were my rocks,' says Tamara, 'the most important people in my life up until I got married and had kids.' So it makes sense to Tamara that she continues to feel and smell the soothing presence of both women – sometimes, it's the woodfire tang of her grandmother's lounge room that envelops her, at other times, her little son will awake from his nap with his warm cheeks smelling of Elsie's signature face powder.

'It's such a beautiful thing. You can be having the worst day in the world, but just to know there is someone there looking after you and watching you, to let you know it's going to be okay, that is the most special thing,' says Tamara, who felt her grandmother cuddle her during her difficult labour. 'Love doesn't stop. Just because you die doesn't mean you ever stop loving your family.'

'My maternal grandmother passed away when I was ten. I was very close to her, she was the centre of my universe,' says Tereza Johnson, a thirty-nine-year-old book-keeper from Sydney. 'Her passing was my first experience of death. It had an enormous impact psychologically on my life then and now – she taught me when she was alive in this world and still does even though she's passed into the next.

'A few weeks after she'd passed, I was lying in bed and I opened my eyes and saw her standing over me. She was not looking at me, but looking out to the backyard through the window. Her apparition was in the form of smoke, but she was clearly defined. I've seen her many times since. I believe she is my guardian angel.'

Adored pets may also return to comfort us, as Amy Shepherd found when she lost her ten-year-old German Shepherd, Jessie, to cancer in 2006. 'I'd gone to work and Mum and Dad called me to say they'd had to put Jessie down. A couple of nights later, I had a dream she was there and she spoke to me [via telepathy and the sound of a male voice]. I've gone out the back and she was there. I said, "Jessie, what are you doing here? You're not supposed to be here!" She was taking me to where she was buried and she laid down on it. She said, "I want to make sure you are okay."'

With tears wetting her face, Amy explains that the experience of learning that her dog was safe, reunited with their other deceased pets, restored her faith in a higher power. 'I woke up the next morning and I was so at peace, 'cause I knew she was okay. That's probably the most amazing experience I've ever had.'

Similarly, Julie Said will never forget the moment she learned that love never dies. It happened in 1973 when she was thirteen. The teenager, her little brother and two friends would often visit a warm-hearted elderly neighbour with eyes the colour of the sky, as she recalls:

'Mr Sydney Hall was a dear old man, like a grandfather figure to us. Gentle, kind and always interested in the trivial things happening in our day-to-day activities. He taught us deep appreciation for plants and showed us the beautiful pansies he would grow. Sometimes, he cut his flowers and we would take them home to our mums. He shared his wisdom and knowledge with us and never tired of our continuous chatter. We would talk, laugh and share our stories. Sometimes, he had a lolly or a cake for us. Although he was maybe in his mid seventies and scuffled about, he had the clearest blue eyes I can ever remember. They looked right through you, and when he spoke, it was always so politely.

'Mr Hall had lost his wife, Lucy, many years earlier and they had never had children. He missed her very much and often talked about her, and what life was like when he was young. Sometimes he would mention how she would "appear" and visit him. We never really believed him, we just thought that this was his way of staying close to her. We thought he may have been going a little senile, but that did not bother us, as he was just a good, nice person. Children are not as judgmental as adults, either.

'He also told us that he often saw his old neighbour across the road sitting on his front verandah in his favourite chair. This man had passed away a while ago! Anyway, we just dismissed it.

'On one visit, all five of us were chatting. I asked if I could please get myself a glass of water. I walked down the hall, which was long and opened up to a small lounge, then into a dining kitchen. The kitchen was more like a little alcove, with the old-style tap on the wall. It was always a little stiff to turn.

'The moment I turned on the tap I was aware of a presence watching me. It really startled me and I felt scared and extremely uncomfortable. I could not see anything, but I knew Lucy was watching me. She was near the dining table, directly to my right-hand side. I could feel that she was smiling at me and thanking me for visiting her husband. I just kept wishing she would go away, as it was very weird.

'I had to walk back through the dining room, lounge and up the hall knowing she was behind me. I said nothing when I re-entered the room with the others, but looked up at the doorway. At that precise moment, Mr Hall stopped talking and stared at the doorway. He was very still. I said, "Your wife is there, isn't she?" He just nodded. Then she was gone.

'This all happened in a matter of minutes, but it was a life-defining moment for me. The feeling was very intense, and although I was scared, I know to this day she meant me no harm. She never appeared to me again. Since then, I have a greater appreciation for energies that we cannot see, and listen to my instincts.'

It's a sweet story, with its quaint details from a simpler time – a time when there simply *was* more time. The gracious Mr Hall lodged in my thoughts for a long time after I read this. I like to think he and Lucy are together again now, holdings hand for eternity.

KEEPING UP APPEARANCES

'Oh hi, Nan, you're back!'

Cherie Frazer couldn't attend her grandmother's funeral, but she knows exactly how her beloved Nan was dressed. The slim seventy-two-year-old looked sharp in her favourite pale yellow pantsuit, as mourners filing past her at the open casket service would have noted. She wore exactly the same outfit when she popped in to coo over her first great-grandchild's cot. Cherie says she looked radiant.

The Sydney nurse was six months pregnant in November 2003 when her maternal grandmother, Gloria, passed away from a haemorrhagic stroke. 'I didn't make it to the funeral because I was so upset about her passing that the doctor said it wasn't advisable,' says Cherie.

'I asked Mum, "What did you bury Nan in? Was it the lemon suit?" She said, "Yes, I did actually bury Nan in the lemon suit, how did you know that?"' Cherie drew in her breath. 'Well, she's wearing it. I can see her in it."' *Wearing.* Cherie emphasised the present tense to her mother, Claire, because in the first three months of baby Ellias's life, she spotted Nan watching over his cot up to four times a week. Sometimes, her sister Danielle, who'd come to help out, would see her too.

The thirty-one-year-old is an earthy, 'can-do' specialist; the kind of friend people count on, the reliable relative who ferries her in-laws around to doctors' appointments, her three small children strapped in the back of her station wagon. As she pulls into my driveway one warm autumn day, I spy only two babies on board, as her eldest, Ellias, is at pre-school. There's Georgiou, a heart-melting two-year-old, and five-month-old Marcella, her olive eyes bordered by a hedge of dark lashes. 'Here,' says Cherie, handing me a photo of Nan, beaming behind glass in a silver-plated frame. Over muffins at my kitchen table, amid chatter about finding a good book of recipes for children, Cherie fills me in on her devoted – and stylish – spirit nanny.

Gloria had been ill for around seven weeks before the stroke. Cherie would keep her updated by phone with progress reports on her study and her growing belly. 'I'd say things like "The baby's kicking," and, "We're going to sign him up to the soccer team," and all these things that I'd later find out put a smile on her face. I rang her the day before she passed to say that I'd handed in my final assignment and that my degree was finished and I would be a fully-fledged nurse. She died the next day. I believe that she actually hung on to hear that I had graduated, because that was something she always looked forward to.'

The first signs of Nan's presence in the unit Cherie shared with her husband, Hanna, a Palestinian-born engineer, were subtle and began in the lead-up to Ellias's birth. 'I would hear somebody walking on the carpet and I'd get up to investigate, thinking, *I'm sure I can hear somebody in the house.* Or out of the corner of my eye, I'd catch a movement, but I still hadn't connected that it was Nan.'

Hush, smiled Nan, a finger to her lips over Elli's cot. An offering of love.

There comes a time when house-guests stop tip-toeing around a host's home, when they finally feel comfortable enough to make a crease in the fabric of a household. For Nan, this moment arrived two weeks after Elli's birth. Cherie has always been a heavy sleeper. She can dream right through a screaming alarm clock, likewise her husband. This night, the couple were out cold, their exhaustion fierce as they navigated the shell-shocked early days of first-time parenthood. Suddenly, someone was yanking Cherie rudely out of sleep, literally pulling her by the lapel of her pyjamas to haul her up and awake. In two strides, she was at her baby's side. Ellias was coughing and coughing, his throat clogged with mucus. The newborn, who'd been sleeping on his back in a cradle by his parents' bed, was choking.

'I thought, *That's strange, somebody has actually lifted me out of my bed*,' recalls Cherie, 'but then I realised it was Nan. She was always very protective. I'm sure it was her saying, "Cherie, you're not hearing him, get up, he needs you, he *needs* you."' After potentially saving her great-grandson's life, Gloria began to materialise clearly by his cot, to her granddaughter's delight. 'She appeared to me in her fifties, when she was probably the best she ever looked, wearing the lemon suit she loved. Once, when Elli was three months old, I walked into the room in the middle of the night and she was looking over the cot. I said, "Hi Nan, you're here! What do you think of your beautiful great grandson?" And she turned and smiled.'

Seeing her dead grandmother in her son's small bedroom in the glow of a dim night light didn't scare Cherie. 'Never,' she states. 'I was never fearful. I was much more frightened when I could hear the footsteps before he was born and would think there was an intruder in the house.'

'She was just so besotted with her great grandchild. She was standing over him and I knew that she was protecting him at night. It got to the point where I'd often say, "Nan, just keep an eye on him for me tonight. That would be really good."'

As much as she adored having her around, Cherie says that when Elli was nearing four months, she felt obliged to send Gloria to her grieving grandfather. 'I'd heard that he wasn't dealing very well with her death, so I went to the room – I could hear the footsteps – and I said, "Nan, you're here, aren't you? If you can hear me, Pop needs you. He's not coping, he's missing you, you need to go to Pop." I didn't see or hear from her after that. I *felt* her leave.' Soon afterward, Cherie's mum phoned to say that her father had heard his late wife calling his name from the lush square acre of gardens she'd cherished and cultivated in life, now sheltering her ashes in death.

The months ambled on for Cherie and her growing brood. The family moved into a house in late 2004 and welcomed Georgiou in May 2006. After feeding her one-month-old late one night, Cherie lowered him back into his cot in her room. Toddler Elli slept in his room across the corridor, around eight steps away, his cot positioned so that Cherie could keep an eye on him from her own bed. A hat dangled from the handle of a linen closet in the hallway connecting the rooms, its bright straw flowers decorating the shadows.

Yawning, Cherie climbed back into bed beside her husband, closed her eyes and was just drifting to sleep when she heard the wooden floorboards in the lounge-room creak, a thunder clap in the soft quiet of the slumbering house. Instinctively, she looked over the top of Georgi's crib at her side to peer down the corridor into Elli's room. 'There was an old lady standing at the straw hat, pulling at it and looking into Elli's room,' relates Cherie. 'So I looked a little further beyond that old woman to see my grandmother looking over the top of Elli's cot like she'd come to see him again. The old lady with her was my great grandmother Ruby, her mother.'

Ruby, or Little Nan, as she was nicknamed, had died in 1999. In her green floral dress and pink cardigan, she stood fingering the pretty hat, as smitten with it as her daughter was with the sleeping Elli, his little chest swelling and dipping beneath his blanket. 'From what I could see, she was saying to my grandmother, "This is a lovely hat, what a lovely hat!" I couldn't hear it, I could just see from the facial expressions and the way she was touching the hat. I could imagine her admiring it because she loved hats,' says Cherie, explaining that Little Nan enjoyed collecting vintage hats, bonnets and pins. 'My Nan was looking back at her, smiling, and I could see this exchange between them.

'Little Nan was more transparent than Nan,' says Cherie. 'I wouldn't have said they were full-bodied and human in their appearance. They were fuzzy, *distinctively* fuzzy.' After watching them for a few seconds, Cherie addressed her visitors. 'Oh hi Nan, you're back! Are you back to meet Georgi?' Little Nan turned to her then, an astonished look on her face, and Gloria, chic for eternity in her lemon suit, looked up too. Cherie noticed her grandmother's scarf, knotted jauntily at the neck just like a character she admired in the British TV show, *Keeping Up Appearances*. Nan grinned, flaunting the even white teeth she displays in the portrait Cherie brought over.

'Yes,' nodded Nan.

'I said, "Georgi's over here when you get around to looking at him." And Little Nan was looking at me, startled! I said, "It's okay, Little Nan, it's lovely to see you," and then I just lay back down and went to sleep.' Hanna hadn't even stirred.

Cherie has a history of maintaining strong family ties with her late elders. Raised on the Sapphire Coast of New South Wales, Cherie was two when her parents separated, and her mother went on to have five more children in her second marriage, her father three. Her family network is vast and complicated but she keeps a skilful track of its tendrils. 'I was very close to my Grandpop Graham,' she says, 'my biological grandmother's father, on my dad's side.' One night, during a turbulent period when Cherie was enduring hard times at school, he came to her. He was the first.

'I remember being asleep in bed and feeling somebody sit at the end of the bed,' says Cherie, then sixteen. 'I remember sitting up – again, there was no fear – and Grandpa Graham's on the bed with his legs crossed. He sort of leaned into me like he's interested in having a conversation. He said, "Cherie, it's so good to see you!" and we sat there and actually had a full-on conversation. Then the fatigue would come over me and I'd just go back to sleep again.' Their chat centred on Cherie's problems at school. 'I didn't seem to connect with friends. I was being bullied and harrassed, hassled and victimised. I think maybe I was a little beyond the people I went to school with, beyond the small town mentality,' she shrugs. 'I did what I wanted when I felt like it, and said what I wanted when I wanted to say it.'

Her Grandpop tut-tutted at this. 'He was saying, "You need to settle down and concentrate on your studies . . . this isn't *your* path you're on . . . what are you doing? You're being destructive."' Cherie agreed: 'I had been lashing out at my stepfather too, causing trouble in the family.' When she woke up, resolved to rethink her attitude, she convinced herself that she'd dreamt the entire episode, yet three years later, when Cherie was nineteen and at a another crossroads in her life, he returned. Just as Nan would do a decade later, when Cherie was in the thick of new parenthood, Grandpop Graham had the knack of coming when he was needed most.

This time, Cherie was living in Sydney with her grandmother Flora, Pop Graham's daughter. It was an exciting yet nerve-wracking time, as she looked forward to overseas travel and teetered on the cusp of maturity. 'I was trying to make decisions for myself, I was trying to become an adult,' she explains. One night, she felt the familiar depression at the end of her bed, and looked up to see the 'fuzzy' figure of her great-grandfather. Cherie, with her excellent memory for the finer points, obliges me with a detailed picture of her friendly dead counsellor: 'Old. Aged in his eighties. He was wearing one of those khaki, knitted cardigans and he had his scarf like a cravat with a high collar. He never wore a tie. He had on his suit pants. Also those 1950s, heavy-rimmed black glasses. And,' she adds with an affectionate giggle, 'the bushy eyebrows!' Her reaction? Utterly grateful: 'Thank God you're here! I really needed to talk to somebody.'

The young mum doesn't consider herself a medium. 'No.' She shakes her head of chestnut curls. 'I don't feel like I'm being given messages to pass on.' As she points out, her encounters have mainly been personal, involving close family members drawing around to offer assistance. Unlike Bev, and other anonymous mediums I've met, the spirits are not flocking to *her* for help. Or perhaps that is yet to come?

Some weeks after we talk, Cherie sends me an email: she was watching TV one night when she looked up to see a small girl, around five years of age, hovering in her hallway. She wore what might have been a Victorian-era dress or nightgown. 'It was shin-length, with puffed sleeves to the mid-forearm,' she said, characteristically precise. Her blonde hair tumbled in ringlets from two pigtails tied with blue ribbon. The apparition appeared 'briefly solid', before she turned and walked away.

If there is anything at all that troubles Cherie about what she has experienced, it is this: why hasn't her Nan visited Marcella yet? Wouldn't she want to meet the baby of the family and the only girl? 'I'm actually surprised,' says Cherie, and I can hear the hurt tilting her words. 'Maybe Nan doesn't feel like I need her anymore.'

Unlikely. Towards the end of November 2008, Cherie called with an update. Her sister, Danielle, had been browsing in an esoteric shop in a suburban mall in Perth when she felt drawn to a woman who was doing tarot card readings. At the end of the reading, as Danielle was scraping back her chair to leave, the woman blurted, 'There is an elderly lady here,' and identified her as 'Gloria'.

Eyes brimming, Danielle asked, 'Where is she?'

'She's with somebody who's had a baby in the last twelve months. She's saying it's her only great grand-daughter,' responded the woman, adding that the elderly spirit was clucking over the baby's burnished skin, and her new teeth.

'She's having trouble pronouncing her name. Is it Marcia, Marci, Marciella?'

'She's keeping an eye on the little girl.'

THE COLOUR OF A FATHER'S LOVE

'Something about this woman's demeanour was familiar.'

Kath Clarke is as bubbly as the champagne that flows at the make-up parties she reigns over. Think of the swarms of perky urban fairies who descend on little girls' birthday celebrations every weekend and Kath could be their dorm mother. As a manager of party plan cosmetics company Nutrimetics, the forty-nine-year-old is a modern-day Camelot, a peddler gliding in her BMW to clients' homes armed with palettes of colour and balms to soften the skin and soothe the soul. With her fizzy red hair, girlish timbre and love of a good lippie, it's easy to think you've got the measure of Kath in the first few minutes that she trains her light on you, but like a nest of Russian dolls – the rosy-cheeked *matryoshka* – she guards secret inner selves.

Beneath the sparkle is a shrewd business woman who's made a motza and travelled the world in eight years of doing the job she loves. Inside the businesswoman there's a story, and within that story there's a memory: a vignette of the day the dead popped into a pampering party.

The Sydneysider loves meeting people, she likes to look after them, and cherishes time with her son, Christian. Those three things propelled her decision to leave her job as a primary school teacher and try her luck as a Nutrimetics consultant. 'I wanted a change, it had taken me ten years to have my son,' says Kath, her characteristic drawl sending each sentence on a downward swoop. 'I didn't want to go back to teaching, I didn't want to be ruled by the school bell. I wanted to be home for him, I wanted to be there for the swimming carnivals and school stuff.'

On a cloudless, late-winter's day in August 2000, she kissed her six-year-old goodbye and loaded the car with the bowls, massaging marbles, lotions and essential oils she'd need for a Peppermint Foot Pamper. She also packed her makeup kit, as the hostess requested. Backing out of her driveway for the short drive to Sylvania, in Sydney's southern heartland, Kath's dark eyes were overcast. 'I'll never forget that Saturday, I'd had this massive fight with Anthony over something trivial,' she says. The argument with her husband soured her mood, but she'd soon be back to her smiling self. After all, she was an independent businesswoman now, with a rainbow of opportunities ahead of her.

Pulling up at the red-brick, double-storey house opposite a pre-school in a sleepy street, Kath checked her teeth and dusted imaginary lint off her navy pants and white dress shirt. 'I was still really nervous, it was only my fourth "pampering",' she recalls. 'The booking was for eleven nurses and they were all stressed out.' Inside, the hum of busy women debriefing was background music to a still-life of dips, crackers, olives, flutes of sparkling wine and the odd mug of tea. Introductions out of the way, Kath set to work filling her bowls with fragrant water for eleven pairs of tired feet.

The pampering worked a treat. Relaxed and settling into their Saturday afternoon, the ladies were keen to buy some makeup. *They're in safe hands with me*, thought Kath. After a bad experience purchasing the wrong shade of expensive foundation one day, she'd resolved to never allow her clients to go home with a base too pink, too yellow, too light or too dark for their complexions. 'Let's face it,' she says, 'nobody wants to have the wrong foundation colour, nobody wants to have that *mask*.'

The trick, she learned, is to try on a base in natural light. So when one of the nurses, a mother of two small children, said 'Oh, I really want some of the Sheer Tint Foundation,' Kath led her out into the sunshine on the front lawn. It was 3 pm. The Nutrimetics consultant dabbed some Sheer Tint in the shade Pine onto her hand and began to blend a streak of it into her customer's jaw line. What happened next was not in the handbook.

'All of a sudden she seizes up, stiffens, and throws her head back like someone had pulled her backwards from the shoulders. It was a very violent jolt,' reports Kath, the fright still potent in her voice. 'I didn't know what to do, I thought, *Oh my God, she's having an epileptic fit or some kind of seizure.*' Another nurse who'd wandered out excused herself now, muttering, 'It's happening again, I'll go inside.' Kath, bewildered, watched mutely as she walked away. 'I got the impression that she'd seen this before, and she knew what would happen.

'So she just disappeared inside and all the others stayed inside, nobody came out, and I didn't know what to do! I was really scared. But the nurse didn't collapse, she was standing up. Then she looked at me, but she wasn't there, if that makes sense? She started talking to me, but her voice was different, it wasn't the same voice she'd used before.'

'She said, "You're doing okay, you're in the pilot's seat. Everything's fine." And it calmed me down, though I couldn't move from the spot on the grass that I was standing on, and I've still got the Pine Sheer Tint in my hand! My heart was beating fast but something told me that I had to stay there, and I had to listen. I didn't run away, because something about this woman's demeanour was familiar.

'She said to me, "You know you can't change them, just let them be." And I said, "Who?" I knew it was a man speaking. It was her voice but it was a man speaking. It was really bizarre, but by this stage I knew it was a man and I knew it was my father.'

Kath's dad, Tom, was sixty-four when he died of lung cancer in 1997.

Oh my God! thought Kath, her hand clapped over her mouth, her eyes tearing. The following week, Kath was expecting her sister to visit from Chicago, so she understood the subtext. 'My sister had been on my mind, and my mother had been on my mind, because my sister riles my mum up. This was my father telling me, "You know you can't change them, you know you can't change the situation. Just let them be."

'The next thing he said to me was, "Be kind to your husband, stop fighting with him, he's a good man, a sweet man." Now, this woman didn't know me from a bar of soap, she didn't know that I was married, didn't know where I lived, didn't know a thing about me, and here she was telling me to be kind to my husband.'

But Tom wasn't done yet. Via the channelling nurse, he advised Kath to '"Enjoy your new business, enjoy the journey, and all the lovely things that will happen along the way, but keep your feet on the ground." When I heard that, I had no doubt it was my father.'

Keep your feet on the ground had been a favourite refrain of Tom's.

'Dad?' she whispered to the stranger in the pretty red and grey frock and cardigan. 'Yes!' answered the woman. 'It's lovely here. It's very peaceful and I'm in the white light. I miss you so much. I have such great remorse that I didn't spend enough time with you all.'

Kath had suffered six miscarriages trying to have a second baby, so she took the opportunity to ask, 'Will I have another child?' The medium lowered her gaze to Kath's belly muttering, 'I can hear gasping. Why can I hear gasping?' Kath felt her womb begin to boil under the psychic's gaze. Explaining that her pregnancies 'just fizzled out', Kath believes the nurse was referencing her lost babies.

The nurse's trance lasted fifteen minutes, and at the end of it, she blinked, then looked around asking, 'Did it happen again?' She explained to Kath that she had no control over the channelling, that it happened spontaneously and the messages were erased from her memory once she'd passed them on. They made their way inside, where someone thrust a mug of strong, sweet tea at Kath, 'but I asked for bubbles instead!'

In retrospect, Kath describes the experience as 'really peaceful', though it had a profound effect on her life. Though she had always had a vague interest in the unknown (her husband, an engineer, is a long-standing member of the UFO Research Society of New South Wales), those fifteen minutes on a classic Sydney winter's day sparked an intense curiosity about a world beyond our own.

Kath accepts she is the last person such a thing should have happened to. 'I'm sane, I bake, I knit!' she says, chortling. 'The trainers never tell you anything like that's gonna happen when you're doing your colour-matching!' The beauty consultant, who has since welcomed other, more subtle, messages from her dad, now reasons that spirits exist in another dimension but that occasionally, our two worlds brush against each other. Knowing that makes her heart beat a little faster, but it's also comforting. Busier than ever these days, with her thriving sideline business doing wedding and formal makeup, Kath often thinks back to the encounter.

'To this day, I still colour match in natural daylight,' she says with a grin. 'And my nurse ended up buying that foundation.'

BUTTERFLY KISSES

'There are too many of these things that people call coincidences.'

Armed with glass-cleaner and paper towels, Sheila Berry was outside wiping the sliding back doors of her Perth home, when she noticed something curious on the glass. Frowning, she peered closer: 'What *is* that?' On her way inside to fetch a camera to photograph it, a thought bloomed inside her, flooding her chest with warmth. She didn't dare voice it, but the mild autumn air snatched it up and seemed to shimmer with the question, *Is this how it feels to be touched by grace?*

'It was an impression of a complete butterfly on the glass,' says Sheila, her voice swelling with wonder, even three years later. 'Everything was so clear; eyes, wings, even the pattern on the wings! It couldn't be missed because it was at eye level. I took one-and-a-half rolls of film trying to get a good picture of it. Friends were astonished by how clear it was.'

It was the twentieth of March 2005, and her beloved daughter, Jackie, had been dead for almost seven months. At the age of thirty-six, she'd succumbed to an inoperable brain tumour.

For Sheila, sixty-nine, the butterfly stamped on her back door sparked her own spiritual metamorphosis. Things began to happen after that, events that the former sceptic could no longer dismiss.

It took the combined efforts of her late husband and daughter, but by the end of 2005, Sheila had come to believe that the barriers of distance, time and physical death could dissolve in a heartbeat.

Or in the flutter of a frail wing.

'When I saw this in the window, I looked in the Yellow Pages to try to find butterfly farms to see if butterflies did this sort of thing,' says Sheila, who searched the floor and surrounds but found no insect culprit, dead or alive. 'My friend said, "No butterfly would leave an impression like that, on glass – every tiny mark, even antennae: they don't fly like that!"

'It is white, like a powder of some sort,' explains Sheila. 'I actually phoned Perth Zoo and spoke to a man there who said it didn't sound like a butterfly could do that. He said, "I don't know what it would be."'

Three months after she found the impression, Sheila was shopping at the local mall. After dropping off her watch for a battery replacement, she strolled next door to a handbag shop. For a few moments, she lost herself in the colourful window display.

Something fluttered around her face.

'I jumped back, thinking it was a wasp. As I watched it go inside the shop, I noticed it was a butterfly! I followed it in and saw it land on a pretty lilac bag with a soft fringe on it, and on the front of this bag was an embroidered butterfly. The next day, she returned and bought the bag, now displayed like a treasure inside a glass cabinet at home.

'That year, 2005, butterflies surrounded me everywhere I went,' says Sheila, who returned from a one-week stay with the youngest of her three children, Melainie, to find a large one perched at her front door, its translucent wings waving, as if in greeting.

Another time, she found a butterfly as beautiful as a child's drawing lying dead at her back door. 'Because it looked so lovely, I couldn't dispose of it,' recalls Sheila, who tenderly placed it in a tiny, plastic container. She covered it and left it on the garden table. 'The next day, I thought, *If it looks terrible, I'll throw it in the bin*, but when I looked inside, it was completely empty!'

Most remarkably, perhaps, the experiences also encompassed Sheila's closest family and friends. 'I was on the phone one day,' recalls Sheila, who emigrated from the UK in 1972 with her husband Bill, Jackie and their son, Mark. 'I was talking to my brother in Cornwall [UK], telling him about these butterflies and he was half-listening, thinking, *Yeah, sure* ... Then, he paused. When he came back on the line, he exclaimed, "You will never guess what has just happened to me!"

'He was in his garden and a butterfly flew straight into his face,' continues Sheila with a laugh. 'He was a non-believer, but he said to me that day, "I am a hundred per cent sure that had something to do with Jackie."'

Jackie, Sheila's middle child, was only eighteen and plagued by chronic headaches when she was diagnosed with a tumour nestled deep in the centre of her brain. Surgery removed most of it, and Jackie had radiotherapy, but three months later, the tumour grew back. 'It nearly killed me and Bill at the time,' whispers Sheila. 'It was so traumatic. But she was a girl that never complained. Ever.'

After more surgery and a second bout of radiotherapy, Jackie pulled through. She survived another eighteen years, her life split in two with a scalpel's precision. When the headaches came back, the doctors shook their heads. 'It was inoperable. She lost sight in her right eye and mobility started to be a problem,' says Sheila, who lived with Jackie. 'Still, she never moaned or groaned.'

The family sought out Sydney brain surgeon Charlie Teo, but Jackie died a month before the appointment. 'She was a great mate to me. We were very, very close, I know she'd be worried about me,' says Sheila, who lost her husband in 1996. 'I still can't believe Jackie is gone.'

Did the kind-hearted, witty young woman find a whimsical way to prove that she was still around? As Sheila reels off the stories, it sounds like Jackie's butterfly effect touched family and friends far and wide: Sheila's sister has spotted butterflies in her garden in the heart of a freezing English winter; another flitted around Melainie and her husband at their home in the stifling heat of Karratha, a mining town in Western Australia; a friend was writing a letter in bed one night when a butterfly glided onto the page . . .

As Sheila talks, I try to think of any memorable encounters I've had with butterflies, and I come up with . . . nothing. I have never chanced upon one in a shopping mall, in the cold or extreme heat and definitely not in bed at night. Even on the sweetest spring day, I'm not exactly swatting them away.

Yet this wasn't Sheila's first feather-light message from the spirit world. Eight years before Jackie passed, Bill died of lung cancer. The sixty-five-year-old had been a keen amateur singer whose deep voice would rumble through the house as he sampled an eclectic repertoire featuring Nat King Cole and Louis Armstrong classics.

With the funeral only a few days away, Sheila and Jackie were at home one morning when Sheila suddenly wilted with panic. Where was her husband's body? It had always been Bill's habit to let Sheila know his whereabouts. If he was at work running his tyre shop and on his way to an appointment, he'd call his wife and put her mind at ease by telling her where he was off to and when he'd be home. But on this day, 'I was so upset that I didn't know where he was,' says Sheila. 'I didn't know if he was still at the hospital or at the funeral parlour.'

As worry gnawed at her, Sheila, who was in the bathroom, heard the opening strains of 'A Wonderful World.' She followed the melody to Jackie's room, where her radio was blaring Nat King Cole's version of the sentimental favourite. 'I thought, *God, it sounds just like Bill singing*,' she remembers. 'It was like he was telling me he was in a wonderful world, and I just broke down. At least I knew where he was. He was happy.'

If she had any doubt that her husband was healing her with music, it faded when she heard the tune that followed it. 'The very next song was my all-time favourite,' says Sheila, explaining how she was struck dumb when the 1970 hit, 'Cheryl Moana Marie', by the New Zealand singer John Rowles started up. 'That was the clincher,' says Sheila. 'It was like magic.'

A month later, Melainie had gone horse-riding. Sheila stayed at home, fretting – she hadn't wanted her to go out that day. As Sheila tried to distract herself by watching a telethon, the phone rang with the frightful news that Melainie had been in a minor accident, but friends were bringing her home. When the doorbell rang, Sheila found that she was literally paralysed with fear, so Jackie let them in: 'Then, on the TV, came the song 'A Wonderful World'. It was like my husband was there saying, *Don't panic, it's going to be okay.*'

For six months, Bill's white utility vehicle was parked in the backyard. 'My son, Mark, said he'd sell it, but he didn't get around to it,' remembers Sheila. Eventually, Mark and Melainie opened the door of their father's car for the first time since his death, turned the ignition to move the vehicle, and gasped in surprise to hear 'A Wonderful World' spill from the radio.

'It happened all the time,' says Sheila, who is ever grateful for how Jackie helped her through her blur of grief. Each week, the women would travel to the cemetery and lay flowers at Bill's grave. 'When I was upset, I'd cry and scream and then I'd think, *I've got to stop this*, switch on the radio and there it was. People ask, "Does it frighten you?" and I say, "No, it is lovely, lovely . . ."'

Is the universe capable of custom-designing a motif to embrace us when we need it most? Yes, according to metaphysics. Philosopher Deepak Chopra dubs it 'meaningful coincidence'. In her book,

Secrets of the Monarch, medium Allison DuBois uses the concept of the Monarch butterfly – which only lives for two months, so takes several generations to complete its annual migration – to illustrate her point that 'our individual lives are part of a bigger story involving our friends and our family.'

Sheila Berry calls it 'simply wonderful'.

Convinced that her husband and her child have comforted her in spirit she directs any doubters to the evidence on her sliding glass door. To mark the spot, she has placed a circle of tiny stick-on butterflies around the outline and forbids anyone to touch it. 'It is still there today, every tiny mark,' marvels Sheila.

'There are too many of these things that people call coincidences,' she says. 'But they are not.'

TIME WILL TELL

'There is no explanation for that clock being there.'

With a yawn, twenty-four-year-old Di Webster unlocked the door of her unit in the eastern Melbourne suburb of Carnegie one summer's night in 1980, and put down her keys and bag. Feeling peckish after a night at the cinema, she walked into the kitchen to fix a late supper. As she pulled out the frying pan to cook bacon and eggs, she glanced at the clock – the ubiquitous eighties starburst with a bronze face – in its usual spot on the wall above the stove and noted that it was 11.15 pm.

After her snack, Di went straight to bed. 'And the next thing I know, I wake up and it was like it is in the movies, when you sit bolt upright in bed because you've had a fright, and I never believed that people really did that,' says Di, a freelance journalist based in Sydney. 'Something frightened me, but I wasn't having a nightmare.'

Her eyes darted about the room, before stopping at the alarm clock: 5.25 am. Her skin answered a shift in the atmosphere, but she rubbed down the goose bumps and lay her head back on the pillow. Ninety minutes later, when she was ready to start her day, Di padded into the kitchen, and her jaw dropped.

'I look up above the stove to the clock, and it's not there. I thought, *That's weird*. It was a U-shaped kitchen and on the other side of the U, on the bench, was the clock. *On the bench*! And its batteries had been removed and were around the corner in the lounge-room. The clock had stopped at 5.25 am.

'There is no explanation for that clock being there. If it fell, it would fall onto the stove. It would have to go *clunk, clunk, clunk* along the floor and climb back onto the other bench. It was quite a distance away! And what of the batteries being around the corner, on the floor in the lounge-room?' says Di, measuring her words and pausing between thoughts, her green eyes wide, still trying to process the anomaly even three decades on. 'But the clock was just sitting neatly on the bench; it wasn't marked in any way, the starbursts weren't bent from dropping. It was just on the bench on the other side of the kitchen.'

The episode came at the close of a difficult chapter in the life of *The Age* newspaper editorial assistant. 'Up until I was twenty-three, it was just one loss after another,' she says in a quiet voice. In January of that year, her mother, Shirley, sixty, died within hours of a cerebral haemorrhage. 'It was horrifying,' shudders Di, who was sixteen when one of her best friends, Colin, was killed in a car accident. Barely a year later, her brother died of cystic fibrosis.

Casting her mind back to the wandering clock opens other doors in Di's past. She polishes a tender memory of Colin, the law student surrounded by towering shelves of books, dwarfing the petite Di, at his parents' house on the eve of his death. 'I pulled out a book of bush poetry by a bloke called Tom Quilty. I was just flicking through it and I came across a poem called *To My Mate*, about what two friends mean to each other. I could recite it for you word for word . . . it makes me tear up to think about it. I said, "Oh, isn't this lovely," and he read it. It ends with the words, "But like the fields of brilliant blooms, we too must fade and perish." He was killed the next day.'

The clock in Colin's mother's living room stopped at the precise moment of his accident, says Di, and the same thing happened at her mum's house when her brother passed. With a flutter in her belly, she picked up the phone to share her own version of the clock saga with Colin's mum, Kate, who had also been her mother's dearest friend.

'What time was on the clock?' asked Kate.

'Twenty-five past five, and the second hand was on the ten.'

'She said, "5.10.25 is my birthday."'

Is it possible that Shirley, understanding her daughter's knowledge of the role clocks had played in recent losses, had chosen the same device to nudge her toward a new mother figure? Di's future wound its way there, regardless. 'The woman whose date of birth was on the clock looked after me after my mother died,' she states.

'She absolutely took me under her wing and became my second mother.'

THE REUNION

'It was the most amazing thing I've ever had happen to me.'

In the pre-dawn hours of the morning, a husband and wife are together in bed. She is still asleep, but he is awake and sitting up, dressed only in his pyjama bottoms. The wife stirs, opens her eyes, smiles and reaches for him. She holds him tight, strokes his familiar skin, lays her cheek against his chest. They exchange a handful of tender words. Love pulses between them. No matter that they are both in their late sixties. No matter that they've been married fifteen years – the third time for him, the second for her. No matter that he has been dead for eleven days.

Eleven days is also all it had taken for them to fall in love. 'Stace and I married in 1990 and I've never known a love like I had for this man,' says retired nurse Lorna Virgo, seventy. 'He asked me to marry him eleven days after I met him and I'd only seen him five days in that time! It was just lovely. Once I asked him, "Why did you marry me so quickly?" and he said, "Because I didn't want anybody else to get you."'

At the age of fifty-two, with seven daughters and the detritus of failed dates behind her, divorcee Lorna wasn't expecting to bump into eternal love at the Mount Gravatt Bowling Club. At a girlfriend's urging, she'd agreed to accompany her to a singles dance for 'Parents Without Partners' at the Brisbane venue. She would have been happy with a laugh, some conversation and maybe a twirl around the dance floor, none of which seemed imminent when Lorna, in her new purple floral frock, arrived to find that her friend had stood her up. 'I sat there and thought, *Please God, open the floor up and swallow me.*'

A little while later, she decided to make her escape, but took a detour to the bar for a soft drink on the way out. The man who would propose to her before the fortnight was through sat, dapper in a suit and tie, with his elbows propped up on the bench, watching a soccer game on TV. In keeping with the mood of the evening, the bartender completely ignored Lorna. The gallant at the bar corrected this with a tilt of his arm that sent the barman scurrying over, and Lorna and the stranger started talking. 'I asked him what his name was and he said, "Jim". I said, "What does your mother call you?" And he said "Stace," and I just looked at him and said, "I'm going to call you Stace."'

Stace turned heads with his movie star good looks: a full head of hair and a dashing moustache, both peppered with grey, a strong jaw and an aquiline nose. Lorna put all thoughts of going home aside when Gilbert 'Stace' Virgo asked her to dance. 'He was six-foot-four-and-a-half and I'm five-foot-three! I said, "You don't want to dance with me, you're too tall for me!" I nearly talked myself out of it.'

Instead, she married the British-born ex-serviceman. At their wedding, the groom stood up and reminisced about the first time they'd locked eyes, all of twelve weeks before: 'This woman there, who I didn't even know, fired four questions off within a few minutes, and the first one was "What's your name?" and the last one was "Guess how many children I've got?"' Perhaps that night at the bowling club, Lorna had stolen a peek into the once-in-a-lifetime partnership in store for her, because she usually kept her abundance of girls close and quiet. 'I didn't tell men how many children I had, because they'd walk away in horror.'

Unlike her first marriage, which had ended in 1982 when her husband walked out on Lorna and their brood, this one proved harmonious and happy. 'We always held hands if we were out. If he was sitting down I'd come up behind him and put my arms around his neck. We were always affectionate, you know? People knew we loved each other.'

Stace introduced his wife to sport, jazz and Margaritas. Every Friday night, when he knocked off from his job as a taxi driver, the couple would dress up and head to the Twin Towns RSL for dinner and a dance. They also shared a love of caravans, and Stace took Lorna on her first trip overseas. They visited England, where he was born, eight times in their fifteen years together. When Stace strode through customs, wearing his trench coat, black hat and signature silver 'mo', others would stop and stare.

'You could see them thinking, *Isn't he that old rocker? Or is it the actor from Tombstone?* He was unaware of the magnetism he possessed,' marvels Lorna. Even her late mother, Bessie, who'd died aged seventy-four in 1984, apparently approved of the match, because she stopped checking on her.

Since the moment she'd originally materialised as a shadowy outline at the foot of Lorna's bed, not long after her first marriage broke down, Bessie had taken to dropping in on her daughter in her dreams. For Lorna, it was comforting to know that her mum was looking after her. 'Sometimes in my dreams there'd be a knock at the door and I'd open it and there was Mum,' says Lorna, in her quick-speaking, matter-of-fact way. 'I was always so pleased to see Mum and she was always in colour. I'd say, "Oh Mum, come in and have a cup of tea." I'd get up the next morning and say to whichever children I had at home, "Oh, I saw grandma last night, it was so lovely." I felt she was always there for me.'

Yet in 1995, Bessie's pop-ins stopped. 'After I'd been married for five years, I dreamt I went to her funeral and I have never seen Mum since,' says Lorna, who attributes the end of the visits to her mum's acknowledgement that she was content in her second marriage. 'The years ticked over and every day it was such a joy to wake up and find him in bed beside me. I now understood what it really meant to be married to someone I loved, and who loved me.'

But events a decade later up-ended their world.

On the twenty-fourth of August 2005, Stace was diagnosed with a malignant high-grade primary brain tumour. 'I'm a nurse; as soon as I read that radiology report I knew he would die,' says Lorna, who coped by switching to professional mode. 'I thought to myself, he's going to be dead by Christmas, and he was. And it was just so hard. We never talked about death, Stace just wanted to live life normally. He died in 14 weeks. He just got weaker and weaker.'

Five days before his death, the active, 102 kilogram giant who never faltered from his routine of rising, pulling on his 'smellies' – paint-spattered old clothes – and working outdoors, had no choice but to take to his bed. But he did it on his terms. 'He said to me, "Lovie, I'm not going to take any more medications, I'm not going to eat, I'm not going to drink." He didn't want to be an invalid.' A local doctor from nearby Tweed Heads, on the northern New South Wales coast, drove to the couple's Burringbar home to administer palliative care. The love of Lorna's life passed away at the age of sixty-nine on the seventh of December 2005, on her youngest daughter's birthday. Surrounded by her girls and their families, Lorna buried her husband on the thirteenth of December. 'I was just devastated,' says Lorna, who returned his ashes to England in 2006. 'Even now, I cry, but you can't live your life crying.'

Her memory of the morning five days after the funeral is a balm for her pain. To hear her tell it is to be reminded of the kernel of truth shimmering in platitudes like 'everlasting love' and 'soul mate'.

'I woke up and Stace was in bed with me. He didn't have a shirt on and he was just sitting up in bed. He had his pyjamas on, and I cuddled into him and I said, "Oh love, you're back!"' says Lorna, smiling through her tears. 'I just cuddled him and the feeling was there and I thought *Oh, he's back, isn't this wonderful?* It was just the same. And then he said, "Lovie, I had to go, I would have had tumours everywhere. You take care."'

'I got up and said to the girls who were home, "I saw Stace this morning, it was so wonderful."' Lorna says Stace appeared to her four more times, in extraordinarily vivid dreams, until early in 2007 when, in an echo of her mother's farewell, she dreamt that she attended his funeral. Except for one occasion at the end of November of that year, when he came to her the day after his grandson was born, Lorna hasn't seem him since.

But she is convinced that the encounter on the eighteenth of December was much more profound than any subconscious meandering. 'Oh, that wasn't a dream!' she exclaims. 'It was an apparition. I know every pore of that man's skin, I've looked at him, I've felt it . . .' she trails off, her voice cracking. 'No, no, it was the most amazing thing I've ever had happen to me in my life. It was so real! I felt the joy in my heart. I just looked at him and I said, "Oh you're back!" There was nothing to be frightened of.'

Lorna has since had the opportunity to meet other men, but she no longer has need of this. In her fifteen years with Stace, she gorged on love, enough to last a lifetime – and beyond. 'Dead or alive,' she says. 'He is the one.'

∽∞∾

In the end, there is only love.

The methods our loved ones select to convey this message ranges from the familiar (Jill Sikorski's dad raking cloud fingers through her hair, and her mum drifting in on her favourite perfume) to the cryptic and symbolic (Di Webster's mother's manipulation of the clock and Sheila Berry's daughter's butterfly motif). It's up to the dead whether we peel back layers of the lesson over time, or learn it in a single moment to topple established notions of life and death.

For Kath Clarke, whose father crashed her Nutrimetics party, it was the latter. Kath first shared this story with me many years ago during a make-up party of my own, and it was one of the first to light the spark that would become *Spirit Sisters*. Not only because it raised gooseflesh, but because it encompassed twin ideas that cut my imagination adrift: the paranormal can upend our ordered lives when we least expect it, and it may happen because those we have loved and lost continue to care for us in spirit.

That is the lesson hidden on every page of my subjects' suffering, the secret note in the music of their sonorous stories.

A SPIRITED DEBATE

'All argument is against it; but all belief is for it.'
SAMUEL JOHNSON

Writing *Spirit Sisters* presented a paradox: the more I learned, the less I felt I knew.

The more my candid and courageous interviewees revealed their hearts, the more questions they birthed in my mind. For a year, their stories haunted me; they shared my pillow, perched on my shoulder as I packed lunchboxes, and rode the 8.38 am train with me to work. Each experience was a maze I lost myself in as I struggled to understand the extraordinary events that had taken place in these women's homes, hearts and minds. *How could it be*, I obsessed, that some among us can see dead strangers, or loved ones who've been wrenched from our arms, dream of the future, lock eyes with their mirror image or be stalked by invisible horror?

Would it even be possible to come close to knowing?

Finally, I think I know the answer, but more on that later.

I arrived at each interview with an open mind, but in keeping with the spirit of the project, if my intuition hinted something wasn't right, I didn't include the story. Having said that, there were also many stories that didn't make it in simply for lack of space.

And so the questions tumbled out, one over the other. *How could it be* that Patricia Turnbull, her parents and eleven brothers and sisters could all hear the laughter of long-dead workers and later the pitiful wails of their dead brother in their seaside cottage in Hobart? My narrow frame of reference could not imagine a house full of children where the ghosts crowded in with the people and the father of the house, a mid-century Australian fisherman unused to shows of emotion, resorts to ripping out the stairwell to thwart the spooks.

Yet Patricia was entirely sure of, and comfortable with, what she'd lived. When I turned to her sister, she too was nonchalant. 'Oh yes. That's the way it was.'

This kind of resignation was common, though the process of reaching such acceptance was not always straightforward. Do you think you might shout from the rooftops if you experienced something you could not explain? I put it to you that you wouldn't. I can still see Amy Shepherd, nibbling at her raisin toast at the coffee shop as she told a ghost story that made my scalp crawl: a tale of a vintage family who materialised at a sleepover and ogled her with unabashed curiosity. Her voice was even, her expression serene and intelligent. 'This is what happened,' her eyes challenged mine. 'Take it or leave it.'

Take it? I dove head first into it.

Amy's story was one of the first to come my way and it's remained with me for that reason, as much as for the head-reeling possibilities it encompasses. You see, the 'family' didn't merely appear and fade away, a blip in time; they *interacted*. They stood, like a museum display come to life, and in a few unforgettable minutes communicated a message of unity to Amy – a family on earth and forever more. The father, noble and a little haughty, was clearly in charge, while his wife and son seemed more openly inquisitive about the living marvel before them. When Amy described how the mother bent down and whispered in her son's ear and how he nodded, before taking a step towards her . . . Oh, my ears trilled and tears stormed my eyes. My mouth was silent, but my skin screamed.

It's a story that suggests the survival of consciousness, or perhaps the possibility of multiple realities. On the way home, I remembered the thriller *The Others*, where the worlds of the living and the dead overlap. I thought of Nicole Kidman's spectral lady of the house, terror etched on her talc-white face as she confronted living intruders.

This idea that ghosts are merely people going about their business in a parallel dimension that some among us are able to glimpse, or are scenes from a life that the universe stores and 'plays' from time to time, particularly intrigued me. Stories like Judith Parker's ghost with the heavy handshake – '*It was like I was a ghost in his world*' – and Rhonda Rice's vision of the bonneted ladies, out for a gambol, still chatting gaily as they vanished through her wall, had me twisting a mental Rubik's Cube.

Marie D. Jones has been trying to piece together the puzzle for a lot longer than I have, and she kindly shared her wisdom with me. The author of *Psience: How New Discoveries in Quantum Physics and New Science May Explain the Existence of Paranormal Phenomena*, is a journalist, author and lifelong student of paranormal and metaphysical studies. The California single mum gave me a crash course in quantum physics, two words that had me quaking in my heels. 'At its most basic,' she reassured me, 'it is really nothing more than the study of energy and matter at the quantum (subatomic) level.'

So what does quantum physics have to do with the paranormal? It's all about energy. 'As the human body is a bioelectric entity, presumably upon death, this energy never dies nor ceases to exist – it simply changes form and transfers from one system to another,' says Marie, explaining a basic tenet of physics, the Law of Conservation of Energy. 'If ghosts and spirits are nothing more than energy that "lives" beyond bodily death, then these spectral apparitions simply may be one or more forms of that changed energy.'

Marie says that theories within quantum physics may even address the specific types of apparitions described by paranormal researchers. 'Imprints or non-sentient ghosts,' like Rhonda's bonneted ladies, Naomi Kalogiros's 11 pm rector walking the Pomeranian and Leonie Hitchenor's Victorian ladies on horseback, 'act as projections, and speak to the concept of a holographic nature of reality, as well as to the possibility of extra dimensions or parallel universes from which these imprints are being projected.'

Is your brain boggling yet? There's much more. 'Ghosts that seemingly have the ability to interact with their witnesses,' such as Amy's colonial trio, Brenda Purden's lonely shopkeeper and Cherie Frazer's watchful grandmother, 'might be actual entities coming through from other dimensions and universes, via wormholes or portals that allow for the synching up of their world and ours.'

Though she stresses that all this is 'strictly theoretical', Marie offers yet another possibility: 'Those who see ghosts may be seeing images, or 'reflections', that are coming from the Zero Point Field (ZPF). The ZPF is thought to be a repository field of all energy, matter and form, as the well as the entire landscape of time, past, present and future . . . and that some of us in *this* reality may be wired to access information from this field.'

'It is possible that the past is recorded in the human unconscious,' agrees parapsychologist Dr. Lance Storm. 'Carl Jung proposed that not only archetypal events (those events common to humanity since the dawn of time), but also individual events, might be stored in the so-called Collective Unconscious. People may have archetypal experiences of the past from time to time,' which paves the way for a Catch Twenty-two conundrum, says Dr. Storm. 'Some skeptics might say these experiences are mere hallucinations, but the lines between fantasy and reality become blurred at this point, because accessing the past that is stored in the collective unconscious is going to look exactly like hallucination!'

It's heady stuff. What is real, and what is not? And if something is not 'real' by our accepted standard, does that mean it is invalid – or that we need to reconsider the definition of reality?

While I found Marie's book and her round-up of theories refreshing and exciting (albeit *Star Trek*-ish), most mainstream scientists aren't sold on a potential link between quantum physics and the paranormal. 'I've yet to have a convincing case presented to me of how the two might be connected,' says Sydney scientist Paul Willis, broadcaster and reporter on ABC TV's *Catalyst* and *Quantum*. While Marie sent me wriggling into wormholes and peeking into portals, Paul did his best to anchor me to terra firma. First up, he introduced the concept of Ockham's Razor, which states that, 'if there are two competing hypotheses, the simplest is most likely to be correct.'

So when I described my moment with the candle-holder falling from our cabinet around the time Anibal saw the ghosts, he shot back: Which is more likely? That spirits from the afterlife are trying to communicate with me by almost knocking me out with bric-a-brac? Or that a rodent (yuck!) scuttled past and tipped it over the edge? That's Ockham's Razor, and Paul wielded it freely – think Johnny Depp in *Sweeney Todd* – as we emailed back and forth.

Paul offered to analyse specific details of each experience, but as this was not possible in the time frame, he had to make do with my overview of what *Spirit Sisters* is about.

'There are several normal explanations for people seeing apparitions . . . They may all be different, normal phenomena. I too regularly see apparitions, particularly of my dead mother, and I frequently wake up in the middle of the night with a sense of dread that there is someone in the room,' says Paul. 'As real as these experiences may seem to me, I accept that they have perfectly normal explanations, such as my abiding love for my mother and hypnopompic and hypnagogic dreams. These are well-understood phenomena and they are well-studied. Again, it comes down to Ockham's Razor; am I really talking to my dead mother or am I experiencing well-known delusions that have a perfectly normal explanation? Again, the latter is the simpler explanation.'

'Memory fabrication and modification, the projection of dreams into reality, or hypnopompic and hypnagogic dreaming and a whole host of other psychological phenomena are all possible within the minds of perfectly rational, sane and intelligent people,' he continues. 'These [experiences] are all the results of psychological flaws in the healthiest of brains.'

Of course, such experiences are also known in the realms of neurology and psychiatry, two vast and separate cans of worms, but it would be remiss of me not to touch on them here. In *Phantoms in the Brain*, neuroscientist Dr. V.S. Ramachandran writes about the bizarre neurological condition, Charles Bonnet syndrome, where damage in the visual pathway turns sufferers completely or partially blind, yet causes vivid and lifelike hallucinations.

Professor Warwick Middleton treats patients with dissociative disorders. People who have suffered severe ongoing childhood trauma may 'dissociate', that is, experience parts of themselves – memories and behaviours – as a separate identity. 'Sometimes it's actually heard as an externalised voice and sometimes seen as a vision,' says the Brisbane psychiatrist. 'They could also smell things or taste things or feel things on their skin.

'Most patients with dissociative disorders will report [psi] experiences such as déjà vu, foretelling the future and feeling a presence,' he adds. I find this astonishing, likewise the fact that questions of a parapsychological nature are used in a questionnaire to help determine the diagnosis. Yet Professor Middleton stresses that his patients are a select group of severely traumatised individuals, and appears to agree with Paul Willis when he adds, 'There are many people who hear voices and see things, who don't have a mental illness and don't have a history of trauma.

'The unconscious is an incredibly powerful entity,' says the professor. When I ask if he believes in an afterlife, he pauses. 'Look, I'm probably with Socrates,' he says. 'I think the only thing I know for certain is that I know nothing.'

Part of the paradox is that science accepts only what can be observed and tested in a laboratory, and most paranormal experiences provide only anecdotal evidence. As Leonie Hitchenor grumbles in 'Ripples in Time', 'I can't perform like a trained seal.' To Paul Willis, that seems too convenient.

Searching for something concrete to put to him, I mention the many interviewees (including Debbie Malone, Leonie Evans and Tamara Warden) who say their presence affects electronics and gadgets. I found it fascinating, because the issue of the malfunctioning TVs and DVDs popped up time and again without any prompting. Related to this, a number of women also mentioned a sense of 'static' or 'static charge' in the atmosphere in the moments preceding a manifestation.

'If such claims are made with tangible and measurable results, then let's test them,' says Paul, adding that there's a 1.5 million dollar international prize in store for anyone who can prove it. (If he uncovers such a psychic star, Paul gets ten per cent, which he's pledged to charity and recommends the 'winner' do the same.) 'I genuinely want to find someone who can make electronic gadgets misbehave when they are in touch with the spirits. But no one has yet been able to demonstrate that they can do anything like this.'

Step up, ladies.

But there *is* evidence for psychokinesis – a person's ability to manipulate inanimate objects – says Dr. Hannah Jenkins, president of the Australian Institute of Parapsychological Research. And here we drift into the grey area of the poltergeist, such as tortured Caroline Laurence in 'Nightmare on Cobra Street'. 'There is some indication that electromagnetic forces could be responsible for some paranormal activity,' says Dr. Jenkins. 'The human body has its own electromagnetic field and perhaps some of these events can be explained by some people's apparent ability to interact with the [electromagnetic field] so that either they experience more force than normally, or they affect objects.'

'It seems natural that a manifestation that involves an energetic change would cause problems with computers, TVs and other electrical objects. These reports are especially prominent in the study of poltergeist activity,' adds Marie D. Jones. 'Just as with the presence of static – which may be indicative of energy or matter moving between dimensions – we are seeing interactions of various forms of energy. We are all made up of vibrating particles, we are energy, and so is everything around us. When two types of energy come into contact, there is a reaction.'

'Poltergeist research is a well-respected field of inquiry in para-psychology,' says Dr. Storm, describing phenomena that has been reported since the 1100s. 'At the very least, we may realistically speak of PK [psychokinetic] effects taking place, but it is often the case that a so-called focus person, usually a young person, is the source of the PK.' That 'noisy ghost' also piques Hannah Jenkins's professional interest. 'Some people interpret it as a spirit possessing somebody, but I think there's a more natural explanation, in that those phenomena are being created by the person, perhaps unconsciously. As I recently read, "You don't find poltergeist incidences in happy family homes."'

Caroline Laurence's experience ticks all the experts' boxes: a young girl, a broken home, and on the night the phenomena peaked, a thick static charge – 'you could feel it in your hair' – was her first sign that something wasn't right, followed by the screeching of her unplugged stereo. There were two other elements of Caroline's story that haunted me: the writing in sludge on the mirror and the hangman's noose that seemingly materialised from nowhere.

Reading British psychic Mia Dolan's 2006 book, *Haunted Homes*, I encountered an eerily similar reference to a sticky substance appearing on a mirror in a haunted house. 'It was thick and gluggy,' said the resident, echoing Caroline's memory: 'It didn't come off easily.'

As for the noose, if it was not a macabre joke, then it may have been what Professor David Fontana calls an 'apport', the 'mysterious arrival of objects of unknown origin.' In *Is There An Afterlife?*, he documents his two-year investigation of poltergeist phenomena in a shop in Cardiff (interestingly, there were no youths involved), where 'apports' such as 1912 pennies frequently manifested. Though he accepts that recurrent spontaneous psychokinesis may explain some poltergeist 'hauntings', Fontana warned against taking it as a blanket explanation. In the Cardiff case, for example, he concluded that it was more likely a spirit survived death and caused the phenomena.

It's impossible to unequivocally state what summoned Caroline Laurence's haunting. Psychic Debbie Malone says it might have been 'a bit of both', – i.e., a spirit *and* the teenager's heightened energy. After all, Caroline was an intuitive sixteen-year-old who'd been playing with the ouija board for years, a never-fail recipe for a nightmare, says Debbie. 'It's dangerous, because a spirit might attach itself to you and you won't know how to get rid of it.'

Various themes threaded through the tapestry of tales. Alongside reports of malfunctioning electronics, static, and homes in strife, the notion that psychic-medium ability runs in families was prominent. Mothers – and fathers – tend to pass 'the gift' onto their children, like a kiss sent on the wind. Descriptions of apparitions tallied:

Emma Snowden's little visitor was 'grey, muted, as if drained of colour.' Emma Rusher realised by his overall 'greyish colouring' that her 'Intruder' wasn't alive, and Anne Kidd speaks of the washed-out tones of the ghosts she sees. And how could I forget my husband's word picture of the little boy in our living room?: 'Washed-out brown from head to toe – his clothes, his skin, his hair . . .' Just like a faded sepia photograph.

A feeling of paralysis was also frequently reported. Ever wary that the medical condition sleep paralysis, not the paranormal, could be behind an experience, I grilled an expert. 'Sleep paralysis is a common condition which is generally benign. It occurs when a person wakes up but his/her body is still asleep,' says Dr. Andrew Ng, director of the Centre for Sleep Disorders and Respiratory Failure at Sydney's St. George Hospital. 'The person's mind is usually fully alert – with eyes opened or closed – but with the body feeling like it is paralysed.'

Almost half of us will experience sleep paralysis at least once in our lives, and about three-quarters of those people will also experience associated hallucinations (known as hypnagogic when going into sleep, and hypnopompic when coming out of sleep). These hallucinations are usually auditory, such as humming, voices or laughter. The next most common type of hallucination is visual, which is where the fear factor amps up a notch. 'Visual examples include seeing people in the room often approaching the paralysed person; and sensory examples include a feeling of throat tightness,' says Dr. Ng. 'A threatening presence may be frequently felt, and this combined with the hallucinations of throat tightening or someone approaching them (when they are "paralysed" and "helpless") adds to the often horrific feelings that the person later describes.'

Rhonda Rice, who regularly sees 'the visitors', as she calls them, was diagnosed with hypnagogic hallucinations but says that as she is able to yell and move her arms when a stranger appears at her bedside, 'I thought that [sleep paralysis] doesn't really cover me,' she says. 'Though I *have* had a couple of episodes of sleep paralysis and that was terrifying.' (Dr. Ng maintains that 'hypnagogic hallucinations may be so vivid that they are remembered clearly even after the sleep paralysis has passed.')

In 'The Force', Simone describes something like sleep paralysis that 'attacked' the members of her share household. 'Each of us living in the house was pinned down to our beds, paralysed and unable to open our eyes or defend ourselves,' she said. 'Multiple household members having sleep paralysis would be very rare,' says Dr. Ng, though he adds it does run in families. 'Having the same hallucination would also be extremely rare. Perhaps there is another explanation.'

What of Kath Campbell who was paralysed from top to toe, leaving only her tears trickling freely down her face, when her little girls visited her in spirit? Or Diane Jakubans who was unable to move as a vision of her late teenage son moved about her room? Dr. Ng says that in a sleep paralysis hallucination, it is 'more common to see an "evil" presence than a familiar face.'

'Sleep paralysis with hypnagogic hallucinations could explain some instances of ghosts or haunted houses, but probably not many,' he sums up. 'People usually work out what is happening after the first or second episode.' In yet another tricky twist, parapsychologist Dr. Storm adds that a person experiencing sleep paralysis is in an altered state of consciousness (ASC), which is 'known to be conducive to psi experiences, but the imagination/dreaming also kicks in at this point too.'

How then, to tell the two apart? Or perhaps paranormal experiences and the imagination or dreaming are two sides of the same coin?

'In the Aboriginal view of the dreamtime, they don't make any difference between waking and sleep,' says author and publisher

Maggie Hamilton. 'After many experiences that I've had, I think they are right. We are in a constant "dreaming".'

Scientist Paul Willis disagrees. 'There is something going on here that is perfectly rational and explicable. It always sounds like a harsh call, but I prefer reality any day to belief in unsubstantiated myths. The preference puts me in contact with the world I live in and provides profound meaning to me. I don't live in fear or awe at the prospect of imaginary influences in my life.'

Marie D. Jones lives in hope that science itself will one day substantiate those very 'myths'. 'But it will only happen when scientists, or at least more of them, start admitting that they don't have all the answers, all the facts and all the knowledge and that there are mysteries in life that beg for study,' she says. 'Not all of these things may be duplicable in a lab setting, or applicable to the scientific method . . . but that does not mean they are not real.'

And I have to say that I agree with her.

I believe that each woman's experience was a powerful force in her world. *It happened*. In my research, I came across the delightful story of the upstate New York town of Lily Dale, where all the inhabitants are mediums. 'One of the great lessons of Lily Dale is the encouragement to listen to yourself,' Christine Wicker, author of *Lily Dale: Adventures in the Town that Talks to the Dead*, told ABC Radio National in 2004. 'I found that lots of people have had these kinds of visions or intimations or feelings, but they are afraid to listen to them because we live in a society that says those things are not true, and that people who listen to them are crazy. People who go to Lily Dale get permission to listen to their own voices, and that means a whole lot to them.'

Here's what my inner voice tells me: I believe there is no definitive answer to explain the paranormal and that that's intentional. I think each of us has our course set out before us and we will solve the riddle when we're supposed to.

'Knowing all the answers only after we die seems to make no sense,' says Sandra James, who tells of visiting a heavenly realm in 'The View From There'. 'But I have learned over time that everything has a reason, and faith is simply accepting and acknowledging this fact.'

When I was a small child, I read a paragraph in a reference book that set fire to my thoughts. The book said that one distant day, the sun would consume the earth and then there would be . . . nothing. At night, I'd lay on the top bunk in our flat at Eastlakes, with the traffic sounds of the main road filtering through the walls, and try to picture this 'nothingness'. Behind my eyelids, shut tight, the light of day would turn cruel and snuff out everything I knew. It was at that point, with the darkness spreading like an ink stain over my imagination, that I'd fail. Always here, I would shudder and have to start again. I just couldn't fathom such emptiness.

Now, I no longer need to.

BIBLIOGRAPHY AND RESOURCES

Bardens, D., *Ghosts and Hauntings*, Middlesex: Senate, 1997.

Braude, S.E., *The Gold Leaf Lady and Other Parapsychological Investigations*, Chicago and London: The University of Chicago Press, 2007.

Browne, S., with Harrison, L., *Visits From the Afterlife*, London: Piatkus, 2006.

Burks, E. and Cribbs, G., *Ghosthunter: Investigating the World of Ghosts and Spirits*, Wiltshire: BCA with Headline Book Publishing, 1995.

Chambers, P., *Paranormal People*, London: Blandford, 1998.

Davies, O., *The Haunted: A Social History of Ghosts*, New York: Palgrave Macmillan, 2007.

Dolan, M., *Haunted Homes: True Stories of Paranormal Investigations*, London: HarperElement, 2006.

Donaghy, B., *Anna's Story*, Sydney: HarperCollins, 2006.

DuBois, A., *Secrets of the Monarch*, New York: Fireside, 2007.

Eldritch, M (ed.), *Ghosts*, Lanark: Geddes & Grosset, 2005

Fontana, D., *Is There An Afterlife? A Comprehensive Overview of the Evidence*, Hampshire: O Books, 2005.

Goodwyn, M., *Ghost Worlds*, Minnesota: Llewellyn Publications, 2007.

Grzelka, A., with Gibb, D., *Life & Beyond*, Sydney: Rockpool Publishing, 2008.

Hamilton-Parker, C., *What to Do When You Are Dead*, New York: Sterling, 2001.

Hill, D., and Williams, P., *The Supernatural*, New York: Hawthorn Book Publishers, 1965.

Holzer, H., *Ghosts: True Encounters With the World Beyond*, New York: Black Dog & Leventhal Publishers, 1997.

Jones, M.D., *PSIence: How New Discoveries In Quantum Physics and New Science May Explain the Existence of Paranormal Phenomena*, New Jersey: New Page Books, 2007.

Kübler-Ross, E., *On Life After Death*, California: Celestial Arts, 1991.

LaGrand, L.E., *Messages and Miracles: Extraordinary Experiences of the Bereaved*, Minnesota: Llewellyn Publications, 1999.

Mishlove, J., *Psi Development Systems*, North Carolina: McFarland, 1983.

Pinkney, J., *Haunted: The Book of Australia's Ghosts*, Victoria: The Five Mile Press, 2005.

Ramachandran, V.S., and Blakeslee, S., *Phantoms in the Brain*, London: Fourth Estate, 1998.

Randles, J., and Hough, P., *The Afterlife: An Investigation Into the Mysteries of Life After Death*, London: Piatkus, 1993.

Rhine, L.E., *Hidden Channels of the Mind*, New York: William Morrow and Company, 1961.

Rule, L., *Ghosts Among Us*, Missouri: Andrews McMeel Publishing, 2004.

Storr, W., *Will Storr vs. The Supernatural*, London: Ebury Press, 2006.

Sutherland, C., *Beloved Visitors*, Sydney: Bantam, 1997.

Sutherland, C., *Within The Light*, Sydney: Bantam, 1993.

Thalbourne, A., (ed.) *Australian Journal of Parapsychology*; Dec. 2002, Vol. 2, No. 2.

Townshend, G. & Ffoulkes, M., *True Ghost Stories*, Middlesex: Senate, 1994.

Underwood, P., *The Ghost Hunters*, London: Guild Publishing, 1985.

Williamson, L., *Ghosts and Earthbound Spirits*, London: Piatkus, 2006.

Willin, M., *Ghosts Caught on Film: Photographs of the Paranormal*, Cincinnati: David & Charles, 2007.

Winkowski, M., *When Ghosts Speak*, Sydney: Hachette Australia, 2007.

HELPFUL WEBSITES

http://www.afterlifenews.com
http://www.aiprinc.org/index.asp
http://www.australianparanormalsociety.com
http://www.betweentwoworlds.net
http://www.castleofspirits.com
http://www.extraordinarygriefexperiences.com
http://www.ghostvillage.com
http://www.hauntedaustralia.com/index.php
http://www.mariedjones.com
http://paranormal.about.com
http://www.paranormal.com.au/public
http://www.paranormalaustralia.com
http://www.Rhine.org/main.shtml
http://www.spr.ac.uk/expcms
http://www.strangenation.com.au
http://www.whatthebleep.com

ACKNOWLEDGMENTS

First and foremost, thank you to all the courageous women who shared their experiences with me. I am honoured and privileged to be entrusted with your stories. I am also indebted to the following people whose input was invaluable: Hannah Jenkins, Lance Storm and Robb Tilley from the Australian Institute of Parapsychological Research, Professor Warwick Middleton, Paul Willis, Dr. Andrew Ng, Kerrie Higgins, Debbie Malone, Mahta Manzouri, Maggie Hamilton and Marie D. Jones, whose breadth of knowledge and willingness to share it with me was inspirational. Thank you to my husband, Anibal, for taking care of everything in 2008 so that I had the space and time to write, and to my lovely children Jasmin and Tabaré for being so understanding. Thanks to my mum for passing on her passion for books, writing and stories; I am ever grateful for what you've given me. To my sister, Natalie, and sis-in-law Dani for the laughs and encouragement, and to all my dear family and friends for being a fabulous and ever-helpful cheer squad. Thanks also to my spirit sister Romina Mandrini for reading the manuscript. To my *Who* editor Nicky Briger and the rest of my *Who* 'family', especially Deb Grunfeld and Annette Dasey, thank you so much for your generous support. Thank you to Emma Rusher, who loved the idea from the beginning and nudged it towards my publisher, Vanessa Radnidge, who luckily felt the same way. Thank you, Vanessa – and my agent, Selwa Anthony – for your guidance, wisdom and reassurance, and to the Hachette team, especially my wonderful editor Kate Ballard. I also appreciate the efforts of everyone who helped in my search for stories, including Marianne Bilkey, Liz Vincent, Rowena Gilbert, Wendy James and my dear friend Suzanne Newton. A round of applause to Janette Doolan, whose swift and careful transcribing is the reason I made deadline. Lastly, I'd like to mention Varuna, the Writers' House, where I spent a productive (albeit spooky!) week losing myself in *Spirit Sisters*.

More Non-fiction from Headline

THE PET PSYCHIC

JOANNE HULL

They speak, she listens
Amazing tales from the world
of animal communication

Joanne Hull always knew there was something that made her different from other children.

While other girls her age were playing with dolls, Joanne was busy collecting any stray animal that came her way, until her parents' backyard resembled a zoo. As she grew older she realised that she was developing incredible powers that allowed her to psychically connect with, and talk to, animals.

For the last ten years Joanne has used the animal spirit world to help owners across the country understand troubled pets, find missing ones and, most amazingly, contact those we've lost to the other side. Joanne has given hundreds of spine-chillingly accurate readings – and for the first time she shares the sometimes heart-warming, sometimes heart-breaking, but always extraordinary stories that have formed her life as The Pet Psychic.

NON-FICTION / AUTOBIOGRAPHY 978 0 7553 1971 8

BEING THE SOHAM PSYCHIC

DENNIS McKENZIE

The remarkable story of one man's paranormal powers . . .

'*I am really sorry but both the girls are dead*'

Dennis McKenzie was brought to the world's attention following his involvement in the tragic Soham murder case. After making stunningly accurate predictions about the deaths of Holly Wells and Jessica Chapman, he was dubbed the 'Soham Psychic'.

Since then, Dennis's expertise has continually been drawn on to help solve many horrific crimes, including the case of the 'BTK' Killer – a serial killer who bound, tortured and killed women in Wichita, Kansas and evaded the police for over 30 years.

An ordinary boy from a working-class background, Dennis never imagined his life would follow such an extraordinary path. From his first psychic sighting at the age of four to his traumatic prediction of a family friend's death, Dennis describes the experiences that have defined his remarkable life in his typically frank and down-to-earth way.

This is the fascinating story of how Dennis discovered his gift and how, with the help of his spirit guides, he has shared his psychic wisdom with the world.

NON-FICTION / AUTOBIOGRAPHY 978 0 7553 1903 9